KETTLE BROTH TO GOOSEBERRY FOOL

Jenny Baker's interest in food began during her childhood in Devon. During the sixties she lived in the Middle East with her husband James – who claims to have taught her how to cook – and on their return to London they started a business catering for functions of up to 400 guests. When their son and daughter left home for college, Jenny began to write about cooking. She divides her time between her two kitchens in London and France.

Kettle Broth to Gooseberry Fool is Jenny Baker's seventh book for Faber.

Kettle Broth
to Gooseberry Fool

A Celebration of Simple English Cooking

JENNY BAKER

Illustrated by James Baker

faber and faber
LONDON · BOSTON

First published in 1996
by Faber and Faber Limited
3 Queen Square London WC1N 3AU
This paperback edition first published in 1997

Photoset by Parker Typesetting Service, Leicester
Printed in England by Clays Ltd, St Ives plc

A CIP record for this book
is available from the British Library
ISBN 0–571–17297–0

2 4 6 8 10 9 7 5 3 1

For Eloise and Oliver

Acknowledgements

Special thanks to Kate Hobson and Bill Akhurst for their recipes, to Lynda Johnson, Gina Raggett, Judith Peppitt and Isabel Radage for recommending and lending me difficult-to-find cookery books, to Pete Hardy and Rupert Truman for their computer skills and to Belinda Matthews for all her support and encouragement.

Contents

Introduction

This is a companion to my two regional French cookbooks. While I was researching them, I began to think it would be interesting to write a book about English food, approaching it almost from the same angle – that is, as if I was discovering a foreign cuisine. Which, in effect, I was, because although I retain wonderful memories of the food of my childhood, like so many people I have tended to turn right away from my roots and to fall in love with the cooking of other countries.

I may have gone into the project full of innocence, sure it was going to be quite an easy task but it wasn't long before I realized that, far from there being only a limited and manageable choice of recipes, there were so many that I had to decide what to put in and what to leave out. And I had to choose between writing a book of nostalgia or one with recipes that would suit today's taste. I opted for the latter, selecting recipes that appealed to me. So there is not too much stodge. No roly-poly puddings, although I couldn't resist a Kate and Sidney. There is plenty of fish and game, seasonal fruits and vegetables, herbs, spices and quite a lot of wine, cider and spirits.

It seemed to me when I was writing *Cuisine Grandmère* that the cookery of northern France had a pattern that was not so dissimilar from my earliest memories of English food. I couldn't really decide if this was wishful thinking but when I began to read old English recipes, I discovered many which were just as imaginative and intriguing as the French recipes I was trying and testing. Like them the English relied on good, fresh produce: aromatic spices and sweet garden herbs, fresh vegetables from the garden, fish caught around our shores, seasonal game. Fruit came from local orchards and meat and dairy produce from rich grazing pastures. Lots of dishes were cooked in wine or cider. Even occasionally, garlic!

They brought back memories of the time when I was a child and lived for a few years with my family in my grandmother's house in Devon. She presided over the kitchen, which was the centre of our lives, cooking all our meals including lunch for us all every day. And just like those French grandmères across the Channel, she hardly ever consulted a cookery book but made the dishes she knew, Devonshire and West Country dishes which had been handed down over the generations as well as the now universally popular ones from other parts of the country, such as Yorkshire pudding and steak and kidney pie.

There were daily dishes ranging from roast lamb and mint sauce, rabbit pie, pork with apples to boiled beef and dumplings, which would be followed by desserts like bramble crumble, creamy rice or bread and butter puddings, fruit fools, junkets, freshly picked raspberries and gooseberry fool. Her garden and that of relations and friends provided her with fruit and vegetables and she grew an array of herbs like mint, parsley, rosemary, juniper and thyme.

But while she and other unsung cooks all over the country were following older traditions, English cooking was being poorly served by works' canteens, school dinners and most kinds of institutional catering. Cookery books which once had contained heartwarming recipes full of spices, herbs and subtle flavourings were now full of bland ingredients with barely a herb in sight.

So when did it all go wrong? Up to and during the eighteenth century, English cooking was considered to be on a par with that of France but by the nineteenth, while French cooking continued to flourish, that of England had already begun its steady decline. The railways didn't help. There were huge advantages but it meant the beginning of the end of regional cooking, as it became possible for produce to be transported all over the country. This contrasts with France, where cooking has retained its character largely because of the size of the country and its inadequate transport system. It has remained rural and very conservative and until recently everyone has taken for granted that their meals would always be just the same as those prepared by their mothers and grandmothers. Even so, things are beginning to change now that France is networked by autoroutes and it seems likely that, in time, it too will lose much of its traditional regional cooking.

Ironically, too, French cooking received an additional boost as a result of the Revolution. Chefs who had been employed by the aristocrats found themselves out of work, but were soon using their skills to produce popular local dishes. Many of them opened small restaurants which flourished all over France among ordinary people.

The opposite happened here. Our industrial revolution sent people migrating from the country into the towns. With the increase in trade and profits came a burgeoning middle class who, keen to be accepted in the right circles, began to adopt prudish and snobbish attitudes towards food. The well-to-do Victorians may have eaten enormously yet at the same time food became a taboo subject which only the ill-bred ever talked about and although a 'lady' might run her household with the efficiency of an Isabella Beeton, she didn't expect to sully her hands by doing anything so menial as cooking.

All sorts of genteel manners emerged, and it is possible that people were only too happy to label things like oysters and mussels poor man's food, not just because they were cheap and therefore possibly nasty, but because they were impossible to eat elegantly. Habits like dunking sops and sippets (bread, either plain, toasted or fried) into soup became uncouth and only became acceptable again comparatively recently when we discovered French *croûtons*. I hope sippets may now be reinstated (see Etceteras). Inevitably our traditions began to die. As time went by food became more and more bland right across the social spectrum and people began to rely not on the cook to provide flavour but on a liberal splash of one of the newly invented bottled sauces.

The decline continued right through most of the twentieth century, the worst moment being after the Second World War when the food allowance was so meagre that it was almost impossible to do anything imaginative. People were tired of austerity and longed for things to get better, to be new and exciting and, when eventually food began to be plentiful, the last thing anyone wanted was to look backwards. So when the great revival of interest in cooking occurred in the fifties and sixties, we were only too eager to be inspired by Elizabeth David and her evocative books and articles full of the heady flavours of Southern France, Italy and the Mediterranean.

In no time at all, England became a country where a great many people loved good food, the taboo of silence imposed by the Victorians at last broken. Everyone talked about meals past, present and future as they sat in restaurants or round the dinner table. More people travelled, ate strange and delicious food in exotic places and when they came home they were eager to reproduce all these new dishes in their own kitchens. They became wonderful cooks, welcoming with glee every cooking tradition but their own, perfectly happy to agree with every foreigner that the English may have wonderful ingredients but they have no idea how to put them together.

Which of course is nonsense, as a trawl of early cookery books reveals. We know just as much about food and cooking as any of our neighbours. Of all countries we have been willing to take on new ideas and flavours and have not been afraid of experimenting, embracing over the centuries the influence of many different cultures. Two of the most influential were the Roman and Norman invaders. The first, with their passion for highly flavoured foods, brought Mediterranean herbs and spices, while the Normans introduced a sophisticated cuisine and a whole new culinary language. The Crusaders brought back aromatic spices, sugar, all kinds of dried fruits, sweet and bitter almonds, rose and orange flower waters. Throughout the centuries as we roamed the globe as explorers, conquerors and merchant traders we gathered new ingredients and new culinary ideas.

This book is a collection of some of them.

A few words on practicalities. All recipes are for 4 people unless the recipe says otherwise. I use olive oil for cooking – we know it is the best and I am encouraged by the fact that, along with all those herbs and spices, the Romans must first have introduced it into our culinary repertoire! As for pastry, I have included recipes for both plain and sweet shortcrust in Etceteras, but I haven't given one for puff pastry, because it is very time-consuming to make and it is so easy to buy it fresh or frozen.

Quantities are given in both metric and imperial. Because they are approximate conversions, you should not mix the two but use one or the other when following a recipe. Usually exact quantities are not, in fact, critical except when making cakes or boiling rice (for which a useful rule to follow is that you need twice as much liquid as volume of rice – for example, for 4 people allow one cup of rice to two cups of water).

Jenny Baker
Wandsworth
1996

The Flavour

If you happen to pick up an English cookery book published in the past hundred years, a quick glance will convince you there isn't any flavour at all. What fun can there be in preparing a recipe like the one I came across recently in a cookery book published in 1932 for mince and macaroni, the list of ingredients being leftover beef or lamb, dripping, flour, a small carrot, gravy, mushroom ketchup, an onion, macaroni and stale grated cheese? Or this one, in another, for shepherd's pie, which called for cooked meat, potatoes, onion, seasoning, milk, dripping, flour, stock or water and gravy browning? We can hardly believe our eyes as we riffle through these sorts of books.

Was English cooking really as dull as all that? Called upon to defend it, all we can lamely say is that our roasts are wonderful, no one can roast meat or vegetables like we do and the rest may be plain and simple but the glory of English cooking is in its use of top quality meat, fish, fruit and vegetables. All perhaps true, but only half the story.

Go back a century or two to Eliza Acton and Hannah Glasse and you are reading the writings of two Elizabeth Davids of an earlier age. Full of seasonal herbs, warmed with spices and alcohol, they express a sensual but practical appreciation of food and how to prepare it. Go back further still and it is the same story. We are the inheritors of a wonderful tradition that changed and developed over the centuries until we betrayed it, not just by adopting new ideas but by embracing them so heartily that we fell into the habit of denigrating completely our own English cooking.

There may be few herbs in those early twentieth-century cookery books, but we have used herbs from the earliest times, at first probably just medicinally, although it is nice to think of those Stone-Age people on the beach, roasting their mussels in the embers of their bonfires and then eating them with a sprinkling of garlic and parsley. More likely it was the Romans who showed us how to use both herbs and spices to give flavour to dishes and we have to thank them for introducing us to many of our most familiar varieties. Even those herbs which we consider peculiarly our own, like parsley, mint and sage, all have their beginnings in the Mediterranean, as do the more obvious sun-loving varieties such as thyme, rosemary and marjoram.

A faggot of herbs or sweet herbs tied in a bundle is a feature in many older English recipes. It consisted of two or three kinds, most commonly parsley, thyme and a bay leaf, which were added to the pot to give flavour and then removed before the dish was brought to the table. Nowadays we tend to use the term bouquet garni as if the idea was purely a French invention. As Tom Stobart rather severely remarks in *Herbs, Spices and Flavourings*, 'The cook who does not habitually use some sort of bouquet garni is probably not worthy of being called a cook . . .'

The choice of herbs varies according to the season and the recipe and ideally they should be fresh. In winter this is not always possible, so it is a good idea to dry herbs from the garden in the summer. If neither fresh nor home-dried is available, then the commercial sort have to do but it is worth remembering that after a few months they lose their pungency so must be replaced fairly frequently.

Spices were widely used in both the Roman and Byzantine Empires. The word stems from the Latin *species*, meaning goods or wares and originally referred not just to aromatic flavourings like cinnamon and nutmeg but to all sorts of other kinds like sugar, milk, honey and herbs. The Romans liked their food highly seasoned and their recipes are packed with strong and pungent flavours. Early English recipes owe a lot to their influence, so that by the time of the Crusaders there was a ready market for the flow of exotic spices which now came in greater abundance from the East. Our appetite for these desirable flavourings was so great that it fuelled our efforts to discover and open the sea routes to the Orient during the Renaissance. Throughout this time and well into the seventeenth century spices were used with reckless abandon but gradually they began to be used with more discretion.

And alcohol? Even before the Romans we were making mead from fermented honey and producing our own crude wine. From them we learnt the art of viticulture and from that time on developed a love for wine which increased with the arrival of the Normans, so that even when our own wine production declined, we imported it in quantity. We learnt cider making from the French, developed our own strong beer-producing tradition, drank sherry and port, brandy and spirits and when the duty was prohibitive we became vigorous smugglers. And naturally we cooked with whatever kind of alcohol was to hand.

So let's begin with simple dishes like Kettle broth and London particular, fish strewn with herbs, chicken with rosemary, pease pudding and gingerbread, followed by dishes laced with alcohol like venison in red wine, stewed pigeons, trifle or tipsy cake and Devonshire junket. And because the roast is so very much part of tradition, we complete this flavoursome part of the book with a whole range of roast meats and vegetables with their accompanying sauces.

Sweet herbs

Kettle broth (leek and bacon soup)

To dry marigold flowers

London particular (dried pea soup)

Snails

Jugged kippers

Poached finnan haddock

Dabs with herbs

Grilled trout

Fried trout

Trout with rosemary

Chicken with rosemary

Chicken pie

Lamb chops with onion sauce

Sausages

Bacon and egg pie

Pease pudding

Forcemeat balls

Herb vinegars

Garlic or shallot vinegar

Kettle broth

This warming and delicious soup coloured a deep gold by marigold petals, the poor man's saffron, is an adaptation of a Cornish recipe which was originally made by simply pouring boiling water from the kettle – a large pot with no spout – into bowls containing sops of bread, some sweet herbs, the chopped garlicky flavoured leaves of wild leeks, a bit of bacon, some butter, pepper and salt. This version is rather more sophisticated but almost as simple to prepare.

50 g (2 oz) butter
450 g (1 lb) leeks, sliced
4 rashers bacon, chopped
2 cloves garlic, crushed
2 or 3 marigold heads
1 or 2 sprigs of thyme or
   1 teaspoon dried

1 bay leaf
600 ml (1 pint) water
salt
freshly milled black pepper
handful parsley, chopped
slices of bread from a crusty loaf

Melt the butter in a saucepan, add the leeks, bacon and garlic, cover and leave to sweat over a low heat for 10 minutes. Add the petals from the marigold flowers and the thyme and bay leaf. Pour over the water, season with salt and pepper and simmer for 30–40 minutes. Just before serving remove the bay leaf and sprigs of thyme and scatter over the parsley. Put a piece of bread into each soup plate and pour the broth on top.

To dry marigold flowers

Marigold flowers can be dried and stored for use during the winter – simply pick them on a sunny day and either leave them whole or pull off the petals and put them in a warm, airy place for several days until dry and shrivelled, store them in jars away from the light so that their deep orange does not fade. Use them to flavour and colour soups and stews.

London particular

Until smokeless fuel became obligatory, London fogs were thick and dense with a tinge of greenish yellow and the term pea-souper was an apt description of them. In *Bleak House* Dickens describes such a one as a London particular and soon this name was applied to the soup as well. The soup, especially if made with the stock left over from boiling a ham, remains rich and satisfying, whereas the fog only lingers as an unpleasant memory.

The dash of Worcestershire sauce gives it a tang which would have been much appreciated in Dickens's day. One of the few survivors of those original sauces introduced by families returning home from the Raj era India, it is made with vinegar, shallots, tamarinds, garlic, molasses and spices to a secret recipe supplied by the one-time governor of Bengal, Lord Sandys. He asked his local chemists, Lea and Perrins, to make him up a batch but the result was so shatteringly fiery that they hid it away in the cellar and forgot it. Ages later, it was rediscovered and tasted again. Still fiery but no longer mind-blowing, the long, slow maturation process had produced the first of the famous sauces we know today.

Make the soup with dried whole or split peas. The latter need no soaking.

225 g (8 oz) dried whole or split peas
25 g (1 oz) butter
50 g (2 oz) streaky bacon, chopped
1 onion, chopped
1 carrot, sliced

1 litre (1¾ pints) stock or water
freshly milled black pepper
salt
1 tablespoon chopped mint
1 teaspoon Worcestershire sauce (optional)

If using dried whole peas, soak them overnight. The next day melt the butter and add the bacon, onion and carrot and let them sweat, covered, for 10 minutes. Add the peas and stock or water and season with pepper. Cover and simmer until the peas are tender (whole peas will take about 2 hours, split peas about 45 minutes). Purée the soup, add salt to taste and sprinkle with the mint. To give an authentic touch, stir in the teaspoon of Worcestershire sauce just before serving.

Snails

And what, you might ask, are snails doing in a book of English food? Well, snails thrive on plants freshly washed by rain and in Somerset, where they were once popular among the lead miners who used to fry them on their shovels, they were euphemistically known as wall fish. It was widely thought that snails were good for the lungs and a kind of broth was fed to glass-blowers and to small children who might be bronchitic. In fact, to make you squirm a little more, Dorothy Hartley in *Food in England* tells how sickly children were thought to benefit from 'dew slugs' which were dissolved in salt or salt broth before being mixed with the children's soup.

Of course it is mostly the English who are squeamish about eating such fare. Other people adore them, beginning with the Romans who introduced the large *Helix pomatia*, now known as the Burgundian snail, into this country, cultivating huge numbers in special enclosures. These are the kind to look out for in tins as they are plump and fat. In fact, if you tend to be adventurous, you can collect and eat our own common garden snail, *Helix aspersa*, which is prized all over southern Europe. The method is given in detail in *Simple French Cuisine*.

One of the nicest ways of eating snails is stuffed with a well-flavoured butter and the recipe below is based on a mixture of summer herbs. Canned snails are sold on their own or topped with a bag of shells. Buy them first with shells, subsequently you can save money by washing the shells and buying snails without them. To wash the shells, put them in a pan with 1 teaspoon baking soda and boil rapidly. Throw away the water and rinse thoroughly.

225 g (8 oz) unsalted butter
2 teaspoons chopped chives
1 teaspoon chopped lemon
   thyme

2–3 tablespoons mixture of
   chopped summer herbs such as
   parsley, dill and tarragon
salt
cayenne pepper
2 cans of snails with shells

Melt the butter and stir in the herbs. Season generously with salt and pepper. Pour a little of the mixture into each snail shell, add a snail and top up with the mixture. Stand the filled shells upright on a baking sheet lined with a sheet of crumpled foil so that they do not fall over. Set aside to allow the butter to solidify.

Heat the oven to Gas 7/425°F/220°C and bake the snails for 10–12 minutes until the butter is melted and bubbling.

Jugged kippers

Kippers, descendants of the heavily salted red herrings which nowadays are hard to find, are one of the joys of English gastronomy, except when they have been subjected to modern methods involving artificial dyes and flavourings. A good kipper should be plump and glistening, its colour somewhere between silver and gold with just a hint of red. They were invented in Northumberland and the best still come from there as well as East Anglia and the Isle of Man.

They are nicest either grilled on a greased grid with no added oil or fat for about 5 minutes, or cooked in a jug. Nowadays, of course, all jugs have handles, but when this recipe was invented a jug was simply a tall jar.

Simply put your kipper(s) into a tall jug or jar, pour over sufficient freshly boiled water to cover and leave for 5–10 minutes. Drain and eat with a knob of butter on top, a squeeze of lemon, a sprinkling of parsley and lots of brown bread.

Poached finnan haddock

Smoked haddock poached in milk flavoured with herbs makes a delicious and substantial breakfast dish or supper. It is sold either whole or in fillets. Whole fish are known as finnan haddock because the method of smoking originated in Scotland in a village called Findon. They are beheaded and split before being cured by salting and cold smoking. Recognize the best by their pale gold colour.

175–225 g (6–8 oz) smoked haddock per person
sprig of thyme or ¼ teaspoon dried
1 bay leaf
1–2 sprigs of parsley

½ teaspoon whole peppercorns
sufficient mixture of milk and water to cover
25 g (1 oz) butter
1 lemon, cut in wedges

Put the fish into a shallow pan with the thyme, bay leaf, parsley and peppercorns. Just cover with the mixture of milk and water. Bring gently to the boil. Let it bubble for 1 minute then remove from the heat. Cover and leave for 4 minutes, until the fish is opaque. Serve each fillet topped with a knob of butter and garnished with lemon.

Dabs with herbs

Sometimes the fishmonger sells what he calls small plaice but which are really dabs and they are worth snapping up because they have far more flavour. You can tell them because they lack the plaice's bony nodules on the head and their dark skin, which is easily removed after cooking, is like sandpaper. The main catch comes from the North Sea, so they are plentiful in East Anglia. In this summer recipe, they are cooked sandwiched between layers of herbs. If you can't find dabs, use small plaice instead or other flat fish like lemon sole.

50 g (2 oz) butter	$\frac{1}{2}$ teaspoon nutmeg
2–3 tablespoons chopped parsley	salt
2–3 tablespoons chopped chives	freshly milled black pepper
2–3 tablespoons chopped tarragon	juice of 1 lemon
4 dabs	150 ml ($\frac{1}{4}$ pint) dry white wine or strong dry cider

At least half an hour before you want to cook the fish, butter a shallow oven dish and sprinkle half the herbs over the base. Lay the fish on top, sprinkle with remaining herbs and add the nutmeg, salt, pepper and lemon juice. Pour over the wine or cider.

Heat the oven to Gas 6/400°F/200°C. Dot the fish with the remaining butter and bake them for 15–20 minutes.

Grilled trout

If, like me, you are lucky enough to have a fisherman in the family who brings home freshly caught trout, they can be cooked in the simplest manner by grilling or frying. Farmed trout, which are plentiful and comparatively cheap, may need a little more elaboration. Make sure they are fresh, their skins covered in a clear film and, if they are frozen, are thoroughly thawed before cooking.

Put a sprig of rosemary, thyme or marjoram into the cavity of each fish. Wrap each one in a rasher of bacon or a vine leaf (or follow Dorothy Hartley's advice in *Food in England* where she suggests 'a single folded leek leaf holds a trout very neatly for grilling'). Brush them with oil or melted butter and grill under a preheated grill (or on a cast-iron grill pan) for 4–5 minutes on either side.

Fried trout

Fry them in the style of the miller's wife, *à la meunière*. Coat each trout in fine oatmeal or flour seasoned with salt and pepper. Fry them in clarified butter (see Etceteras). Turn them over after 3–4 minutes and fry the other side. Put them on a warm serving dish. Wipe out the pan with kitchen paper, add a knob of butter and when it has melted squeeze in the juice of half a lemon and pour it sizzling over the fish. Sprinkle with chopped parsley or dill.

Trout with rosemary

This simple dish of trout is delicious served hot or cold. If serving cold, remove the trout from the dish in which they were cooked and carefully remove the skin. Put them on to a platter, pour over the cooking juices and, when cold, garnish the dish with a sprinkling of fresh parsley and lemon wedges.

4 trout	150 ml ($\frac{1}{4}$ pint) dry white wine
50 g (2 oz) butter	salt
4 sprigs of rosemary	freshly milled black pepper
	4 tablespoons chopped parsley

Heat the oven to Gas 6/400°F/200°C. Lay the trout in a shallow oven dish and put a knob of butter and a sprig of rosemary into the cavity of each. Pour over the white wine, season with salt and pepper and strew with parsley. Dot the remaining butter on top and bake for 25 minutes.

Chicken with rosemary

This adaptation of an eighteenth-century Northumbrian recipe is an attractive way of serving chicken breasts. They emerge from their pastry crusts deliciously flavoured with rosemary, valued as a cooking herb until the nineteenth century, and garlic, which the Romans brought to Britain.

4 boned chicken breasts   4 sprigs of rosemary
freshly milled black pepper   350 g (12 oz) puff pastry
juice of 1 lemon   salt
1 clove garlic, chopped   1 egg yolk, beaten

At least an hour ahead, put the chicken breasts into a dish, season
them with pepper, sprinkle over the lemon juice and garlic and lay a
sprig of rosemary on each. Divide the pastry into four and roll each
out into a square large enough to wrap one of the breasts.

When ready to cook, heat the oven to Gas 6/400°F/200°C. Lay a
chicken breast diagonally across each pastry square, season with salt
and more pepper and sprinkle over the lemon juice from the marinade.
Brush the edges of the pastry with water and fold the corners over to
form parcels, pressing the edges together. Turn them over and put
them on a damp baking sheet and brush them all over with the egg
yolk. Bake for 25–30 minutes until puffed and golden.

Chicken pie

This West Country pie can be eaten hot but is especially good eaten
cold on a warm summer's evening or perhaps at a picnic. Make it
when you have some left-over chicken, first making a stock from the
bones of the carcase which sets into a thick jelly when the pie is cooked
and left to cool. For a touch of luxury, add 2 or 3 tablespoons of sour
cream with the chicken stock.

450 g (1 lb) cooked chicken cut   1 clove garlic, chopped
   in pieces   3–4 tablespoons chopped parsley
150 g (6 oz) bacon or ham,   salt
   chopped   freshly milled black pepper
2 hard-boiled eggs, sliced   225 g (8 oz) shortcrust pastry
300 ml (½ pint) chicken stock (see 1 egg yolk, beaten
   Etceteras)

Put a pie funnel in the centre of a deepish pie dish. Surround with the
chicken, bacon or ham and the hard-boiled eggs. Mix well. Pour over
the chicken stock, scatter with the chopped garlic and parsley and
season with salt and pepper.

Roll out the pastry to make a lid and cut the trimmings into strips
the width of the edge of the pie dish. Brush this edge with a little water

and lay the strips all round, then brush this pastry edging with water and put the pastry lid on top, crimping the two layers together. Mark all round with the prongs of a fork. Set the pie aside for 30 minutes or so before cooking.

Heat the oven to Gas 6/400°F/200°C. Brush the pastry with the beaten egg yolk and bake the pie for 30–35 minutes until the pastry is golden brown.

Lamb chops with onion sauce

Onion sauce and lamb chops go together and this is how my grandmother used to serve them. The chops come out of the oven full of flavour, juicy and tender.

450 g (1 lb) onions, sliced
50 g (2 oz) butter
1 teaspoon sugar
1 tablespoon flour
150 ml ($\frac{1}{4}$ pint) milk
salt

freshly milled black pepper
4 chump chops
4 sprigs of rosemary, thyme or
    marjoram
1–2 tablespoons chopped parsley

Boil the onion slices in a little water in a small saucepan for ten minutes. Drain them well but keep 150 ml ($\frac{1}{4}$ pint) of the liquid. Wipe out the saucepan and melt the butter in it. Add the drained onions and sugar and cook them very gently for 10–15 minutes, until they are soft and pale gold. Stir in the flour and cook for 2 minutes, stirring all the time, before adding the reserved cooking liquid and the milk. Stir until the sauce boils, season with salt and pepper and set over a very low heat to reduce and thicken a little.

Heat the oven to Gas 7/425°F/220°C. Lay the chops in a flameproof gratin dish with the sprigs of herbs on top. Season them with pepper and put them into the oven for 5–10 minutes, until they are beginning to brown. Remove the herbs, turn the chops over and pour the sauce on top. Return to the oven for a further 10–15 minutes. Sprinkle with the parsley and serve

Sausages

Real sausages, as opposed to the characterless mass-produced variety, are going through something of a renaissance. They can be found in good butchers and some enterprising farm shops, often made by the proprietor. There are even specialist shops opening, not perhaps in their droves, but in sufficient numbers to make it possible for most of us to get hold of anything from the traditional fat Cumberland, sage- and ginger-flavoured Lincolnshire, herby Oxfordshire and a host of new inventions, imaginatively spiked with ingredients like garlic, spices, all kinds of herbs, leek and apple. Pork is the most likely meat to be used, but it is also possible to obtain ones made with wild boar, lamb, pheasant or venison. Henrietta Green lists over a hundred suppliers in her *Food Lover's Guide to Britain*, some of whom will despatch orders by post.

If all else fails, it isn't hard to make your own. The difficulty is getting the skins to put them in. If you have a friendly butcher, he might oblige but for those who shop in the supermarket, there is very little hope. If you can get sausage skins, soak them for a couple of hours in water to rid them of their salt. A sausage maker is a useful buy for those who intend to make a lot of sausages, otherwise use a forcing bag as in the method below. On the other hand, you can make skinless sausages. Either roll the mixture into sausage shapes or form it into flat cakes, which are perhaps easier to control.

This recipe is based on one from Gloucestershire. The finished sausages can be grilled or fried for 10–15 minutes in very little fat until golden brown all over and cooked right through or baked for 25–30 minutes in an oven heated to Gas 5/375°F/190°C. Grilled, fried or baked, sausages have an affinity with fried apple rings or apple sauce and as a change try them with stump, which is a mixture of potato, carrot and swede all mashed together (see Roots).

450 g (1 lb) lean pork, minced	$\frac{1}{4}$ teaspoon each dried thyme and
150 g (6 oz) beef or vegetarian	marjoram
suet	salt
100 g (4 oz) white breadcrumbs	freshly milled black pepper
freshly grated nutmeg	sausage skins or flour for coating

Mix the pork, suet, breadcrumbs, nutmeg and herbs together very thoroughly and season generously with salt and pepper. If using sausage skins, knot one end of a 50 cm (20 in) length and fill it by using a forcing bag with a wide nozzle. To do this, place the open end over the nozzle and push the skin over the nozzle like a sock. Force in the meat, opening up the length of skin as you go until it is filled. Knot

it and twist the skin at 8 cm (3 in) intervals to form the sausages.
Repeat the process with another length of sausage skin and remaining
sausage meat. Set aside for 1 hour to firm up.

If sausage skins are not available, form the sausage meat into a long
roll and cut into sausage lengths, or form it into flat cakes about the
size of a hamburger. Coat evenly with flour.

Bacon and egg pie

Perfect for a picnic, bacon and egg pie is best eaten with the fingers – a
piece in one hand, a ripe tomato in the other. For me it epitomizes the
reward earned, sitting wrapped in a towel on a stony beach like
Devon's Budleigh Salterton, after having been encouraged by the
grown-ups (who remained clad in their wind-cheating clothes) to take
a dip in a far from calm sea. The pie can be eaten cold although it is
nicest when warm. As it takes not much longer to make than a pile of
sandwiches, it can be made on the day of the picnic itself.

225 g (8 oz) shortcrust pastry   freshly milled black pepper
4 rashers back bacon   freshly grated nutmeg
4 eggs   2 tablespoons chopped parsley
150 ml ($\frac{1}{4}$ pint) single cream   little milk
salt

Divide the pastry into two and roll each piece out into a circle large
enough to cover a pie plate or flan tin 20 cm (8 in) diameter. Use one
circle to line the dish and brush the edges all round with a little water.
Lay the bacon rashers on top and break the eggs over the bacon,
taking care that the yolks remain intact. Pour over the cream and
season with the salt, pepper and nutmeg. Sprinkle over the parsley.
Cover with the remaining pastry circle, pressing the edges together and
mark all round with the prongs of a fork. Cut a slit in the top and
brush all over with a little milk. Set aside for 30 minutes. Heat the
oven to Gas 6/400°F/200°C. Bake for 25–30 minutes until the pastry is
golden brown.

Pease pudding

If pease pudding had reached us via the Continent those English who
are a little snobbish about food would treat it with the same respect as

those from the North-East who invented it – though this respect was not felt by sailors, who called it dog's body. It is eaten with any kind of pork dish. Try it with roast pork, ham, sausages or saveloys. Of course on its home ground it can be bought ready prepared from butchers' shops and is also sold in cans all over England. Don't be surprised if the colour of your home-made pease pudding bears no resemblance to the ready-prepared variety. This is sometimes intensified with the aid of green dye, although rumour has it Brussels is trying to put an end to this.

450 g (1 lb) dried split peas	2 tablespoons chopped mint
50 g (2 oz) butter	salt
1 egg, beaten	freshly milled black pepper

Soak the split peas overnight in cold water. The next day, drain them, cover with fresh water, bring to the boil and simmer, covered, for 1 hour. Drain them and purée them in a food processor or liquidizer. Add the butter, beaten egg and mint, mix well and season with salt and pepper.

The pudding now needs to be either steamed or baked. To steam, put the mixture into a buttered pudding basin, cover with foil and stand it in a saucepan half filled with water. Simmer, covered, for 40–45 minutes, until the pudding is firm. Alternatively, turn the mixture into a buttered oven dish, cover with foil and bake for 30 minutes in a pre-heated oven at Gas 4/350°F/180°C.

Forcemeat balls

Traditionally served with game dishes, either roasted or stewed, or roast meats like pork, forcemeat balls are easy to prepare. The name has nothing to do with forcing, it derives from the Latin *farcire*, to stuff, and forcemeat balls are made when the meat with which they are to be served is not suitable for stuffing. It is an old-fashioned name for what we call stuffing but sounds more elegant in this context! The herbs can be varied to suit the meat the forcemeat is to accompany.

50 g (2 oz) fresh breadcrumbs
25 g (1 oz) beef or vegetarian
  suet
1 tablespoon chopped parsley
½ teaspoon dried thyme or sage
finely grated peel of 1 lemon

1 rasher bacon, finely chopped
salt
freshly milled black pepper
1 egg, beaten
oil for frying

Mix all the dry ingredients together and bind with the beaten egg.
Form into balls 2–3 cm (1 in) across. Heat the oil in a frying pan and
when it is hot fry them for about 5 minutes, turning them over as they
cook, until they are golden brown.

Herb vinegars

Vinegars flavoured with herbs like tarragon, basil, dill, rosemary, mint
and sage add a subtle flavour to salads. Rose or violet petals can also
be used and nasturtium flowers make a particularly attractive vinegar
packed in a bottle with a clove or two of garlic, a chopped shallot, salt
and cayenne pepper.

   Pack a jar with your chosen herb or mixture of herbs. Pour over 600
ml (1 pint) of white wine or cider vinegar. Cover and leave for 2–3
weeks. Strain into a clean bottle and add a fresh sprig of herbs.

Garlic or shallot vinegar

For something tangier, make garlic or shallot vinegar, which custom
decreed should be done between Midsummer and Michaelmas when
the new season's crop are at their sweetest. You can use these vinegars
to flavour salads, or add a sprinkling to sauces or gravies.

1 head of garlic or 2–3 shallots

600 ml (1 pint) white wine or
           cider vinegar

Peel and chop the garlic or shallots. Put them in a jar and cover with
the vinegar. Leave for 10 days. Strain and bottle.

Spices

Likky (leek) tart

Scotch woodcock

Potted trout or salmon

Potted shrimps

Potted game

Bloater paste

Crab ramekins

Grey mullet with cream

Stuffed herrings with mustard

Stargazy (sardine) pie

Haddock in cream

Devilled whitebait

Hen on her nest (pot-roast chicken with eggs)

White devil (spiced leftover chicken)

Gilded apples (pork meatballs)

Pheasant with mushrooms

Kedgeree

Ginger cream

Spiced pears

Million (pumpkin) pie

Treacle tart

Cinnamon toast

Rice pudding

Gingerbread

Mulled and spiced ales

Likky tart

Leek pies appear all over England from the North-West to Cornwall where they were eaten on feast days and known as likky pies. This modern version dispenses with the pastry lid and so becomes a tart. It is light with a subtle flavour of nutmeg, puffed and golden, the top dotted with little pieces of crisp bacon. Eat it warm as a starter or as a simple lunch or supper dish.

225 g (8 oz) shortcrust pastry
450 g (1 lb) leeks, chopped
salt
2 eggs
150 ml ($\frac{1}{4}$ pint) single cream
freshly milled black pepper
generous pinch of nutmeg
6 rashers streaky bacon, chopped

Roll out the pastry and line a 20 cm (8 in) loose-bottomed flan tin and set it aside to rest.

Blanch the chopped leeks for 5 minutes in boiling, salted water and drain well.

Heat the oven to Gas 6/400°F/200°C.

Beat the eggs until frothy and beat in the cream. Season with salt, pepper and nutmeg. Bake the pastry shell blind for 15 minutes (see page 42). Spread the leeks over the base of the pastry. Pour on the egg and cream mixture and scatter the bacon pieces over the top. Bake for 30–35 minutes until puffed and golden.

Scotch woodcock

Just as Welsh rabbit has no rabbit and doesn't come from Wales, so this savoury of anchovies on toast, topped with a rich sauce made with cream and egg yolks doesn't come from Scotland and contains no woodcock. The name is a play on the fact that the English regard the Scots as perhaps a little too careful with their money and that woodcock are rather rare and expensive. Once eaten towards the end of a meal, nowadays Scotch woodcock is more likely to be served as a starter or as a light lunch or supper dish.

Cayenne pepper became popular in the eighteenth century. Made from the ground seeds and flesh of dried red peppers, it is less coarse than chilli powder which is made in the same way. The name originates from the South American Tupis who called it *kyinha*.

4 anchovy fillets, chopped
4 slices of buttered toast
3 egg yolks
150 ml (¼ pint) double cream

freshly milled black pepper
cayenne pepper
1–2 tablespoons chopped parsley

Lay the chopped anchovies on the buttered toast and put them on a plate in a warm oven. Beat the egg yolks with the cream and season with pepper and cayenne – no salt, the anchovies are salty enough. Pour the mixture into a small saucepan and heat gently, stirring all the time until it thickens, taking care it does not boil or it will curdle. Pour over the anchovy toasts and serve piping hot.

Potted trout or salmon

In the Lake District, especially around Windermere, potted charr was a great delicacy. It used to be sold in special dishes decorated with fish. Nowadays the charr, a close relation to the trout and salmon, have all but disappeared and the dishes themselves have found their way into the antique shops. However, all is not lost because trout or salmon, either fresh or smoked, can be potted instead. Make the day before and serve with thin slices of toast and quartered lemons as a starter.

Mace, the dried aril covering the nutmeg, came to England in the fourteenth century and from then on featured widely in cooking. Bright scarlet and fleshy when fresh, this fibrous covering is flattened and dried and sold either as blades or ground into a yellow-ochre powder. It is more expensive than nutmeg, with a sweeter, delicate flavour. Powdered mace should be kept tightly covered as it soon loses its aroma.

225 g (8 oz) trout fillets
¼ teaspoon powdered mace
1 clove
1 bay leaf

½ teaspoon crushed whole black
   peppercorns
salt
100 g (4 oz) unsalted butter
clarified butter (see Etceteras)

Heat the oven to Gas 4/350°F/180°C.
   Lay the fillets in a shallow dish with the mace, clove, bay leaf,

peppercorns and salt. Cut the butter into slices and lay them over the fish. Bake for 10–15 minutes until the fish is just cooked. Remove the fish and strain the liquid into a deep dish or jug and set aside in a cool place.

Skin the fish and remove any lingering bones. As soon as the butter has risen to the top of the liquid, put the fish into a processor with just the melted butter (a bulb baster helps to remove it easily, or spoon it out carefully). Process until the mixture is smooth. Taste and if necessary add more seasoning, the mace flavour should be quite pronounced. Put into small pots and when cold cover each with a thin layer of clarified butter. Covered with foil or food-wrap and refrigerated, it will keep for two to three days.

Potted shrimps

Morecambe Bay has been famous since the eighteenth century for its potted shrimps and if you go to the Lakes or to the Lancashire coast, you will still find them being served for tea in the local cafés or sold at the fishmongers.

The dividing line between shrimps and prawns is a narrow one. Because they are fiddly to peel, very small, brown shrimps are best eaten as they are, shells and all, with lemon juice and brown bread and butter, although they can be pulverized in a food blender and mixed with melted butter and spices to become a sort of shrimp paste. For potting, it is better to use the larger pink prawns, which are easier to peel.

If you don't want to eat your potted shrimps for tea, serve them as a starter instead, with thin slices of brown bread and butter.

100 g (4 oz) unsalted butter
¼ teaspoon each mace, nutmeg
  and cayenne pepper
450 g (l lb) peeled prawns
salt

freshly milled black pepper
clarified butter (see Etceteras)
bunch of watercress
1 lemon, cut in wedges

Melt the butter with the mace, nutmeg and cayenne pepper. Stir in the prawns. Season to taste with salt and pepper. Put into small pots and cover each with a layer of clarified butter. Allow to cool and refrigerate.

Before serving, stand the pots in a bowl of very hot water; as soon as the butter softens, turn them out on to individual plates, surround with the watercress and garnish with the lemon wedges.

Potted game

Seasoned with mixed spice (a mixture of cinnamon, coriander, dill, ginger, cloves and nutmeg), potting is a delicious way of using up the remains of a pheasant or other kinds of game. Spread it on canapés to serve with drinks or eat it with toast as a starter. It should be kept for a week before it is eaten.

cooked pheasant or other game
one-third of its weight in
    softened butter
lemon juice
1–2 teaspoons sherry
salt

freshly milled black pepper
mixed spice
25 g (1 oz) concentrated or
    clarified butter, melted (see
    Etceteras)
1 bay leaf

Remove the meat from the bones and discard all skin and gristle. Weigh it before chopping or mincing it. Mash it with the butter and mix in a squeeze of lemon juice, the sherry, salt, pepper and mixed spice to taste. Put it into a jar and pour over the concentrated or clarified butter. Garnish with a bay leaf. Keep in a cool place for a week and, once started, eat within two days.

Bloater paste

Great Yarmouth and Lowestoft in East Anglia were made famous by their herring industry. Once caught, herrings deteriorate quickly so the people became skilful in salting and smoking the fish, producing red herrings, kippers, buckling and bloaters. Bloaters are soaked in brine and cold-smoked and, because they are left ungutted, they have a distinctive gamy taste. They are nice split open, spread with butter and lightly grilled, or they can be eaten raw with sour cream or yoghurt. In this recipe they are turned into a paste to be eaten with buttered toast or scrambled eggs, or made into sandwiches. If you can't get bloaters, use smoked haddock or kippers instead.

2 bloaters
unsalted butter (see method)
juice of ½ lemon

¼ teaspoon cayenne pepper
1 slice lemon

Put the bloaters into a bowl and pour over sufficient boiling water to cover. Set aside for 5–10 minutes, then drain well, remove the skin and all the bones. Weigh the flesh and mash it with an equal weight of unsalted butter. Add the lemon juice and cayenne pepper and mix well. Transfer to a small bowl and put the slice of lemon on top.

Crab ramekins

Serve this West Country recipe as a starter followed by a light main course. The crab meat is mixed with spices, anchovies and lemon juice before being piled into ramekin dishes (or you could use scallop shells) which are then put under a hot grill.

Crab are not something to prepare in a hurry but their flavour is so rich and luscious, some people think even better than lobster, that they are worth every bit of trouble. They are sold either live or boiled and, if you don't mind paying a bit more, already dressed. Make sure you buy from a reliable fishmonger and that, if already cooked, the crab has been freshly boiled.

You will find detailed instructions on how to boil and prepare crab in my book *Simply Fish*, but for this recipe all you need to know, if you are unfamiliar with the process, is how to extract the meat from a ready-cooked crab. To do this, lay it on its back with the head towards you and twist off the legs and claws. Extract the meat from legs and claws by cracking them either with a rolling pin or nutcrackers and using a skewer to pull out the stubborn bits. Next, twist off and discard the tail flap. Using a knife prise the central portion away from the main shell. Split the central piece in half and scoop out all the meat, only discarding the gills and stomach sac near the mouth and the greenish lungs known as dead man's fingers. Now tackle the main shell, removing all the white meat and the brown meat under the rim, throw out the rubbery red bits which are the beginnings of the new shell.

2 cooked crabs	juice of $\frac{1}{2}$ lemon, plus 1 lemon,
cayenne pepper	quartered
mace	50 g (2 oz) butter
4 tablespoons breadcrumbs	1 tablespoon chopped parsley
4 anchovy fillets, chopped	

Mix the crab meat with the cayenne pepper, mace, breadcrumbs, anchovy fillets and lemon juice. Turn on the grill to heat. Melt the butter in a saucepan, add the crab meat and stir until piping hot. Pile into 4 warmed ramekin dishes and put under the hot grill until the tops turn golden brown. Sprinkle over the parsley and serve each with a lemon quarter.

Grey mullet with cream

This method of cooking grey mullet comes from the Cornish port of Penzance. The fish is flavoured with lemon juice and spices before being smeared with clotted cream and baked in the oven.

Grey mullet (which, incidentally, is no relation of the red mullet) is not always available, although it is a delicious fish and relatively cheap. It lives on plants growing in the mud and has a very long gut, so make sure the fishmonger thoroughly cleans it for you and removes the gills. At the same time ask him to scale it and remove the fins. The fish vary in size so it is difficult to give exact quantities, but as a rule of thumb allow 225–300 g (8–10 oz) per head.

1 or 2 grey mullet, depending on
  size
2 lemons
salt
$\frac{1}{2}$ teaspoon mace

pinch of cayenne
2–3 tablespoons clotted or
  double cream
1–2 tablespoons chopped parsley

Heat the oven to Gas 5/375°F/190°C.

Lay the fish in a buttered ovenproof dish. Add the grated peel and juice of one lemon and season with salt, mace and cayenne. Smear over the cream and bake the fish in the oven for 15–20 minutes for small fish, 25–30 minutes for large. (When it is done the eyes will be white and the flesh of the fish opaque.)

Serve garnished with remaining lemon cut in quarters and sprinkled with the parsley.

Stuffed herrings with mustard

Mustard was introduced to us by the Romans. Made from the crushed seeds of plants related to the cabbage family, the pungency is obtained by mixing them with cold water which releases an essential oil. If mixed with hot water or vinegar, the enzymes are killed and the taste can be unpleasantly bitter. If using powdered mustard, mix it and allow to stand for about 10 minutes to develop the flavour. It does not keep and should be made as and when needed.

Mustard and bacon go well with herring, as does oatmeal, and this Kentish recipe for stuffed herrings combines all three. There is no doubt these are bony fish and it is a pity that this can be enough to prevent people ever enjoying their unique, slightly bitter flavour. To overcome this drawback cooks all over the country devised recipes in which the fish were first boned and then stuffed.

A good fishmonger will bone the herrings for you but if you have to do it yourself, first slit the fish along the belly to the tail. Lay it belly-side down on a board and press all along the backbone with the ball of your thumbs. You'll feel the bone coming away from the flesh as you do so. Turn the fish over and carefully, using your fingers and the point of a knife, ease out the backbone with all its thread-like ribs, cutting it away from the head and tail with scissors. Drape the fish over the back of your hand and use tweezers to remove any small bones that lurk behind.

4 tablespoons breadcrumbs	salt
handful of parsley, chopped	freshly milled black pepper
25 g (1 oz) butter	4 herrings
juice and finely grated peel of 1 lemon	4 rashers streaky bacon
	4 tablespoons fine oatmeal
1 teaspoon ready-made mustard	

Heat the oven to Gas 6/400°F/200°C.

Make the stuffing by mixing the breadcrumbs with the parsley, butter, grated lemon peel and juice and the mustard. Season with salt and pepper. Fill the cavity of each fish. Lay them in a buttered ovenproof dish. Cut the rashers of bacon in half lengthwise, roll them up and put them around the fish. Scatter over the oatmeal and bake for 25 minutes.

Stargazy pie

Stargazy pasties containing pilchards (just another name for adult sardines) used to be sold in the markets in Truro and other Cornish fishing ports. The fish were laid in a line on a strip of pastry, encased by another with just their heads and tails protruding. They were sold hot, the fishmonger cutting off only the number of fish each customer demanded.

The same fish were also made into stargazy pies, and Jane Grigson relates how there is a tradition in Mousehole to serve them on 23 December, which they call Tom Bawcock's Eve in memory of a fisherman whose catch on that particular day saved the villagers from a hungry Christmas. The romantic-sounding name reflects the fact that the fish are gazing at the stars, but the more basic reason for serving them so is because although the heads are inedible they contain rich oil, so this way none of it was lost and nor was any of the space between the layers of pastry.

Sardines are full of flavour. They should be spanking fresh, with bright eyes. Wash and clean each fish and remove the backbone by slitting along the belly with a sharp knife. Open out the fish and lay it on its back, gently press all along the backbone with the ball of your thumb to loosen it. Turn the fish over and ease out the bone, cutting it away from the head.

8 sardines	1–2 tablespoons chopped thyme
mustard	and parsley
1 onion, finely chopped	225 g (8 oz) shortcrust pastry
	1 egg yolk, beaten

Clean and bone the fish but leave on the heads. Fill each cavity with a little mustard, chopped onion and herbs. Divide the pastry in half and roll out each piece into a circle the size of a pie plate. Line the plate with the first circle and brush the outside edge with the beaten egg. Arrange the fish around the plate like the spokes of a wheel, their heads overlapping the rim. Cover with the second circle of pastry, letting the heads hang out, but sealing the pastry between each fish. Set aside for 30 minutes. Heat the oven to Gas 6/400°F/200°C. Cut a slit in the centre, brush all over with the remaining egg and bake for 30–35 minutes.

Haddock in cream

This is a quick and easy way with haddock fillets though not for the diet-conscious because they are poached in cream which right at the end is flavoured with mustard and lemon juice. Eat it with a dark green vegetable like spinach or broccoli and steamed parsleyed potatoes.

2 tablespoons flour

salt

freshly milled black pepper

4 haddock fillets

25 g (1 oz) butter

150 ml ($\frac{1}{4}$ pint) double cream

1 teaspoon ready-made mustard

juice of 1 lemon

Put the flour on to a plate, season it with salt and pepper and coat the fillets in it. Melt the butter in a shallow flameproof dish, remove from the heat, lay the fillets in it and turn them over and over so they are coated in butter. Pour over the cream. Bring just to the boil, then reduce the heat and let it barely simmer for 15–20 minutes, until the fish turns opaque and is cooked.

Transfer the fish to a warm serving dish. Stir the mustard into the creamy cooking liquid, raise the heat and let it boil until it thickens and reduces by half. Stir in the lemon juice, pour over the fish and serve.

Devilled whitebait

Whitebait are not a species of fish but the small fry of other fish like herrings and sprats. The Thames was once famous for them and they used to be served up in droves at feasts held in Dagenham and Greenwich to celebrate the draining of the Essex marshes. Nowadays, strict controls abound as to the size of the catch and you are most likely to come across them frozen rather than fresh. Make sure they are completely defrosted before cooking.

450 g (l lb) whitebait

milk

6 tablespoons flour

1 teaspoon salt

1 teaspoon cayenne pepper

oil for frying

2 lemons, cut in quarters

brown bread and butter

Put the fish into a bowl and cover them with cold milk. After a few minutes, drain them in a sieve. Put the flour into a bag with the salt and cayenne pepper. Add the fish and shake the bag gently until the fish are coated all over in the seasoned flour. Heat the oven to Gas 2/ 300°F/150°C and line a baking sheet with greaseproof paper.

Half fill a deep frying pan with oil and when it is piping hot, put a handful of the fish into the frying basket, shake it to remove excess flour and deep-fry the whitebait for 2–3 minutes, until they are golden. Transfer them to the baking tray and put into the oven. Repeat this frying operation until all the fish are cooked.

Serve the fish garnished with the quarters of lemon and a plate of brown bread and butter. Hand round more cayenne pepper separately.

Hen on her nest

Dating from the nineteenth century, this Norfolk farmhouse recipe has a large fowl flavoured with spices and herbs served on a nest of mashed potatoes or rice, surrounded by a ring of hard-boiled eggs. The children would be given the eggs while the adults ate the chicken.

Fowls, egg-laying birds which have ceased producing, are hard to come by nowadays, but the recipe works well with a pot-roasted chicken, although I doubt if the children will be satisfied with just the eggs! Half an hour or so before the dish is ready, prepare some boiled rice or mashed potatoes.

1 carrot, chopped	salt
1 onion, chopped	freshly milled black pepper
1.5 kg (3½–4 lb) chicken	6 eggs
2 tablespoons oil	50 g (2 oz) butter
1 teaspoon mace	25 g (1 oz) flour
1 sliver root ginger or 1 teaspoon	cayenne pepper
ground	3–4 tablespoons double cream
sprigs of parsley and thyme	350 g (12 oz) boiled rice or
300 ml (½ pint) stock or water	900 g (2 lb) mashed potatoes

Heat the oven to Gas 5/375°F/190°C.

Put the chopped carrot and onion into a flameproof casserole in which the chicken will sit comfortably and lay the bird on top. Sprinkle with the oil and add the mace, ginger, parsley and thyme. Pour over the stock or water and season with salt and pepper. Bring to the boil on top of the stove, put on the lid and put into the oven for 1 hour. Remove the lid and raise the heat to Gas 7/425°F/220°C and cook for a further 10 minutes or so to brown. Put the bird on to a serving dish, cover with foil and keep warm. Measure 300 ml (½ pint) of the cooking liquid into a jug.

Hard-boil the eggs for 10 minutes. Make the sauce by melting the butter, stir in the flour and let it cook for 2 minutes, stirring all the time. Gradually mix in the liquid from the jug and let it simmer gently for 5–10 minutes. Season with salt, pepper and cayenne. Stir in the cream and pour into a sauce boat. Shell the eggs.

Serve the chicken on a nest of rice or mashed potatoes, arrange the hard-boiled eggs around and decorate with the sprigs of parsley. Serve the sauce separately.

White Devil

Devilled or Mephistophelian sauces were very popular in the nineteenth century, especially among the officer classes. They were created to give spice to leftover pieces of poultry or game which could be served hot or cold, as in this recipe from Romano's in the Strand which was famous for its private dining rooms and intimate suppers. It is coloured with turmeric which originally was exported from India overland via Arabia and used to dye cloth. It has a strong, distinctive flavour.

The quantities in this recipe are for two, but of course it can be adapted for larger numbers. Although chicken breasts are specified in the recipe, you could use cooked drumsticks or thighs. If you want to try this recipe using fresh chicken breasts, poach them first in a little water, flavoured with lemon juice, a bay leaf and a sprig or two of parsley or thyme. Give them about 5 minutes, until they feel springy to the touch.

2 cooked chicken breasts, each divided into two fillets
2 teaspoons ready-made English mustard
$\frac{1}{4}$ teaspoon cayenne pepper
$\frac{1}{4}$ teaspoon turmeric
150 ml ($\frac{1}{4}$ pint) double cream
salt
freshly milled black pepper

Heat the oven to Gas 6/400°F/200°C.

Lay the pieces of chicken breast in a buttered ovenproof dish. Mix the mustard, cayenne pepper, turmeric and cream together. Season with salt and pepper. Spread this mixture over the chicken and put the dish at the top of the oven for 10–15 minutes until hot through, bubbling and golden brown.

Gilded apples

A grand name for meatballs the size of small apples made from the remains of a joint of roast pork, which from medieval times were known as *pommes dorres* (sic). They were spit roasted and served well sprinkled with parsley or 'gilded' with saffron. In this recipe they are dipped in batter and deep-fried in oil. If you prefer you could shallow fry them without batter but dipped in beaten egg and rolled in breadcrumbs.

Popular with the Romans who introduced it to the English, ginger originated in Asia but it was taken to Jamaica by the Spanish and it is there that the best ginger is grown. It was immensely popular in the Middle Ages, being used very much as we use pepper today. Ground ginger is most useful for adding to cakes and sweet dishes but root ginger, which is widely available, gives a fresher and more interesting flavour to dishes like this one. Buy a 'hand' that looks firm and fresh and cut off slivers as you need them; the root heals itself and will keep for some time.

2 tablespoons flour	sliver ginger, finely chopped or
salt	$\frac{1}{2}$ teaspoon powdered
1 tablespoon olive oil plus oil for	1 clove garlic
frying	1 teaspoon mace
150 ml ($\frac{1}{4}$ pint) water	2 tablespoons chopped parsley
450 g (l lb) cooked pork	and sage
	freshly milled black pepper
	3 eggs

Make the batter by mixing the flour with a pinch of salt, 1 tablespoon oil and the water. Beat well and set aside for 30 minutes.

Mince the pork with the ginger and garlic. Stir in the mace, parsley and sage. Season with salt and pepper. Bind with two of the eggs plus the yolk of the third, saving the egg white for the batter. With damp hands, form the mixture into 8 small balls.

Beat the egg white until stiff and fold into the batter. Heat the oil for deep-frying until very hot. Dip the pork 'apples' into the batter and fry until golden.

Pheasant with mushrooms

It is the mace which proclaims this recipe's Englishness, which reminds me of the sort of dish I've come across in France bearing the title hunter's or even poacher's pheasant. Quick and easy to prepare, the bird is moist and tender and delicious served with steamed potatoes scattered with parsley and perhaps a dish of jugged celery (see Apples) or glazed turnips (see Roots).

50 g (2 oz) butter
1 tablespoon oil
1 pheasant
1 onion, chopped
2–3 rashers streaky bacon,
   chopped
225 g (8 oz) flat mushrooms,
   sliced
salt

freshly milled black pepper
$\frac{1}{2}$ teaspoon ground mace
$\frac{1}{2}$ teaspoon dried thyme
1 bay leaf
sprig of parsley
150 ml ($\frac{1}{4}$ pint) dry white wine or
   strong dry cider
watercress for garnish

Heat the oven to Gas 4/350°F/180°C.

Melt the butter with the oil in a flameproof casserole and brown the pheasant all over. Remove to a plate. Add the onion and bacon to the casserole and fry them gently until golden. Add the mushrooms and continue cooking over a low heat until they have absorbed all the moisture. Set the pheasant on top, breast side down. Add the salt, pepper, mace and herbs. Pour in the wine or cider, let it bubble, put on the lid and transfer the casserole to the oven for 1 hour.

Put the pheasant and mushrooms on to a serving dish and keep them warm. Return the casserole to the hob and boil the sauce hard for a few minutes until it thickens and reduces by about half. Pour over the bird and serve garnished with the watercress.

Kedgeree

As just about everybody knows, kedgeree originated in India, the name being an anglicized corruption of the word *kicheri*, the staple peasant dish of rice and beans. The Victorians turned it into a fashionable breakfast dish, adding fish and eggs and leaving out the beans. If you want to be truly traditional make it with smoked finnan haddock, although it can be made with almost any sort of white fish or salmon, fresh or canned. It is a great way of using up leftover fish. If using raw fish, poach it for 5 minutes or so (in milk, if using haddock, or water for other fish), flavoured with a little lemon juice, parsley, a bay leaf and peppercorns.

1 tablespoon oil

1 onion, chopped

150 g (6 oz) long-grain rice

300 ml (½ pint) boiling water

salt

4 eggs

150 g (6 oz) cooked fish

50 g (2 oz) butter

grated nutmeg

cayenne pepper

2 tablespoons chopped parsley

2 tablespoons snipped chives

Heat the oil in a heavy-based saucepan and fry the chopped onion over a low heat for about 5 minutes, until golden. Add the rice and ½ teaspoon salt, stir well and pour over the boiling water. Cover and put over a very low heat for 20 minutes. Then remove from the heat and set aside for 10 minutes.

Meanwhile, hard boil two of the eggs for 9 minutes, drain them and put under running cold water for a few minutes. Shell and chop them finely. Flake the fish and discard any skin and bones.

Melt the butter in a large frying pan, add the fish and let it heat through gently, add the chopped eggs and nutmeg. Fork in the hot rice, season to taste with the cayenne pepper and salt. Beat the remaining 2 eggs and stir them into the mixture. As soon as it is piping hot turn on to a warm serving dish, sprinkle over the parsley and chives and serve at once.

Ginger cream

The use of ginger in cooking goes back to the Romans but ginger preserved in syrup only came to England at the beginning of the eighteenth century. Nowadays it usually appears around Christmas packed in Oriental china pots in upmarket food shops, although it is possible to buy it much more cheaply all the year round in glass jars. It is delicious chopped and eaten with bananas or made into this spicy cream which only takes seconds to prepare.

4 pieces preserved ginger   300 ml (½ pint) whipped cream

Chop the ginger and put a little into 4 cocotte dishes or wine glasses. Top with the whipped cream. Chill. Just before serving, pour a little of the juice from the jar over each.

Spiced pears

Ever since the Middle Ages, the English have enjoyed stewed pears flavoured with spices and stained crimson by the wine in which they are cooked. There are many variations on the theme. One sixteenth-century method suggests layering them in vine leaves and among Hannah Glasse's recipes she has one to turn them purple. As this effect is achieved by cooking them rather riskily covered with a pewter plate, she obviously didn't know about lead poisoning, although she warns you must watch to make sure it doesn't melt!

Wine seems safer. If you haven't got wine, follow the Devonshire custom and use a good dry cider instead. The fruit turn to pale gold which darkens to amber the longer they are kept. Pears like this were sold at the Barnstaple autumn fair.

The spices vary but nearly always include a cinnamon stick and often ginger or cloves. It is a perfect way of dealing with those hard little Conference pears which, because they never seem to ripen, are sold quite cheaply. Cook the pears either on top of the stove or in an earthenware pot in a low oven. They are delicious warm or cold with a good dollop of thick cream or yoghurt.

6–8 small, hard pears	4 tablespoons caster or soft
150 ml ($\frac{1}{4}$ pint) red wine or	brown sugar
strong dry cider	2 or 3 whole cloves
150 ml ($\frac{1}{4}$ pint) water	piece of root ginger or 1
	teaspoon powdered
	1 stick cinnamon

Peel the pears with a swivel-bladed peeler, leaving the stalks on. Stand them in a saucepan or earthenware casserole and pour over the red wine or cider and 150 ml ($\frac{1}{4}$ pint) water. Add the sugar, cloves, ginger and cinnamon. Either bring them to the boil on top of the stove, cover and simmer for 1–2 hours until tender (the time will vary according to the ripeness of the pears); or put the casserole in a cool oven, Gas 2/300°F/150°C, when they will take at least 2 hours.

Transfer the cooked pears to a serving bowl and boil the liquid hard until it is reduced by half. Strain over the pears and set them aside to cool slightly and absorb even more of the colour of the wine or cider.

Million pie

Norfolk's pilgrim fathers took pumpkin pie to America where it became part of the annual Thanksgiving feast. The name 'million' comes from the old East Anglian word for a gourd and the pie can also be made with marrow. This version is for an uncovered tart which makes a filling and comfortable dessert on a chilly autumn evening when eaten hot or warm with cream.

Before cutting the flesh into cubes, the pumpkin must be peeled, de-pithed and seeded which is made easier if you first cut it into manageable segments. A pumpkin yields about half its weight in flesh once it is prepared for cooking. When fresh pumpkins are not available, canned can be used instead.

225 g (8 oz) shortcrust pastry	1 teaspoon grated nutmeg
350 g (12 oz) pumpkin flesh, cut into cubes	1 teaspoon ground cinnamon
	$\frac{1}{2}$ teaspoon ground ginger
1 egg	2 tablespoons dried mixed fruit
50 g (2 oz) brown sugar	4 tablespoons apricot jam

Roll out the pastry and line a flan tin about 20 cm (8 in) in diameter. Set aside to chill.

Put the cubes of pumpkin flesh into a pan with a little water. Simmer them for 10–15 minutes until soft. Drain very well in a colander, pressing a saucer or small plate on top to squeeze out as much moisture as possible, then mash.

Heat the oven to Gas 6/400°F/200°C. Partially bake the pastry shell blind for 10 minutes, first covering it with a sheet of foil weighed down by either rice or dried beans.

Beat the pumpkin flesh with the egg, sugar, nutmeg, cinnamon and ginger. Stir in the dried fruit. Spread the jam over the pastry base followed by the pumpkin mixture. Bake for 10–15 minutes, lower the heat to Gas 4/350°F/180°C and continue baking for a further 15 minutes.

Treacle tart

If you want this traditional North Country tart to be authentic you must make it in a pie plate, which can still be found in some iron-mongers. Otherwise, use a flan tin. It is a true nursery pudding, gooey and sticky and not for the diet-conscious.

150 g (6 oz) shortcrust pastry   6–8 tablespoons golden syrup
50 g (2 oz) white breadcrumbs   juice of ½ lemon
pinch of powdered ginger or
   cinnamon

Heat the oven to Gas 5/375°F/190°C.

Roll out the pastry to line a 20 cm (8 in) pie plate. Pinch the edge all round to make a fluted effect. Reserve the trimmings. Sprinkle over the breadcrumbs and the powdered ginger or cinnamon. Pour over the golden syrup and sprinkle with the lemon juice. Roll out the remaining pastry into thin strips and use these to make a criss-cross pattern over the top of the tart, pressing them firmly into the edge. Bake for 25 minutes. Eat warm or cold with cream or yoghurt.

Cinnamon toast

True cinnamon, which reached England in the fifteenth century, comes from Sri Lanka. It is the inner bark of a small tree, which is peeled and dried, forming thin, pale quills which are used whole to give flavour and a delicate pungency to dishes. In its powdered form it is most useful in cakes and puddings. Cassia, which comes from Burma and is sometimes confused with cinnamon, is coarser, with a stronger flavour.

This tea-time treat takes only minutes to prepare. It was a great favourite among Oxford students and is the sort of thing you might find on the menu of an olde worlde tea shoppe. There are two ways of making it. Either spread slices of toast with butter and sprinkle with cinnamon and caster sugar, or toast the bread on one side only, sprinkle with sugar and cinnamon and put under the grill until the sugar and cinnamon melt into each other. Whichever method you choose, cut off the crusts, cut the toast in squares and eat immediately.

Rice pudding

In my grandmother's recipe book, a baked rice pudding is described as 'a nice pudding for children' and I certainly found it so. It was one of my favourites, along with tapioca and sago. I loved the creamy, soft cereal and the dark, crisp skin which formed on top. I still do. These sorts of puddings should be eaten with a good dollop of jam and, for a treat, a spoonful or two of clotted cream. My grandmother always used to sprinkle her puddings with nutmeg but some people prefer to use cinnamon instead. Although it is nicest eaten hot, there is something appealing, too, about cold rice pudding, at least to fans like me.

butter
3 tablespoons pudding rice
2 tablespoons soft brown sugar

600 ml (1 pint) full cream milk
grated nutmeg or cinnamon

Heat the oven to Gas 2/300°F/150°C.

Butter a shallow ovenproof dish and put in the rice, sugar and milk. Stir to mix. Sprinkle grated nutmeg or cinnamon over the top and dot with small pieces of butter. Bake for 2 hours, stirring the pudding after 15 minutes and once more after a further 15 minutes. Bake undisturbed for the last $1\frac{1}{2}$ hours until a golden brown skin has formed on top and the rice is soft and creamy.

Gingerbread

In very early times, gingerbread was a sort of sweetmeat made with honey flavoured with ginger and spices, plumped out with breadcrumbs and patterned with gold leaf. Over the years it evolved and came to mean different things to different people. At Grasmere, in the Lake District, it became a crumbly cake handed round at the annual rush-bearing ceremony in August, which goes back to the days when the earth floors of churches were carpeted with straw. In Yorkshire, it metamorphosed into parkin, rich and sticky, dark with treacle and more than a hint of oatmeal, served especially on Guy Fawkes' night, sometimes with cheese or topped with stewed apples. In the West Country it is traditional to serve gingerbread with spiced ale at country fairs, only this time the gingerbread has become a small, crisp biscuit.

The following version is based on an eighteenth-century recipe and includes ginger, cinnamon, honey and black treacle, augmented with almonds and chopped candied cherries. It is a soft, gooey cake which should be made well ahead because it improves on keeping. The ingredients are many but the gingerbread itself is prepared in minutes.

100 g (4 oz) butter	$\frac{1}{2}$ teaspoon bicarbonate of soda
1 tablespoon honey	$\frac{1}{2}$ teaspoon ground ginger
150 g (6 oz) black treacle	$\frac{1}{2}$ teaspoon cinnamon
50 g (2 oz) dark brown sugar	1 tablespoon ground almonds
150 ml ($\frac{1}{4}$ pint) milk	2 tablespoons chopped candied
2 eggs	cherries
225 g (8 oz) plain flour, sifted	

Grease an 18 cm (7 in) square cake tin. Heat the oven to Gas 2/300°F/ 150°C.

Put the butter, honey, treacle, brown sugar and milk into a saucepan and warm over a low heat until they melt into each other. Remove from the heat.

Beat the eggs in a mixing bowl and pour in the melted treacle mixture and mix well. Stir in all the remaining ingredients. Pour into the cake tin and bake for 1–1$\frac{1}{2}$ hours until it feels springy and is leaving the sides of the tin. Allow to cool and remove from the tin. Wrap in foil and keep for at least 2 days before eating.

Mulled and spiced ales

These were warming drinks to be taken at any time to give strength to the weary labourer or traveller. Mulled ale contained eggs beaten in a large bowl with a little cold ale. This was then mixed with heated ale and the drink sweetened with sugar and flavoured with nutmeg. It was removed from the heat before it could curdle and a lump of butter was beaten into the mixture. Spiced ale, flavoured with cloves, ginger, allspice and cinnamon and laced with brandy, is a lighter drink and if you like beer you will enjoy its pungent flavour. It makes a change from mulled wine and is a cheaper alternative in freezing winters.

Cloves, which come from south-east Asia and were used by the Chinese long before Christianity, are the buds of an aromatic tree. They need to be used with discretion. Allspice, also known as Jamaica pepper, is the berry of a West Indian tree. Dried, the flavour is reminiscent of a mixture of cloves, cinnamon and nutmeg.

1.2 litres (2 pints) light ale
2 whole cloves
$\frac{1}{4}$ teaspoon powdered ginger
$\frac{1}{4}$ teaspoon ground allspice

1–2 cinnamon sticks
150 ml ($\frac{1}{4}$ pint) brandy
1 tablespoon soft brown sugar

Put the ale and spices into a saucepan and heat gently until just below boiling. Remove from the heat and stir in the brandy and sugar. Ladle into warmed glasses and serve at once.

A *dash of alcohol*

Scallops in their half shell

Trout with sorrel

Rack of lamb

Pheasant with celery

Chicken in red wine

Quail in vine leaves

Roasted guinea fowl with grapes

Farmer's wife partridges

Stewed pigeons

Venison in red wine

Parson's venison (marinated and casseroled leg of lamb)

Berkshire jugged steak

Oxtail

Cottage and shepherd's pie

Kate and Sidney (steak and kidney) pud or pie

Trifle or tipsy cake

Syllabub

Poor knights of Windsor (bread dipped in milk)

Devonshire junket

Egg nog

WINE, SHERRY, BRANDY ET AL

Wine-making goes back at least three millennia to the Mesopotamian and Egyptian civilizations but it was the Greeks who first produced it on a grand scale. Wine was finding its way to England well before the Roman occupation, but during this time vineyards were planted in many places including Silchester, Boxmoor in Hertfordshire and Gloucester, and the Emperor Probus in AD 280 designated Britain an official wine-producing area. Even so, not enough was produced to satisfy the Roman settlers so wine was imported from Italy, Spain and later from France, in particular from Bordeaux and Moselle.

The Romans probably gave us our first taste for wine in cooking and this was certainly encouraged by the Normans who planted vines in southern and eastern England; records even show wine-making around Lincoln and York. However, the vines' days were numbered from the time of Henry II. He was married to Eleanor of Aquitaine and soon the market was flooded with cheap wine from her Gascony vineyards. Decline in wine growing was exacerbated by the Wars of the Roses and later still by the dissolution of the monasteries (monks were enthusiastic wine growers). By Elizabethan times, hardly any native wine was produced. This further encouraged us to import it from all over France and the rest of Europe.

Sherry, so enthusiastically adopted by the English, originated in the wine-growing area around Jerez in Spain, and it is here that the only genuine sherry is made, although there are of course many excellent imitations. It was not considered a refined drink until the eighteenth century but was sold in quantity in the taverns, where it was known as *sherris sack*, sack being the general name for Spanish wines which became so popular in the time of Henry VIII. Originally known as *wyne seck*, a corruption of the French *vin sec*, these wines were dry on arrival in this country, too dry for popular taste, so they were liberally sweetened with sugar before being sold.

Fine Spanish sherry is far too good for cooking, better to use montilla, a sherry-type wine which in Spain is produced around Córdoba. It has a good flavour but is cheaper than sherry.

Port came to be known as the Englishman's wine in the eighteenth century when the duty on wines from Portugal was much less than on those from France, with whom, remember, we were frequently falling out. Originally just a simple red wine, the wine we shipped from Portugal was fortified with brandy to make it travel well and in time variations were invented, ranging from the cheaper ruby through to tawny ports and the expensive vintage varieties which are only made in exceptional years. For cooking use one of the less expensive kinds or, if not available, cheat a little by substituting red wine with a tablespoon of brandy.

Brandy, or *brandewijn* (burnt wine), made its appearance in Europe around the fourteenth century, the art of distilling having been invented a couple of centuries before by apothecaries in search of ever more effective medicines. Brandy is referred to as brandywine in old recipes. It, along with other distilled drinks, were known collectively as aqua vitae, which the French translated as *eau-de-vie* and the English as spirits. They seem to have gained popularity around the time of the Black Death when they were prescribed to lift the spirits of the survivors. Was it part of some folklore memory that made my grandmother keep a bottle of brandy in her wardrobe to be brought out only for medicinal purposes?

And of course wherever wines and spirits are drunk, so they find their way into the cooking. England is no exception.

Scallops in their half shell

Scallops, with their bright orange coral, are available from autumn to early summer. They can be expensive but cooked in their half shells in a white sauce flavoured with mushrooms, mustard and sherry, they make a splendid starter. Allow 1–2 per head, depending on their size and the state of your purse. Scallops are normally served open, attached to their flat shell. Make sure they are very fresh with a distinct smell of the sea, avoiding those which look damp and pallid. Ask the fishmonger to give you their rounded shells too, and to remove the frilly membrane and black thread of gut, leaving just the nut and the coral.

4–8 scallops
300 ml (½ pint milk)
salt
freshly milled black pepper
50 g (2 oz) butter
50 g (2 oz) mushrooms, finely
 chopped
50 g (2 oz) flour

½ teaspoon ready-made mustard
1 tablespoon dry sherry or
 montilla
50 g (2 oz) breadcrumbs
50 g (2 oz) Cheddar cheese,
 grated
1–2 tablespoons chopped parsley
1 lemon, cut in wedges

Wash the scallops under running cold water and cut each in half, leaving the corals whole. Put them into a small saucepan with the milk and season with salt and pepper. Bring slowly to the boil and as soon as the milk bubbles, remove from the heat and leave covered for 3–4 minutes. Drain the scallops, but keep the liquid to make the sauce.

Wipe out the saucepan with kitchen paper. Melt the butter in it, add the mushrooms and cook them for a few minutes, stirring all the time. Stir in the flour and continue to stir and cook over a low heat for 2 minutes. Stir in the mustard and sherry or montilla and gradually add just sufficient of the liquid in which the scallops were cooked to make a thick, creamy sauce.

Lay the scallops on four of the half shells and spoon over the sauce. Sprinkle with the breadcrumbs and cheese and put under a preheated grill or hot oven until the sauce bubbles and the cheese is golden brown. Serve garnished with the chopped parsley and lemon wedges.

Trout with sorrel

This adaptation of a recipe by Charles Carter comes from *The Complete Practical Cook*, first published in 1730. The trout are poached in wine with herbs and their delicate flavour is given some oomph by serving them with a sorrel and anchovy sauce. Sorrel is one of those herbs which is not easy to find unless you make a place for it in your garden, but spinach can be used instead.

4 trout fillets
salt
freshly milled black pepper
sprigs of thyme or $\frac{1}{2}$ teaspoonful
    dried
1 bay leaf
150 ml ($\frac{1}{4}$ pint) white wine

50 g (2 oz) butter
handful of young sorrel or
    spinach leaves, chopped
2–3 anchovy fillets
2 tablespoons double cream
1 lemon, quartered

Lay the trout fillets flat in a shallow pan. Season with salt and pepper. Add the thyme and bay leaf, pour over the wine and just enough water to cover. Bring slowly to the boil and poach for 5–7 minutes, until the fish turns opaque.

Meanwhile, make the sauce. Melt the butter in a saucepan, add the sorrel or spinach leaves and when they slacken and soften, break them up with a wooden spoon. Add the chopped anchovy fillets and stir in the double cream. When it bubbles add 2–3 tablespoons of the liquid in which the fish was poached. Put the fish fillets on to a warm dish, pour the sauce over and garnish the dish with the lemon quarters.

Rack of lamb

A rack of lamb makes the perfect roast for a romantic evening for two. Sweet and succulent, in a gravy flavoured with sherry and redcurrant jelly, it needs nothing more complicated than roast potatoes and something green, like Savoy cabbage with nutmeg.

For a party of four you will need two racks and can ask your butcher to form them either into a crown roast or a guard of honour. The tip of each bone topped with a paper frill, the racks are turned outwards and formed into a crown, or they are presented facing each other, the bones interlaced like the swords in a real guard of honour.

In the spring, serve with a selection of new vegetables (potatoes, diced carrots and turnips, peas and broad beans) which have been gently steamed together until tender and a dish of puréed potatoes. In fact, a crown roast can be brought to the table with the centre filled either with the vegetables or potatoes.

1 prepared rack of lamb
1 clove garlic
sprigs of rosemary
6 tablespoons oil or 75 g (3 oz)
   butter, cut in small pieces

1 tablespoon flour
300 ml ($\frac{1}{2}$ pint) stock or water
2 tablespoons sherry
1 tablespoon redcurrant jelly

Heat the oven to Gas 7/425°F/220°C.

Remove the paper frills if the meat is already dressed. Cut slits in the lamb and insert slivers of garlic. Set it in a roasting dish, put the sprigs of rosemary on top and pour over the oil or surround with the pieces of butter. Roast for 45–60 minutes (depending upon whether you want the meat rare or well done), reducing the heat after 10 minutes to Gas 5/375°F/190°C. Transfer the cooked meat to a warm serving dish and return to the turned-off oven while you prepare the gravy.

Pour away most of the fatty juices in the roasting pan, stir the flour into the remaining juices and let it cook for a minute before stirring in the stock or water, sherry and redcurrant jelly. Lower the heat and simmer gently until it has reduced a little. Pour into a sauce boat. Top each bone with its paper frill.

Pheasant with celery

In this recipe pheasant is braised in port with bacon and celery until it almost melts in the mouth. Right at the end, the sauce is enriched with cream and egg yolk. One pheasant will serve two; if feeding four, you will need two birds. (Don't forget a hen, though smaller, is meatier than a cock pheasant.) Try the same recipe with guinea fowl or chicken and if you feel port is just too extravagant use red wine instead, with perhaps a dash of brandy.

50 g (2 oz) butter
1–2 pheasants
2 rashers streaky bacon, chopped
150 ml ($\frac{1}{4}$ pint) stock
150 ml ($\frac{1}{4}$ pint) port
salt

freshly milled black pepper
1 head celery, sliced
1–2 tablespoons chopped parsley
1 egg yolk
150 ml ($\frac{1}{4}$ pint) double cream

Heat the oven to Gas 4/350°F/180°C.

Heat the butter in a flameproof casserole which will hold the bird(s) comfortably and brown the pheasant all over. Add the bacon, stock and port. Bring to the boil and season with salt and pepper. Cover with foil and the lid and put into the oven for 30 minutes. Remove and pack the sliced celery all round the bird(s). Return to the oven for a further 45 minutes or until the pheasant is cooked – tested with a skewer, the juices should run clear.

Put the cooked bird(s) on to a serving dish surrounded by the celery and sprinkle over the parsley. Beat the egg yolk with the cream, add a little of the hot stock to it and then tip it into the pot containing the rest of the stock, stir until hot but don't allow to boil or it will curdle. Serve separately.

Chicken in red wine

This is an adaptation of an eighteenth-century recipe which Hannah Glasse calls 'To stew chickens'. The name gives no idea of how good the dish is. The quartered bird is simmered in red wine with herbs and spices. I have cut down on the amount of liquid that she uses and am suggesting the egg yolks are optional because, as she says, 'if you don't like it; leave them out'.

50 g (2 oz) butter
1 chicken, divided into quarters
1 onion, chopped
100 ml (4 fl oz) red wine
100 ml (4 fl oz) water
$\frac{1}{4}$ teaspoon mace or nutmeg
salt

freshly milled black pepper
sprigs of thyme, sage and parsley
   tied in a bunch
25 g (1 oz) flour
2 egg yolks (optional)
1 lemon, cut in slices

Melt half the butter in a heavy-based casserole and fry the chicken pieces all over, removing them to a plate as you go. Add the chopped onion and fry for a few minutes until golden. Return the chicken pieces. Pour in the wine and water and add the mace or nutmeg. Season with salt and pepper and lay the bunch of herbs on top. Cover and simmer for 45 minutes.

Mix the remaining butter with the flour to form a paste. Take the lid off the pan and add the butter and flour mixture in small pieces. Cover and cook for a further 10 minutes. Put the chicken on a dish, discarding the herbs. Stir the egg yolks, if using, into the sauce and when it thickens, pour it over the chicken pieces. Serve garnished with the lemon slices.

Quail in vine leaves

This delicious way of roasting quail is based on a traditional recipe which perhaps has its origins in the cooking of the Romans. The birds are stuffed with either grapes, cherries or crushed juniper berries before being wrapped in brandy-soaked vine leaves and bacon. If you have no access to fresh vine leaves, they can be bought preserved in brine from shops selling products from Greece. They should be soaked for a few minutes to rid them of their salt.

4 quails
8 grapes, cherries or crushed
  juniper berries
vine leaves
100 ml (4 fl oz) brandy
8 rashers streaky bacon

25 g (1 oz) butter
4 slices of bread, 1 cm ($\frac{1}{2}$ in)
  thick, crusts removed
salt
freshly milled black pepper

Heat the oven to Gas 6/400°F/200°C.

Put 2 grapes, cherries or crushed juniper berries into the cavity of each bird. Soak the vine leaves in the brandy for a few minutes, then wrap one round each bird, followed by 2 rashers of bacon. Secure with string. Lay the birds in a shallow ovenproof dish and dot them with the butter. Roast for 30 minutes.

Using a pastry cutter, cut each piece of bread into a circle on which to sit a quail. Remove the dish from the oven and place a circle of bread beneath each bird. Pour over the brandy in which the vine leaves were soaked and season with salt and pepper. Return to the oven for 10 minutes.

Roasted guinea fowl with grapes

This tasty bird originally came from Africa and was brought to England by the Romans who called it *gallina africana*, which explains why in some parts of England it is known as gliny or gleeny. It can be a bit dry, so when roasted it is usually covered in fat bacon and must be basted at intervals. Guinea fowl used to run wild and although nowadays the birds are completely domesticated, they are still half-regarded as game and can be prepared in many of the ways that pheasant is cooked. When roasted they can be stuffed, but in this recipe the cavity is simply filled with a lump of butter and a handful of grapes. Failing grapes, add an apple, peeled, cored and finely chopped. Traditionally, roast guinea fowl is served with redcurrant jelly, bread sauce and a green vegetable such as Brussels sprouts.

1 guinea fowl	freshly milled black pepper
handful of seedless grapes	4 rashers streaky bacon
50 g (2 oz) butter	150 ml ($\frac{1}{4}$ pint) red wine
salt	150 ml ($\frac{1}{4}$ pint) stock or water

Heat the oven to Gas 6/4005°F/200°C.

Put the grapes and half the butter into the cavity of the bird and season inside with salt and pepper. Lay the bird in a roasting tin, cover with the rashers of bacon and smear with the remaining butter. Roast for $1\frac{1}{4}$ hours. After 15 minutes, turn the bird on its side and baste. Turn and baste every 15 minutes. Fifteen minutes before the end of the cooking time, turn breast-side up and push the bacon to one side to allow the breast to brown. Transfer the bird to a warm dish and put into the turned-off oven for 10–15 minutes before serving. Make the gravy by pouring the wine and stock or water into the roasting pan and stirring over a medium heat until it thickens a little and reduces by half.

Farmer's wife partridges

This is a Norfolk recipe for partridges which is well worth doing if you live in an area where partridges are cheap. For most of us they are a luxurious treat, but it is an excellent way of cooking quail or even chicken pieces.

25 g (1 oz) butter	2–3 sprigs of fresh thyme or
4 partridges	$\frac{1}{2}$ teaspoon dried
4 rashers streaky bacon, chopped	225 g (8 oz) mushrooms,
2 cloves garlic, chopped	quartered
3–4 skinned and chopped	1 whole clove
tomatoes, or 2–3 tablespoons	salt
canned chopped tomatoes	freshly milled black pepper
	150 ml ($\frac{1}{4}$ pint) dry white wine

Melt the butter in a flameproof casserole, add the birds and the bacon and brown all over. Add the garlic, tomatoes, thyme, mushrooms and clove. Season with salt and pepper and pour over the wine. Cover and simmer for about 30–35 minutes, until tender. Put the birds on a hot serving dish and boil the sauce hard to reduce by half. Pour over the partridges and serve.

Stewed pigeons

Based on Hannah Glasse's recipe, this is a satisfying dish for dinner. In the original, the birds are cooked in wine with herbs and spices, pickled mushrooms and oysters. Nowadays mushrooms are always available, and if you want to pickle some there is a recipe in the chapter called Pickled Pears to Hodgkin. Otherwise use ordinary flat field mushrooms instead. As for the oysters, it is easier on the pocket if they are left out. The pigeons still come out rich and dark and very tasty. Hannah Glasse thickens the final sauce with egg yolk and cream but if you are diet-conscious, simply leave them out.

50 g (2 oz) butter	100 g (4 oz) pickled or fresh
2–4 whole cloves	mushrooms
powdered mace	1 lemon
sprigs of fresh herbs such as	salt
thyme, rosemary and sage	freshly milled black pepper
4 pigeons	1 egg yolk (optional)
1 onion, chopped	2 tablespoons double cream
100 ml (4 fl oz) dry white wine	(optional)
100 ml (4 fl oz) stock or water	

Put a sliver of butter, a clove, a pinch of mace and small sprigs of herbs inside the cavity of each bird. Melt the remaining butter in a heavy-based casserole and when it is sizzling add the birds and the chopped onion. Brown the birds all over and let the onion soften. Pour in the wine and stock or water and add a further large pinch of mace and more sprigs of herbs tied in a bunch, together with the mushrooms, sliced if large, and a strip of lemon peel. Season with salt and pepper, cover the pan and simmer for $1\frac{1}{2}$–2 hours, until the pigeons are tender.

Just before serving, discard the bunch of herbs, remove the birds, split them in two and put on to a warm serving dish. Boil the sauce hard until reduced by half and stir in the egg yolk and cream, if using. Take care not to let the sauce return to the boil or it will curdle. Pour over the pigeons and serve garnished with the lemon cut in quarters.

Venison in red wine

Venison is a rich, dark meat and because it is so lean a relatively small amount provides an ample serving. Cooked in a casserole in red wine it is delicious served with forcemeat balls (see Sweet Herbs), a thinly sliced orange salad (see Oranges and Lemons), watercress and potatoes mashed with celeriac. This recipe is for young venison. Old venison will need at least 1–2 hours longer cooking time. Like most casseroles, this one can be made the day before and then reheated at Gas 4/350°F/180°C for 30 minutes.

2 tablespoons flour
700 g (1½ lb) venison, cubed
2 tablespoons oil
3–4 shallots
¼ teaspoon allspice

¼ teaspoon mace
300 ml (½ pint) red wine
cayenne pepper
salt

Heat the oven to Gas 4/350°F/180°C.

Put the flour on to a plate and roll the pieces of venison in it until they are evenly coated. Heat the oil in a frying pan and fry the meat until brown, in two or three batches, transferring them as you go to an earthenware casserole. Peel the shallots by steeping them for a few minutes in boiling water – their skins will then come off much more easily. Chop them and fry for a few minutes but don't let them brown or they will be bitter. Add the allspice and mace and pour over the wine. Bring to the boil and pour the contents of the frying pan over the meat in the casserole. Season with cayenne pepper and salt. Cover the casserole with a layer of foil and put on the lid. Transfer it to the oven for 1½–2 hours until the meat is tender.

Parson's venison

This could just as well be called poor man's venison because it isn't venison at all, but lamb dressed up to play the part. Venison used to be just for the rich landowner and his friends so the humble parson had to make do as best he could with a tender and succulent leg of lamb liberally seasoned with such aromatic flavours as juniper, coriander, herbs and wine. The meat is marinated for several days and the recipe calls for quite a lot of wine. If you are skint, you could follow the example of my Kentish friend, Bill Akhurst, who discovered that if you put the meat and all the marinade ingredients into a plastic bag, you could make do with about half the amount of wine. The trick, he said, is to suck out all the air, secure the bag with a twist tie and put it into the fridge. Turn the bag over every day to make sure all the meat comes into contact with the wine.

1 leg joint of lamb weighing about 1½ kg (3 lb)
2 cloves garlic, cut in slivers
2 onions, sliced
2 carrots, sliced
1 teaspoon juniper berries, crushed
1 teaspoon coriander, crushed
1 teaspoon peppercorns, crushed

2 bay leaves
sprigs of thyme, parsley and rosemary
300 ml (½ pint) red wine
2 tablespoons oil
100 g (4 oz) streaky bacon, chopped
2 leeks, sliced

Four or five days ahead of time, score the fat on the lamb all over in a criss-cross pattern and press slivers of garlic into each intersection. Put the leg into a bowl in which it fits comfortably with one each of the sliced onions and carrots. Add the crushed juniper berries, coriander seeds and peppercorns with one of the bay leaves, some sprigs of herbs and the wine. Cover and put into a cool place to marinate for 4–5 days, turning the meat over once or twice a day.

To cook, heat the oven to Gas 4/350°F/180°C.

Dry the leg of lamb with kitchen paper. Choose a large flameproof casserole in which it will fit comfortably and heat the oil. Brown the lamb all over, then remove to a plate. Fry the second sliced onion and carrot with the bacon and leeks for 5–10 minutes. Lay the lamb on top, strain over the liquid from the marinade and season with salt and pepper. Lay the second bay leaf and sprigs of fresh herbs on top. Cover and put into the oven for 1½ hours. Transfer to a warm serving dish and keep warm for at least 15 minutes before carving, to allow the meat to compact.

Berkshire jugged steak

This simple stew flavoured with wine, cloves and redcurrant jelly is prepared in a few minutes. Originally it was cooked in a tall pot which was stood in another of water and set over the fire until the meat was tender and the celery, onions and mushrooms had melted almost to a purée. Nowadays it is simpler to use a casserole and the oven. Serve the dish with steamed or mashed potatoes and perhaps a green vegetable.

700 g (1½ lb) braising steak, cut in cubes
2 onions, each stuck with 3 cloves
4 sticks celery, chopped
100 g (4 oz) mushrooms, chopped

salt
freshly milled black pepper
150 ml (¼ pint) red wine
1 tablespoon redcurrant jelly
2 tablespoons chopped parsley

Heat the oven to Gas 2/300°F/150°C. Lay the braising steak in a deep earthenware casserole with the onions, celery and mushrooms. Season with salt and pepper, pour in the red wine and add the redcurrant jelly. Cover with foil and put on the lid. Put into the oven for 2–3 hours. Serve garnished with the parsley.

Oxtail

An oxtail, jointed and braised for several hours with leeks, carrots and onions and flavoured with spices and herbs, provides a rich, satisfying meal during the winter months. The meat becomes meltingly tender and the vegetables cook to a rich purée. In this recipe I use red wine or strong dry cider instead of the water which the more frugal English cook would probably have used. Most old recipes tell you to cook the dish the day before in order for the fat to rise to the top and be skimmed off before the dish is reheated. Nowadays cattle are reared to be leaner than previously and when I cooked an oxtail recently I found there was very little fat to skim. As you can't be absolutely sure, it is still a good idea to cook it a day ahead because, like many slow-cooked dishes, the flavour improves with keeping.

Oxtail is usually sold by weight, ready jointed, so if you have the choice, go for the larger, meatier pieces rather than those from the thin end of the tail. Eat this dish with something simple such as baked jacket or mashed potatoes and perhaps a green vegetable like spinach.

2 tablespoons oil
900 g (2 lb) joints of oxtail
1 onion, sliced
2 leeks, sliced
450 g (1 lb) carrots, sliced
2 tablespoons flour
1 bay leaf
$\frac{1}{4}$ teaspoon powdered mace
$\frac{1}{2}$ teaspoon dried marjoram

sprigs of parsley and thyme
1 teaspoon peppercorns
3 whole cloves
1 clove garlic, crushed
300 ml ($\frac{1}{2}$ pint) red wine or
    strong dry cider
salt
2 tablespoons chopped parsley

Heat the oven to Gas 2/300°F/150°C.

Heat the oil in a flameproof casserole and brown the pieces of oxtail all over. Transfer the pieces of meat to a warm plate. Fry the onion, leeks and carrots in the fat in the pan for several minutes. Roll the meat in the flour and return to the casserole. Add the bay leaf, mace, marjoram, sprigs of parsley and thyme, peppercorns, cloves and crushed garlic. Pour over the wine or cider, bring to the boil and transfer to the oven. Cook for 3–4 hours until the meat is soft and tender. Leave to get cold and transfer the casserole to the fridge.

The next day, skim off any fat which has risen to the top, bring the casserole to the boil and transfer to the oven heated to Gas 4/350°F/180°C for 30 minutes. Season with the salt, sprinkle over the parsley and serve.

Cottage and shepherd's pie

Cottage pie and shepherd's pie, two childhood favourites, are designed to use up the leftovers of a joint; the one was made with beef, the other with mutton. Original recipes call for the meat to be put into a dish with an onion and some stock thickened with flour. This doesn't enthral me, so my version is jazzed up with tomatoes, herbs and wine! If you have no leftover meat, make the pie using fresh beef or lamb mince, frying it for a few minutes at the same time as the onions.

700 g (1½ lb) potatoes, peeled and
   cut in even-sized pieces
2 tablespoons oil
1 onion, chopped
350 g (12 oz) cooked beef or
   lamb, minced
1 400g can chopped tomatoes,
   drained
½ teaspoon dried thyme

½ teaspoon dried oregano
¼ teaspoon mace
100 ml (4 fl oz) red wine or stock
salt
freshly milled black pepper
50 g (2 oz) butter
milk
paprika

Put the potatoes into a pan of boiling water and simmer them until soft. While they are cooking, heat the oil in a frying pan and fry the onion until golden. Transfer it to a buttered shallow oven dish and mix in the meat, tomatoes, thyme, oregano, mace and the wine or stock. Season with salt and pepper.

Heat the oven to Gas 6/400°F/200°C. Drain the potatoes when they are soft and mash them well, beating in half the butter and enough milk to make a soft consistency. Season to taste. Spread the mashed potatoes over the top of the meat, mark it all over with a fork, sprinkle with paprika and dot with the remaining butter. Put the pie into the oven and bake for 30–40 minutes until the top is golden brown.

Kate and Sidney pud or pie

This is the Cockney name for those most English of dishes, the steak and kidney puddings or pies which were produced all over England, at least since early in the nineteenth century. Puddings or pies made with just steak and no kidneys were known as John Bulls. Puddings were usually made in deep basins except in Kent and Sussex where they used special wide-mouthed bowls which meant they had a greater area of light upper crust.

However they were made and wherever they come from, it didn't take the Victorians too long before predictably they thought them just a little bit common, perhaps because oysters, poor man's food, were used to give richness to the sauce! (If you want to add this authentic touch, add a dozen or so when you assemble the pudding or pie.) Forget snobbery, there is nothing more warming in the depths of our dreary winters than a well-made Kate and Sidney, served with a simple green vegetable like Brussels sprouts, Savoy cabbage or spinach.

Pickled walnuts are a traditional accompaniment.

There are two methods of assembling puddings and pies. The first is to cook meat and crust all together in one operation. The second is to cook the filling on its own before adding the crust. Although this second method appears a bit more trouble, it means you can be sure you have a pudding or pie with tender meat and a light and digestible crust. This is because a pudding filled with raw ingredients must be steamed for several hours to ensure the meat is properly cooked, which means the crust is heavy and sodden; and as for a pie, if the filling is raw, the pastry will pass its peak and be burnt and tough long before the meat is tender.

2 tablespoons flour	2 tablespoons oil
salt	1 onion, chopped
freshly milled black pepper	225 g (8 oz) mushrooms, sliced
450 g (1 lb) fat-free stewing steak, cut in small cubes	100 ml (4 fl oz) red wine
	100 ml (4 fl oz) water or stock
100 g (4 oz) ox kidney, cut in small cubes	1 bay leaf
	sprigs of parsley, thyme and sage tied in a bunch
50 g (2 oz) butter	

Heat the oven to Gas 2/300°F/150°C.

Season the flour with salt and pepper, put on to a plate and roll the steak and kidney in it until well coated. Heat half the butter with the oil in a frying pan and fry the chopped onion until soft and golden, then transfer it to a casserole. Brown the meat in the frying pan, in several batches, transferring it to the casserole as you go. Add remaining butter to the pan and fry the mushrooms for a few minutes. Add them to the meat and onions. Pour the wine and water into the frying pan, stirring over a medium heat and scraping the bottom of the pan to mix well. When it boils, pour it into the casserole. Add the bay leaf, tuck in the bunch of herbs, cover and cook in the oven for 1½–2 hours, until the meat is tender but still holds its shape. Remove the herbs and set aside to cool either for several hours or until the next day.

The pudding

First make a suet crust (see Etceteras), flavouring it with ¼ teaspoonful each of mace and thyme and a little freshly ground black pepper. Cut a circle of foil 10 cm (4 in) bigger than the diameter of a ½ litre (2 pint) pudding basin and grease both it and the basin with butter.

Flour a board. Reserve a quarter of the dough for the lid. Roll the larger piece into a circle big enough to line the pudding basin and drop it into it, pressing it gently into place, allowing a 2–3 cm (1 in) overhang. Add the filling, which should come about 2 cm ($\frac{3}{4}$ in) below the top. Brush the overlapping edges of the lining with water, roll out the remaining dough to form the lid and lay it on top of the pudding. Press the edges firmly together.

Cover the pudding loosely with the foil to allow the pudding to rise, but press the sides tightly against the basin and secure with string, tying it over the top to make a lifting handle. Half fill a large saucepan with boiling water and when it returns to a steady boil, lower in the pudding. The water should come about two-thirds up the side of the basin. Put on the lid and let it gently boil for $1\frac{1}{2}$–2 hours. Check once or twice and if necessary add more boiling water.

The pie

Use 225 g (8 oz) puff or shortcrust pastry and roll it out thinly into a piece to make a lid with sufficient over to cut into thin strips to line the edges of the pie dish. Put the cooked filling into the pie dish and set a pie funnel in the centre. Brush the edges of the dish with water, lay the thin strips of pastry all round, allowing a little overlap and brush them with a little more water. Settle the lid on top and trim the two layers of pastry evenly all round, using a sharp knife. Press the two edges firmly together, before marking them with the prongs of a fork or the blunt edge of a knife. Use any remaining bits of pastry to make leaves and arrange them on the lid. Brush the top of the pie all over with the beaten yolk of an egg. Set aside for 30 minutes.

Heat the oven to Gas 7/425°F/220°C and bake the pie for 15 minutes. Lower the heat to Gas 5/375°F/190°C and cook a further 20 minutes.

Trifle or tipsy cake

Everyone has their own version of trifle, or tipsy cake as it used to be called on account of the lashings of alcohol which it contained. Trifle is practically our national pudding, but can vary from being ghastly to sublime. The former, disguised with a layer of imitation cream, is likely to be made with a base of those dreary trifle sponge cakes, which my dear brother revoltingly called dog-lick, stingily sprinkled with cheap sherry before being swamped in lots of sweet jelly and vivid yellow custard of the powdered or canned variety.

To make a truly sublime tipsy cake, you need good sponge cake, macaroons, brandy and reasonable sherry or similar fortified wine and a freshly made egg custard, all topped with freshly whipped cream or, as a treat, with a light-as-air syllabub (recipe below). Not perhaps a trifle for the children, but served at a dinner party you will have your guests reeling with delight.

Begin the preparations for the trifle the day before.

1 stale sponge cake, sliced	2 eggs plus 1 yolk
100 g (4 oz) macaroons	450 ml ($\frac{3}{4}$ pint) full cream milk
2 tablespoons brandy	2 tablespoons caster or vanilla
150 ml ($\frac{1}{4}$ pint) sherry or montilla	sugar (see Etceteras)
3–4 tablespoons apricot or	300 ml ($\frac{1}{2}$ pint) double cream or
raspberry jam	syllabub (see below)

Arrange the slices of sponge cake and the macaroons over the base of a large glass bowl. Sprinkle over the brandy and sherry. Spread the jam over the top.

Beat the eggs and yolks in a heatproof bowl. In a saucepan heat the milk until just below boiling point. Pour the milk over the eggs and return the mixture to the pan, over a very low heat. Using a wooden spoon, stir the custard constantly until it thickens and coats the back of the spoon, taking great care it does not boil or it will curdle. Stir in the sugar, allow to cool for 5–10 minutes before pouring the custard over the cake and macaroons. Cover and leave in a cool place until the next day.

Begin the preparation for the syllabub, if using.

The next day, whip the cream and spread it over the custard, or finish the syllabub and carefully spoon it over the top of the trifle.

Leave the top quite plain or, if you prefer, decorate it with ratafia biscuits, slivered almonds or candied peel.

Syllabub

Popular since Elizabethan times, the earliest syllabubs were really a drink of sweetened wine made light and frothy with freshly drawn milk from the cow and flavoured with spices. There were all sorts of variations, some made with cider, others with beer, sometimes a mixture of the two. Everlasting syllabubs, of which this recipe is one, were creamy, light confections which could be eaten with a spoon. In Devonshire, of course, they would top it with clotted cream.

When not making a trifle topping serve this syllabub in small custard glasses and sprinkle with a little powdered cinnamon.

150 ml ($\frac{1}{4}$ pint) white wine	3 tablespoons caster sugar
2 tablespoons brandy	300 ml ($\frac{1}{2}$ pint) double cream
grated peel and juice of 1 lemon	

Put the wine, brandy and the grated peel and juice of a lemon into a bowl and leave overnight.

The next day, strain the wine, brandy and lemon mixture into a large bowl. Stir in the caster sugar and when it has dissolved, carefully stir in the cream. Whip with a balloon whisk or, if you have an electric beater, begin whipping the mixture using a high speed but as soon as it begins to thicken, lower the speed and finally completely the whipping by hand, watching all the time that the syllabub doesn't over-thicken and begin to curdle. It should be light and airy and form soft peaks.

Poor knights of Windsor

Introduced to England by the Normans who knew it as *pain perdu*, this is a deliciously unpretentious pudding. Quite why it came to be known by its present name is a mystery. The bread is coated in a mixture of milk, egg yolk, sugar and sherry and fried until golden brown and crisp. It is eaten sprinkled with sugar and cinnamon and can be made even more attractive with the addition of a little jam or honey. Kent has a delicious variation, sandwiching the fried bread with cherries which have been heated with a little sugar until just below boiling point.

4 tablespoons milk	1 egg yolk
3–4 tablespoons caster sugar	50 g (2 oz) butter
1 tablespoon sweet sherry	cinnamon
4 slices stale white bread	

Put 3 tablespoons of the milk, 1 tablespoon of sugar and the sherry into a shallow dish and stir until the sugar dissolves. Dip the slices of bread into this mixture. Drain them. Beat the remaining milk with the egg yolk in the dish and dip the bread into it. Heat the butter in a large frying pan and, when it sizzles, fry the bread quickly on either side. Eat piping hot sprinkled with the rest of the sugar and a little cinnamon.

Devonshire junket

In Eliza Acton's *Modern Cookery for Private Families*, she remarks: 'junket is merely a dish or bowl of sweetened curds and whey, covered with a thick cream of scalded milk . . .' In her day, the milk was curdled by adding a small piece of salted and dried rennet, whereas now rennet is sold in liquid or tablet form. Junket has gone out of fashion but it is easy to make and simply delicious. It is a perfect summer dessert because it needs a warm place in which to set.

It is the scalded, or clotted, cream with which it is served which gives the Devonshire handle to this recipe, but variations on the theme were made all over the country and it was a familiar street food of Victorian London. A Cornish version makes it with two parts of milk to one of cream, sweetened with sugar lumps rubbed over the surface of a lemon until yellow and adds not 2 tablespoons but half a cup of brandy. In Somerset you might come across a rather cloying version known as damask cream, which is decorated with crimson rose petals and served with pouring cream scented with rosewater. Another west of England variation suggests lining the bowl with broken ginger biscuits before adding the other ingredients. If brandy or rum seems too extravagant, use coffee essence or instant coffee instead. Devonshire junket is served with clotted or thick cream which can either be spread over the top or offered in a separate bowl, but if you prefer, you can serve it unadorned or eat it with a spoonful or two of jam.

Whatever you do, don't move the bowl until the junket has set or the milk will separate into curds and whey.

1 pint creamy milk	1 teaspoon (or 1 tablet) rennet
2 teaspoons caster sugar	cinnamon or nutmeg
1½ tablespoons brandy or rum	

Heat the milk to blood heat. (The test is made by dipping your finger into it and counting to ten before you need to withdraw it.) Put the sugar and brandy or rum into a wide, deep bowl and stir to mix and dissolve the sugar. Pour in the heated milk and gently stir in the rennet. Leave undisturbed for at least two hours in a warm place to set. Sprinkle with cinnamon or freshly grated nutmeg.

Egg nog

A marvellous pick-me-up after a bout of heavy drinking, egg nog is not for the faint-hearted as it is made from raw egg yolk and, ideally, a squirt of milk straight from the cow.

For each person, beat together in a glass 1 egg yolk, 1–2 tablespoons of rum or brandy and 4 tablespoons of warm milk. Drink while still warm.

That roast

Roast beef

Yorkshire pudding

Horseradish sauce

Gravy

Roast pork with crackling and apples

Roast lamb

Mint sauce

Onion sauce

Roast onions

Laverbread sauce

Roast chicken

Herb and bacon stuffing

Bread sauce

Roast duckling

Sage and onion stuffing

Apricot and hazelnut stuffing

Apple sauce

Roast turkey

Chestnut stuffing

Cranberry sauce

Roast goose

Prune stuffing

Giblet stock for gravy

Everyone associates English cooking with the Sunday roast. No one can roast meat like we do – although, if we want to be strictly accurate, true roast meat is something that belongs to the past, when the meat was speared on a spit turning over an open fire. Nowadays, because we cook in an enclosed oven, our roasts are actually baked. Even so, what could be easier than sticking a piece of meat in the oven and taking it out some time later, perfectly cooked, succulent and full of flavour? Nothing, especially if we follow a few simple rules.

• Buy from a reputable butcher or supermarket where the meat has been properly hung for a few days before it is sold.

• As a general rule, larger joints roast better than small ones, so it makes sense to buy more than you need and eat the surplus cold or made into something like cottage or shepherd's pie.

• All meat should be firm but springy to the touch. Beef should be deep red. Lamb should be pink to deep red. Despite today's fashion for lean meat, there is no doubt that fat gives it much more flavour, so favour beef and lamb with a fine marbling of firm, white fat. Pork should be pale pink and the fat surrounding it should be white and smooth.

• If the meat is sold pre-packed, remove the plastic covering, wipe the joint with kitchen paper and leave on a plate for the air to circulate before you cook it.

• If the meat has been frozen, it must be completely thawed before it is cooked. Let it thaw either in the fridge or a cool place. Each 500 g (1 lb) will take about 5 hours in the fridge, about half that time in the kitchen.

• Meat should be at room temperature before it is cooked, so remove from the fridge at least 30 minutes, but up to 2–3 hours, before cooking. Chilled meat going into a hot oven will never be tender.

• Weigh the meat before you start cooking and calculate the cooking time (see individual recipes) adding an extra 10–15 minutes to heat the oven and at least 15 minutes at the end. During this last period, the joint is transferred to a dish and kept warm to allow the meat to compact and be easier to carve. This waiting time also allows the juices to be released into the interior, making the meat more tender and tasty. As ovens vary, it is worth using a meat thermometer if you have one. Roast beef should be pink and rare inside with the outside crisp and

brown. We prefer our lamb well done, but the inside is most tender if it
is slightly pink. Pork must always be well cooked because there is a
danger of infection: the juices should run clear when the meat is
pierced; if they are pink, it is not sufficently cooked and must be left for
a little longer.

• Always preheat the oven. Arrange the shelves when you light the
oven. Never roast meat in a tin directly on the floor of the oven,
because the heat will not circulate properly.

• Heat 3–4 tablespoons of oil or fat in the roasting tin before you add
the meat then baste the joint with the heated oil or fat when you put it
into the preheated oven. This will ensure that the outside is
immediately seared and sealed and juices are contained.

• Lean meats need basting frequently, usually about every 20–30
minutes. Remove the joint from the oven when you do so and close the
oven door so that not too much heat escapes. A bulb baster comes in
handly for this job, but a large spoon will do.

So let's begin with the most famous of them all.

Roast beef

This dish, synonymous with English cooking, has become such an
expensive luxury that few of us can afford to eat it. But when we do,
we have to agree it is superlative. The ideal cuts are sirloin or rib,
preferably on the bone for the best flavour. To be truly authentic, it
must be eaten with Yorkshire pudding, horseradish sauce and a good,
brown gravy. For a change try inserting thin pieces of anchovies into
slits cut in the surface. Roast beef is delicious with potatoes and
parsnips roasted around the meat and perhaps glazed carrots or a
green vegetable.

Heat the oven to Gas 7/425°F/220°C.

Follow the roasting procedure described above, using oil or beef
dripping, allowing a cooking time of 15 minutes per 450 g (1 lb) and
15 minutes over for rare, and 20 minutes per 450 g (1 lb) and 30
minutes over for well done meat. However, a joint under 1 kg (3 lb)
should be roasted for 1¼ hours. Put it into the hot oven for 15 minutes
before lowering the heat to Gas 6/400°C/200°F. Baste every 20
minutes. When the meat is done, transfer it to a dish, cover loosely
with foil and keep in a warm place while the Yorkshire pudding is
cooking.

Yorkshire pudding

No matter where you live in Britain, it is almost heretical to eat roast beef without Yorkshire pudding. It wasn't always so. It was originally invented by some enterprising northern housewife to be cooked under a roast shoulder of mutton and it was only later that it came to be associated, at least in southern minds, with roast beef. In Yorkshire, they still eat their puddings with any kind of meat and continue the habit of turning it into a sweet course by cooking it filled with sliced apples or serving it plain and simple with a good dollop of treacle or cream. In the north this pudding is usually served at the start of the meal with plenty of gravy to take the edge off the appetite before the meat itself appears, but in the south it accompanies the meat.

100 g (4 oz) plain flour, sieved	2 eggs, beaten
pinch salt	300 ml ($\frac{1}{2}$ pint) low-fat milk

If you have a food processor put in all the ingredients and blend until light and frothy. If not, put the flour and salt into a basin, make a well in the centre and add the beaten egg and a little milk. Mix using a wooden spoon and gradually add the remaining milk. Beat well until smooth. Whichever method you use, set aside for 1 hour before cooking.

When the meat is removed from the oven raise the temperature to Gas 8/450°F/230°C. Pour sufficient fat from the roast to cover a baking tin with a thin layer. Put into the oven near the top. Add 2 tablespoons of cold water to the batter and process or beat again. After 5 minutes, remove the tin from the oven and pour in the batter. Set it at the top of the oven and bake for 25 minutes until the batter is risen and golden brown. If you prefer, you can make individual puddings in small tart or bun tins; allow them 15 minutes' baking time.

Horseradish sauce

This traditional accompaniment to roast beef is also delicious eaten with smoked fish. In the old days it would be made with freshly grated horseradish root but this vegetable is now nearly impossible to find. Instead, adapt a good commercial brand of horseradish sauce as follows:

1 tablespoon horseradish sauce   squeeze of lemon juice
200 ml (8 fl oz) double cream,   pinch of sugar
  whipped   pinch of salt

Mix all the ingredients together and put them into a small serving
bowl.

Gravy

Make the gravy by pouring off most of the fat from the roasting tin.
Into the remaining pan juices, stir 1 tablespoon of flour and mix
thoroughly over a low heat, blending in all the brown juicy bits from
the meat. When it is thoroughly mixed and has turned a light brown,
remove from the heat (this will help prevent lumps) and gradually stir
in about 300 ml ($\frac{1}{2}$ pint) of vegetable stock (this can be from the water
in which you have cooked any accompanying vegetables). Return to
the heat and gradually bring to the boil, stirring all the time and set
over a low heat to reduce a little and thicken. As soon as the meat is
ready to serve, pour the gravy into a warm sauce boat.

Roast pork with crackling and apples

When the English roast their pork, the skin is deeply scored to
produce, crisp, golden brown crackling. The best crackling comes
from the hindquarters, so choose either a leg or loin joint and ask the
butcher to score it for you. (Supermarket ready-packed joints may
need scoring at home. Do this with a very sharp knife, a scalpel or
Stanley knife, at 5 mm ($\frac{1}{4}$ in) intervals.)

In this recipe whole apples are cooked with the meat but if you
prefer you could serve the joint with apple sauce baked in the oven (see
later on in this section, below roast duckling). Any leftover pork can
be made into gilded apples (see Spices), a dish with medieval origins.

$1\frac{1}{2}$ kg ($3–3\frac{1}{2}$ lb) joint of pork, the   salt
  skin scored   8 Cox's apples
oil

Heat the oven to Gas 5/375°F/190°C.

Thoroughly dry the meat, rub the skin all over with oil and sprinkle
it with salt – all this will ensure the crackling will be crisp. Follow the

roasting procedure at the beginning of this section, putting the joint into the roasting tin skin side up. Allow 30 minutes per 450 g (l lb) and 30 minutes over.

An hour before the end of the cooking time, score the apples round their middles and put them in the roasting tin with the pork. Then, 10 minutes before the end of the cooking time, check the meat. If the crackling is not sufficiently brown, raise the heat to Gas 7/425°F/ 220°C. Test the meat is done by piercing with a skewer: when the meat is cooked the juices will run clear; if not, allow a little extra time.

Set the cooked meat, surrounded by the apples, on a serving dish and put it back into the turned-off oven for 10–15 minutes before carving.

Make the gravy by pouring away most of the fatty juices from the roasting tin. Sprinkle 1 tablespoon of flour into the pan and gently stir into the remaining pan juices for a minute or two before pouring in 300 ml ($\frac{1}{2}$ pint) of stock or strong dry cider. Continue to stir until it thickens and reduces. Serve in a sauce boat.

Roast lamb

Roasting joints include the leg, shoulder and loin. Follow the roasting procedure at the beginning of this section, allowing 20 minutes per 450 g (l lb) and 20 minutes over at Gas 5/375°F/190°C.

Before putting the meat in the oven, sprinkle it with pepper cover it with sprigs of herbs like rosemary, thyme or mint; for a delicious garlicky flavour, make slits in the lamb with the point of a sharp knife and insert slivers of garlic into them. The meat should be basted every 30 minutes with the juices in which it is cooking. These can be augmented by pouring a little wine or orange juice into the pan half way through the roasting time. Allow the joint to rest in the turned-off oven for 15–30 minutes before carving.

Make the gravy by simply pouring a glass or two of wine, strong dry cider or water into the roasting tin from which most of the fat has been discarded. Stir it for a minute or two over the heat before pouring into a sauce boat.

Serve the lamb with garden peas or runner beans and roast or new potatoes.

Mint sauce

If you like mint sauce, just a whiff of it will set your mouth watering in anticipation of the roast lamb which it invariably accompanies. It takes only minutes to prepare but don't leave it to the last minute – steep the mint and sugar in boiling water at least an hour before the meat is ready, to let the flavours develop.

2 or 3 tablespoons fresh mint leaves, chopped	1 teaspoon sugar 150 ml (¼ pint) vinegar

Put the mint and sugar into a sauce boat and pour over enough boiling water barely to cover. Stir until the sugar has dissolved. Set aside for 1 hour. Just before serving, stir in the vinegar.

Onion sauce

Although mint sauce is the most usual accompaniment to lamb, just as traditional, though rarer, is an onion sauce like the one my mother used to make.

50 g (2 oz) butter	300 ml (½ pint) milk
350 g (12 oz) onions, finely chopped	salt
2 tablespoons flour	freshly milled black pepper 2–3 tablespoons single cream

Melt the butter in a saucepan and add the chopped onions. Cook them gently for 15 minutes covered, until soft and golden. Stir in the flour and cook for 2 minutes stirring all the time. Gradually add the milk and stir until it begins to bubble and the sauce thickens. Season with salt and pepper. Put over a very low heat for 30 minutes, covered, stirring from time to time and making sure it does not burn. Stir in the cream just before stirring, reheating gently.

Roast onions

Nothing could be simpler than roasting a few onions alongside the meat; they come out meltingly soft and sweet. Put them, whole and unskinned, in the same pan as the roast if there is room, or in a separate roasting pan lined with foil, root-side down and bake at Gas 6/400°F/200°C for 1–1½ hours until soft and tender. Eat like jacket potatoes with butter, sprinkled with salt and pepper and a little chopped parsley.

Laverbread sauce

Laver or sea spinach is a seaweed which grows on rocks. It used to be eaten nationwide but is now confined to the West Country and Wales. Washed and boiled to a pulp it is known as laverbread and is eaten with roast lamb, or for breakfast mixed with oatmeal and formed into cakes which are fried with bacon and eggs. If you come across laverbread either canned or in a market or fishmongers, buy some and make this intriguing sauce to go with your next joint of roast lamb.

25 g (1 oz) butter	juice and finely grated peel of 1
225 g (8 oz) laverbread	Seville orange (or a sweet
freshly milled black pepper	orange and add squeeze of
	lemon juice)

Melt the butter in a small saucepan, add the other ingredients and stir until well mixed and piping hot.

Roast chicken

Roast chicken stuffed with a herb and bacon stuffing and served with roast potatoes and parsnips and a green vegetable like Brussels sprouts is for me a Sunday lunch full of childhood nostalgia. Serve it with traditional brown gravy if you like, although I prefer a simple sauce made with cider or wine stirred into the buttery juices right at the end. Of course if you are fat-conscious you can roast the bird in oil rather than butter.

herb and bacon stuffing (see below)	50 g (2 oz) softened butter
$1\frac{1}{2}$–2 kg ($3\frac{1}{2}$–$4\frac{1}{2}$ lb) free-range chicken	300 ml ($\frac{1}{2}$ pint) strong dry cider or a mixture of wine and water

Heat the oven to Gas 6/400°F/200°C.

Make the stuffing and fill the cavity of the chicken. Weigh the stuffed bird, then put it in a roasting tin and spread butter all over the skin. Put it in the oven and allow 20 minutes per 450 g (1 lb) and 20 minutes over. Baste it every 30 minutes. Test it is cooked either with a meat thermometer, or by inserting a skewer into the thickest part of a leg – the juices should run clear. When the bird is done, put it on a serving dish and return it to the turned-off oven for 15 minutes to firm up and become easier to carve.

To make the sauce, pour away all but 1 tablespoon of the cooking juices from the roasting tin, pour in the cider or the mixture of wine and water and boil rapidly until the liquid reduces by about a half. Pour into a sauce boat and serve separately.

Herb and bacon stuffing

This simple stuffing adds a delicious flavour to roast chicken. You can vary the herbs at will and when Seville oranges are in season, use one of these instead of the lemon.

50 g (2 oz) butter
4 rashers unsmoked streaky
  bacon, chopped
1 onion, chopped
100 g (4 oz) fresh white
  breadcrumbs

1 teaspoon dried thyme
2 tablespoon chopped parsley
juice and grated peel of 1 lemon
salt
freshly milled black pepper
1 egg, beaten

Melt the butter in a small frying pan and fry the bacon and onion until soft but not brown. Mix with the breadcrumbs, thyme, parsley, grated peel and juice of the lemon and season with salt and pepper. Stir in the beaten egg.

Bread sauce

A classic accompaniment to roast chicken or game, bread sauce is easy to make. Don't waste time turning the bread into crumbs but put a thick slice into a pan with all the other ingredients and break it up with a wooden spoon. Once cooked it is then left to infuse to absorb the flavours of onion and cloves before being gently reheated.

450 ml ($\frac{3}{4}$ pint) milk
1 onion, stuck with 2 cloves
75 g (3 oz) slice of bread, crusts
  removed

salt
freshly milled black pepper

Put all the ingredients into a small saucepan (leave the onion whole) and set it over a low heat, half covered. Keep an eye on it and, as it heats, break up the bread with a wooden spoon. Once the sauce boils, whisk it until well mixed. Remove from the heat, cover and set aside for 30 minutes. Reheat gently, adding a little more milk if it seems too thick.

Roast duckling

Golden brown and succulent, roast duckling filled with sage and onion stuffing and served with an apple or gooseberry sauce is one of the classics of the English kitchen. A duckling may look large in comparison with chicken or guinea fowl but one will only just feed four. Use the giblets to make a gravy or, if they are not obtainable, then make it with a little wine or strong dry cider mixed with water.

1 duckling including the giblets	$\frac{1}{2}$ teaspoon black peppercorns
1 bay leaf	$\frac{1}{2}$ lemon

Heat the oven to Gas 6/400°F/200°C.

If the duck has been frozen, make sure it is thoroughly defrosted and dry it thoroughly using kitchen paper. Put the giblets, if available, into a saucepan, cover with water and add the bay leaf and peppercorns. Bring to the boil and simmer gently while the duck is roasting. If you are stuffing the duck, make the stuffing (see below) and fill the cavity; secure with string or toothpicks.

Weigh the duck with its stuffing and calculate the cooking time, allowing 20 minutes per 450 g (1 lb). Prick the duck all over with a fork to allow the fat to escape as the bird roasts, and rub the breast all over with the cut side of the lemon. Stand the duck on a rack in a roasting pan and baste every 30 minutes.

Put the cooked duck on a serving dish and return it to the turned-off oven. Pour away most of the fat from the pan, stir the strained giblet stock into the remaining pan juices, bring to the boil and stir until the gravy is reduced by half. Serve in a sauce boat.

To carve the bird, first cut off the wings with a small piece of breast, then carve the breast in slanting slices working from the wing to the breast bone, finally remove the legs.

Sage and onion stuffing

225 g (8 oz) onions, chopped
6–8 fresh sage leaves, chopped or
    1 teaspoon dried
100 g (4 oz) breadcrumbs
50 g (2 oz) butter, melted

freshly grated peel of 1 lemon
1 egg, beaten
salt
freshly milled black pepper

Put the chopped onion into a saucepan with just sufficient water to cover, bring to the boil and simmer, covered, for about 10 minutes. Add the sage leaves to the onions and steep for 1 minute, then strain, discarding the liquid. Put the drained onions and sage into a bowl and mix in the breadcrumbs, butter, the lemon peel and the egg. Season well with salt and pepper.

Apricot and hazelnut stuffing

As a change from sage and onion stuffing, try this one made with apricots and hazelnuts flavoured with orange.

50 g (2 oz) butter
1 onion, finely chopped
150 g (6 oz) breadcrumbs
100 g (4 oz) dried apricots,
    chopped
50 g (2 oz) hazelnuts, chopped
1 tablespoon chopped parsley

1 teaspoon dried thyme
salt
freshly milled black pepper
finely pared peel and juice of 1
    orange
1 egg

Melt the butter in a frying pan and fry the chopped onion for a few minutes until golden. Stir in the breadcrumbs, apricots, hazelnuts, parsley and thyme. Season with salt and pepper and add the peel and juice of the orange. Beat the egg and add sufficient to bind the mixture together.

Apple sauce

When apple sauce is called for, it is child's play to cook it in the oven. Eliza Acton thought this a far superior way to making it in a saucepan on top of the stove, when it has to be watched and stirred in case it scorches. She added sugar to her recipe but this is only necessary if you are using sour cooking apples. I prefer the flavour of an eating variety like Cox's.

450 g (1 lb) firm eating apples, peeled, cored and sliced
25 g (1 oz) butter, cut in pieces

generous pinch of cinnamon
1 tablespoon water

Put the sliced apples into a small ovenproof dish with the butter, cinnamon and water. Cover and bake in the oven (temperature between Gas 5/375°F/190°C and Gas 6/400°F/200°C) for 40–45 minutes. Mash and serve.

If you prefer to make the apple sauce on top of the stove, melt the butter in a small pan, add the prepared apples, cinnamon and water and cook over a low heat until the apples are soft, stirring frequently.

Roast turkey

As we all know, the turkey came to us from America and long ago replaced goose as our Christmas bird. It has the advantage of being much meatier and therefore more economical but unfortunately, if factory farmed, it has hardly any flavour and tends to dryness. The solution is to go for a free-range bird like the Bronze or Norfolk Black. It will be more expensive but is well worth it for that one festive day in the year. A hen bird has more flesh for its weight and is tenderer than a cock turkey. If your turkey is frozen, it is important to make sure it is completely defrosted before cooking – read label instructions carefully.

Turkey is often served with bacon rolls and small sausages which are roasted with it for the last 30 minutes. Other traditional accompaniments are bread or cranberry sauce, roast potatoes, parsnips, carrots and Brussels sprouts, together with a gravy made with the giblet stock.

The following recipe is for a $5\frac{1}{2}$ kg (12 lb) drawn weight turkey which will give 9–12 servings. If the bird you are buying is offered at the undrawn weight (i.e. with its innards still in place), ask your supplier to calculate accordingly.

5½ kg (12 lb) turkey, drawn
   weight
chestnut stuffing (see below)
50 g (2 oz) butter
1 carrot

1 onion
1 lemon
sprigs of thyme
oil

Heat the oven to Gas 5/375°F/190°C.

Loosen the skin around the breast and insert a thin layer of the stuffing under it. This will help to keep the bird moist as well as looking attractive when the meat is carved. Use the remaining stuffing to fill the breast cavity, that is through the neck. Put the butter, carrot, onion, the lemon and sprigs of thyme into the body cavity.

To calculate the cooking time, weigh the bird after it has been stuffed: allow 15 minutes per 450 g (1 lb) and 15 minutes over. Allow a further 30–40 minutes at the end, when the bird comes out of the oven and, wrapped in foil, is allowed to compact before it is carved.

Pour sufficient oil into the roasting tin to the depth of 2–3 cm (1 in) and set the tin in the heated oven for 5 minutes. After this time, put the turkey on its side in the tin, baste it and cover very loosely with foil. Just before half-time, turn the bird over on to its other side, baste again and re-cover loosely with the foil. Half an hour before the end of the cooking time, turn the turkey breast-side up, remove the foil and baste well. Test to see if the turkey is done by inserting a skewer in the fleshiest part of the leg; if the juice runs clear it is done; if pink, give it a little longer.

Transfer the cooked turkey to a warm serving dish and wrap completely in foil. Keep in a warm place for 30–40 minutes. It will be easier to carve and the flesh will be firm and juicy.

Chestnut stuffing

This is just about the simplest chestnut stuffing you can make – it takes just a few minutes to prepare using canned, unsweetened chestnut purée mixed with whole, prepared chestnuts which are obtainable either in vacuum packs or cans. It makes a perfect stuffing for that Christmas turkey, or halve the quantities and use it to fill a chicken, guinea fowl or pheasant.

450 g (1 lb) can unsweetened
   chestnut purée
225 g (8 oz) packet or can
   prepared whole chestnuts

50 g (2 oz) butter, melted
salt
freshly milled black pepper

Turn the chestnut purée into a mixing bowl and mash it well. Mix in the whole chestnuts and melted butter and season generously with salt and pepper.

Cranberry sauce

Cranberry sauce has become an alternative to bread sauce as the traditional accompaniment to turkey. It can be made well in advance and stored in a screw-topped jar in the fridge. It is important not to add the sugar until the berries are cooked or their skins will remain tough.

225 g (8 oz) cranberries   juice of 1 orange
150 g (6 oz) granulated sugar

Put the cranberries into a saucepan and just cover with water. Bring to the boil and simmer uncovered until the berries start to pop. Continue to simmer for about 5 minutes and remove from the heat. Stir in the sugar and when it has all dissolved add the orange juice. Store in a screw-topped jar in the fridge until ready to use.

Roast goose

On quarter days the squire expected his tenants to bring him a present as well as the rent. At Christmas it would be a capon, a castrated cock fattened for the table, while on Lady Day (25 March) it might be fish. On Midsummer's Day, 24 June, the offering would be a fowl or two and on Michaelmas Day, 29 September, it would be a stubble goose. A stubble goose was a green goose, so called because it had fed all summer on pastures and then additionally been fattened by feeding on the stubble of the harvested wheat and barley. Tradition has it that green geese are served with a sorrel and bilberry sauce, whereas stubble geese were eaten with one of apples, onions and barberries, the berries of the berberis. Other traditions have the goose stuffed with either sage and onion (recipe on page 80 but double the quantities), or prunes (see below).

To feed four, choose a goose weighing 4–5 kg (9–11 lb) and make up the stuffing that most appeals to you.

Heat the oven to Gas 6/400°F/200°C.

Weigh the goose after it has been stuffed and calculate the cooking time, allowing 15 minutes per 450 g (l lb) and 15 minutes over. Stand the stuffed goose in the roasting tin and rub it all over with flour and season it with salt and pepper. Put it in the oven and roast for 30 minutes. Remove from the oven and reduce the heat to Gas 4/350°F/180°C. Prick the goose all over with a fork, taking care to penetrate just the skin and not the flesh, paying especial attention to the fatty areas around the thighs and carcase. Return to the oven.

After 1 hour, remove the goose and repeat the pricking process. If the bird is browning too quickly, cover loosely in foil. Near the end of cooking time, test the goose is cooked by inserting a skewer in the thickest part. If the juice runs clear it is done; if pink, leave for a little longer.

Take the cooked bird out of the roasting tin and put it on a warm plate. Cover with foil and keep in a warm place for 30–40 minutes for the flesh to compact. Serve with apple or gooseberry sauce and a gravy made by pouring away most of the roasting fat (keep it and use to roast potatoes and other vegetables) and stirring in 150 ml ($\frac{1}{4}$ pint) of the stock from the giblets and 150 ml ($\frac{1}{4}$ pint) of strong dry cider. Add 1–2 tablespoons redcurrant or other tart fruit jelly. Stir well until it has reduced by about half.

Prune stuffing

This makes a sweet and delicious change from sage and onion stuffing.

450 g (l lb) prunes, soaked and stoned	$\frac{1}{4}$ teaspoon dried thyme
4 tablespoons soft brown sugar	100 g (4 oz) breadcrumbs
1 tablespoon parsley	1 egg yolk
sprig of sage	salt
	freshly milled black pepper

Mix all the ingredients well together and put into the cavity of the goose.

Giblet stock for gravy

The stock can be made the day before and kept in the fridge until needed.

turkey, goose or chicken giblets $\frac{1}{2}$ teaspoon black peppercorns
1 small onion   1 teaspoon dried mixed herbs
1 bay leaf

Put the giblets with the onion, bay leaf, peppercorns and herbs into a saucepan and cover with water. Bring to the boil, cover and simmer for 1–2 hours. Strain into a bowl and, when cold, cover and put in the fridge. Use to make gravy by adding to the meat juices in the roasting pan.

Spring and Summer Vegetables

Not so very long ago, the arrival of the first spring and summer vegetables brought a touch of excitement to our lives, their transitory moment something to be enjoyed and indulged. Yet it is an enjoyment and indulgence we're in danger of losing, because we have become so reliant on imported and frozen vegetables that we take for granted it is possible to eat things like asparagus and French beans all the year round. As for those bright green frozen peas, we consume them in such quantities there must be more than one generation of people who have no idea they first come in a pod. You may think this doesn't matter. But imported or frozen vegetables can't compare in texture and flavour with our seasonal English varieties which, because they haven't had to travel far, are in as perfect a condition as possible when they reach the greengrocer or supermarket. And of course if you grow your own, you don't need to be told how much more enjoyable they are when freshly picked.

The first of the early broad beans appear in the shops in May, soon to be followed by home-grown French beans, and with any luck there are garden peas in time for Whitsun weekend, when traditionally they are cooked with lamb or duck. At the same time the first English asparagus appears and, if you live in the right places, you may come across hop shoots and samphire. Perhaps, though, nothing tastes quite as good as those first new potatoes, simply steamed or simmered with a sprig of mint and served with oodles of butter and parsley.

These spring and summer vegetables are delicious eaten on their own as a light starter, made into soups, or served as perfect accompaniments to simple grills, roasts and barbecues.

Pods

Broad beans

Broad beans and parsley sauce

Beans and collops

Garden peas, mange-tout and sugar snaps

Buttery peas

Peas with onions

Pea soup

Lamb with peas and onions

Duck with peas

French beans

French beans with parsley

French beans with tomatoes

French beans with lemon juice and cream

French bean salad

Runner beans

Broad beans, the 'beans of antiquity' as Jane Grigson describes them, have been cultivated in Europe and Asia since the Stone Age and the blossoming of their sweet-scented flowers is one of the first indications that spring has arrived. The first are ready to pick in May, although it is not until June that they arrive in any great number in the shops.

Bear in mind that the pods are heavy so you will need at least 225 g (8 oz) per head. Buy them young (a black seam along their length indicates they are past their prime) and to prevent blackening your hands use rubber gloves to shell them. Frozen broad beans can be used instead, in which case use only 450 g (1 lb) to feed four people.

Broad beans and parsley sauce

Traditionally, broad beans are eaten with parsley sauce but if you are pressed for time, simply serve them with lots of butter and a generous sprinkling of chopped parsley, summer savory or snipped chives.

1–1.5 kg (2½–3½ lb) broad beans	freshly milled white or black
salt	pepper
300 ml (½ pint) milk	4 tablespoons chopped parsley,
25 g (1 oz) butter	summer savory or snipped
25 g (1 oz) flour	chives

Shell the beans and put them into a saucepan, just cover with water and season with salt. Bring to the boil, cover and simmer briskly for 5–10 minutes or until the beans are tender. (If using frozen beans follow instructions on packet.)

Meanwhile, make the parsley sauce. Put the milk into a small saucepan, add the butter and flour. Put over a medium heat and bring to the boil, whisking all the time to prevent lumps forming. As the sauce thickens, lower the heat. Stir for 2 minutes and season with salt and pepper. Put over a very low heat until the beans are done. Drain them well but add a little of their cooking liquid to the sauce, just enough to thin it to a creamy consistency. Stir in the chopped herbs. Put the beans into a vegetable dish and pour over the sauce.

Beans and collops

Collops were thin slices of meat or bacon and in the north of England were always served on the Monday before Shrove Tuesday, which was known as Collop Monday. In this adaptation of a seventeenth-century recipe, the saltiness of bacon nicely complements the somewhat bland flavour of broad beans. The addition of tarragon is an idea from Kent.

900 g (2 lb) broad beans   salt
25 g (1 oz) butter   freshly milled black pepper
1 onion, chopped   1–2 tablespoons chopped
50 g (2 oz) back bacon, chopped   tarragon
chicken stock to cover

Shell the beans. Melt the butter in a saucepan and gently fry the onion and bacon for 5 minutes. Add the beans and sufficient stock to cover. Simmer, covered, for 10–15 minutes, until the beans are tender. Remove the lid and boil the liquid hard until it has reduced to 2–3 tablespoons. Season to taste with salt and pepper and strew with the chopped tarragon.

GARDEN PEAS, MANGE-TOUT AND SUGAR SNAPS

The garden pea can trace its ancestry back to neolithic times, whereas the mange-tout (otherwise known as the sugar pea, or in America as the snow pea) is a baby in comparison, having been developed about three centuries ago. Nowadays its sweetness is probably the closest we get to sample the flavour of the garden pea our grandparents used to know – that is, unless you grow your own. Nearly all the best of our commercial crop of garden peas, bright green and bland, go to the frozen food giants or canning factories. It is true it is possible to buy peas in the pod for a short time in the summer but make sure they are fresh and young, or you may be disappointed.

Snap peas or sugar snaps (usually imported from Africa) look like particularly bright, plump young pea pods but, like mange-tout, are eaten in their entirety. All of them are nice with lashings of butter or cream, either as a starter or as an accompanying vegetable.

Buttery peas

450 g (l lb) young garden peas,   sprig of mint
   mange-tout or sugar snaps   50 g (2 oz) butter or 2–3
salt   tablespoons single cream
freshly milled black pepper

Shell the peas or top and tail the mange-tout or sugar snaps. Either steam or boil them with very little water, salt and the mint, covered, until tender but still with a bite. Allow 10 minutes for steaming, 5–7 for boiling. (Old garden peas will take at least twice as long and mange-tout may take rather less.) Drain well, add pepper, stir in the butter or cream and shake the pan vigorously until they are coated all over.

Peas with onions

If your peas are not so young, try this recipe in which they are cooked with spring onions, nutmeg, sugar, mint and parsley and served coated with cream.

450 g (l lb) peas, shelled   1 teaspoon flour
3 spring onions, sliced   2–3 sprigs of mint
1 teaspoon caster sugar   1 tablespoon chopped parsley
$\frac{1}{4}$ teaspoon nutmeg   150 ml ($\frac{1}{4}$ pint) boiling water
salt   2 tablespoons single cream
25 g (1 oz) butter

Put the peas, spring onions, caster sugar, nutmeg and salt into a saucepan. Mash the butter and mix with the flour, form into a ball. Put this on top of the peas with the mint and parsley. Pour over the boiling water, cover and simmer for about 20 minutes, until the peas are tender. Remove the sprigs of mint, stir in the cream and serve.

Pea soup

A pretty soup which can be eaten hot or chilled. When fresh peas are not available make it with frozen peas.

1 kg (2¼ lb) peas or 450 g (l lb) frozen
50 g (2 oz) butter
1 bunch spring onions, chopped
freshly grated nutmeg

sprig of mint
1 litre (1¾ pints) stock or water
150 ml (¼ pint) single cream
2 tablespoons chopped parsley
1 tablespoon snipped chives

Shell the peas, if using fresh. Melt the butter in a saucepan and fry the chopped onions until golden but not brown. Add the shelled peas (plus 2 or 3 pods if using fresh), grated nutmeg, the sprig of mint and the stock or water. Simmer for 30 minutes and put through a food processor or liquidizer.

If you are serving the soup hot, stir in the cream and garnish with the parsley and chives. Alternatively, put the puréed soup into a bowl and chill in the fridge. Before serving, test the seasoning (when chilled, food can become bland), stir in the cream and garnish with the herbs.

Lamb with peas and onions

A joint of lamb seasoned with herbs and spices is roasted on top of little onions simmering in cider in this succulent West Country dish. Towards the end of the cooking time, small garden peas and sprigs of mint are added. Use fresh peas when they are in season but frozen *petits pois* work almost as well.

450 g (1 lb) pickling or small onions
600 ml (l pint) cider if using fresh peas or 300 ml (½ pint) if using frozen
1 kg (2¼ lb) knuckle end of lamb leg
1 teaspoon dried thyme

1 teaspoon dried marjoram
1 teaspoon crushed coriander seeds
½ teaspoon mace
freshly milled black pepper
450 g (1 lb) fresh peas, shelled, or 350 g (12 oz) frozen
2–3 sprigs of mint

Heat the oven to Gas 6/400°F/200°C.

Peel the onions by steeping them for several minutes in boiling water, when their skins should come off easily. Put them in the bottom of a buttered gratin or roasting dish which will hold the lamb comfortably. Pour in 300 ml ($\frac{1}{2}$ pint) of cider. Put a rack on top and sit the lamb on it. Sprinkle the meat with the thyme, marjoram, coriander seeds and mace. Season it with pepper. Put the dish into the oven and roast for 1 hour, basting the lamb half way through with the cidery juices.

At the end of this time, baste the lamb again and, if using fresh peas, bring the remaining 300 ml ($\frac{1}{2}$ pint) of cider to the boil, pour it into the dish and add the peas. If using frozen peas, simply add them to the dish. Add the sprigs of mint. Continue cooking for 20–30 minutes, until the peas are tender. Turn off the oven and transfer the joint and vegetables to a serving dish. Leave in the warm oven while you boil the liquid hard to reduce it by about half. Serve this sauce separately.

Duck with peas

Duck with peas was a traditional dish for Whitsunday in the north of England. In this version it is cooked in cider or stock with the heart of a lettuce and a bunch of herbs – mint, parsley and marjoram – giving zest to the flavour.

1 duckling
2 tablespoons oil
25 g (1 oz) butter plus 1 tablespoon
150 ml ($\frac{1}{4}$ pint) cider or stock
salt
freshly milled black pepper

450 g (1 lb) fresh garden peas
sprigs of mint, marjoram and parsley tied in a bunch
$\frac{1}{4}$ teaspoon mace
1 lettuce heart, finely sliced
1 tablespoon flour

Heat the oven to Gas 5/375°F/190°C.

Prick the duckling all over with the prongs of a fork – this will make the fat run. Heat the oil and 25 g (1 oz) butter in a heavy, flameproof casserole in which the bird will sit comfortably. Fry the duckling all over until golden brown, this will take about 10 minutes and is part of the cooking process. Remove the duckling and discard all the fat, wipe out the pan with kitchen paper and return the duckling. Pour over the cider or stock and season with salt and pepper. Put on the lid and transfer to the oven for 30 minutes. Remove the casserole from the oven and add the peas, herbs, mace and shredded lettuce. Lower the heat to Gas 4/350°F/180°C. Cook for a further 35 minutes. Remove the duckling to a serving dish, surround with the peas and discard the herbs. Put the dish into the turned-off oven while you thicken the sauce. Mash the flour with the tablespoon of butter and add this mixture in small pieces to the cooking liquids in the casserole, stirring all the time over a low heat. Bring to the boil and boil hard, continuing to stir, until the sauce thickens and reduces. Pour some of the sauce over the duckling and put the remainder into a sauce boat.

FRENCH BEANS

Like most beans, the kind grown for their pods which we call French came to Europe from America. They reached England via France, hence their name.

French beans need to be topped and tailed but are cooked whole. If using runner beans in their place, they must also have the stringy fibres along their sides removed and should be cut into lengths of about 5 cm (2 in).

In the following recipes they can be eaten on their own as a first course or as an accompanying vegetable.

French beans with parsley

450 g (1 lb) French beans
salt
25 g (1 oz) butter

freshly milled black pepper
2–3 tablespoons parsley

Cook the beans, uncovered, in salted boiling water for about 10 minutes, until tender. Drain well and return to the pan. Add the butter, season with salt and black pepper and strew over the parsley. Put over a low heat and, when the butter has melted, put on the lid and give the pan a good shake so that all the beans are nicely coated.

French beans with tomatoes

Cook the beans as in the recipe for French beans with parsley. Drain them and keep warm. Heat 2 tablespoons of oil in the saucepan and add 3–4 quartered tomatoes, lower the heat, cover the pan and let them gently stew for about 5 minutes. Stir in the drained beans and season with salt and black pepper and chopped chives.

French beans with lemon juice and cream

Cook the beans as in the recipe for French beans with parsley. Drain well. Put a generous knob of butter in the pan and return the beans, toss them over a medium heat until well coated. Stir in 2 tablespoons of single cream and a generous squeeze of lemon juice. Season with salt and black pepper and strew with chopped parsley.

French bean salad

Cook the beans as in the recipe for French beans with parsley. Drain well and mix with 3–4 tablespoons of olive oil and a squeeze of lemon juice. Add 2 tablespoons parsley and the same amount of snipped chives. Season with pepper and salt. When cold put into a serving dish and strew over a little more parsley.

RUNNER BEANS

Originally these beans were grown for the beauty of their scarlet flowers and if you live in the country or grow your own, you will probably defend their taste and flavour avidly. They are easy to grow and look spectacular covering a trellis or a wigwam of bamboo canes, and it is extremely satisfying picking just enough for supper on a summer's evening. If you have to rely on buying them, as I do, from a greengrocer or supermarket, you may find them rather tough and uninteresting.

To prepare them, remove the stringy fibres along their sides and either cut into chunks of about 5 cm (2 in) or cut them into thin strips or shreds. This last is the traditional method and devotees say it guarantees a superior flavour.

Cook them as in any of the recipes for French beans above.

Sparrowgrass to hop tops

Asparagus or sparrowgrass

Cream and lemon sauce

Sparrowgrass with scrambled eggs

Asparagus peas

Asparagus soup

Spinach

Spinach soup

Watercress

Watercress and leek soup

Samphire

Hop tops

ASPARAGUS OR SPARROWGRASS

Have you ever wondered why this vegetable, especially the thin, young shoots which some people call sprue, is referred to as 'grass' by many established greengrocers? Cultivated in England since Elizabethan times, it was known by its Latin name, *Asparagus*, which over a period of time was corrupted to sparagus. It is not hard to see how, with our passion for turning the uncomfortable into something homely, it became known as sparrowgrass and grass.

The English season is short, from May until the end of June, and we favour green asparagus as opposed to the white which the French and Italians prefer. Prepare by trimming off the hard, woody end of the stalks and scrape the entire stem with a swivel-bladed peeler.

Cook tied in manageable bundles, standing upright, either in an asparagus kettle or in a tall saucepan, with the water coming half way up the stems. If cooking in a regular saucepan, improvise a lid out of foil. The point to remember is that the stalks take longer to cook than the tips, which will be steamed while the stalks boil. Include the trimmings from the stalks in the pot and, when the asparagus is done, save them and the cooking liquid to make soup. Cooking time depends on the thickness of the stalks, anything between 15 and 45 minutes. Drain them well and eat warm or cold with the fingers, dipping the tips into melted butter or olive oil mixed with a little lemon juice – or with the following sauce.

Cream and lemon sauce

This sauce is not only delicious with asparagus but with other kinds of vegetables, too, such as French beans, mange-tout, sugar snaps or samphire, especially when served as a starter.

50 g (2 oz) butter	freshly milled black pepper
150 ml ($\frac{1}{4}$ pint) double cream	juice of $\frac{1}{2}$ lemon
salt	1–2 tablespoons chopped chives

Melt the butter in a small saucepan and stir in the cream. Let it heat gently but do not boil. When it is hot, season with the salt and pepper, squeeze in the juice of the lemon and stir in the chives. Serve immediately.

Sparrowgrass with scrambled eggs

If you want a supper or lunchtime treat, make this dish which turns scrambled eggs into something really special. Of course, if you can't get hold of fresh asparagus, cheat and use canned pieces instead.

450 g (l lb) young asparagus	50 g (2 oz) butter
8 eggs	4 slices buttered toast
salt	1–2 tablespoons chopped parsley
freshly milled black pepper	

Tie the asparagus into bundles and cook until tender (see page 103. Drain well and, when cool enough to handle, chop into small pieces (save the water and tough end of stalks for soup).

Beat the eggs well, stir in the asparagus and season with salt and pepper. Melt the butter in a heavy-based saucepan and when it is piping hot pour in the egg mixture. Lower the heat and cook, not too fast, stirring from time to time until the eggs scramble and become thick and creamy. Pile on to pieces of hot buttered toast and serve sprinkled with parsley.

Asparagus peas

This is not a recipe for those little winged pods known as asparagus peas, but an adaptation of Eliza Acton's 'Asparagus points dressed like peas'. It is perfect for those small, green tips of asparagus which appear on the supermarket shelves from time to time. Serve as a starter with crusty bread and butter.

225 g (8 oz) asparagus tips	2 egg yolks, beaten
50 g (2 oz) butter	salt
1 teaspoon cornflour	freshly milled black pepper
$\frac{1}{2}$ teaspoon sugar	2 tablespoons chopped parsley

Cut the asparagus into 1 cm ($\frac{3}{4}$ in) lengths. Steam them for 5–7 minutes until they are just tender. Reserve the cooking water.

Melt the butter and stir in the cornflour and sugar. Add the pieces of asparagus and stir them over a low heat for 2 minutes. Pour in sufficient of the cooking water barely to cover (keep the rest for soup). Raise the heat and boil rapidly for 4–5 minutes, until almost all the liquid has evaporated. Remove from the heat and stir in the beaten egg yolks. Season with salt and pepper and serve on warm plates garnished with the parsley.

Asparagus soup

Make this with the trimmings from cooked asparagus and about 600 ml (1 pint) of the liquid from the pot in which it was cooked. Melt 50 g (2 oz) butter in a pan, add a chopped onion, 2 chopped potatoes and a clove of garlic, cover and let them sweat for 10 minutes over a low heat. Add the asparagus liquid and the trimmings. Simmer for 30 minutes. Purée the soup and put it through a sieve to get rid of the fibres. Add salt and pepper to taste, a little freshly grated nutmeg and a squeeze of lemon juice. Reheat, stir in 2–3 tablespoons cream and serve sprinkled with snipped chives.

SPINACH

Spinach is definitely an acquired taste and unfortunately it is one that a lot of people never do acquire because they equate its flavour with bitter childhood memories – not even Popeye could make it palatable for them. Ironically it has been discovered that it contains oxalic acid and so is no longer recommended for young children!

Spinach has a romantic past, having been developed by the Persians and, by way of Nepal, arrived in China in AD 647 as a present to the emperor, where it was called *poh ts'ai*. It reached Europe with the Arabs, who took it to Spain and from there it travelled, in the sixteenth century, via France to England. A favourite way of serving it was in a sweet tart mixed with dried fruits soaked in *eau de vie*, a tart which is still made in Provence to be eaten on Christmas Eve (there is a recipe in *Simple French Cuisine*).

Ready-packed spinach needs only to be rinsed before cooking but loose spinach can be very dirty and must be washed in several changes of water. Young spinach is delicious raw in salads, especially with small pieces of bacon and bread fried until crisp in olive oil. It shrinks dramatically in cooking and 225 g (8 oz) is only enough for one serving.

Cook spinach with no added water and a little salt in a covered pan over a lowish heat for 5 minutes. As it heats, it exudes a lot of liquid, turns limp and darkens. Remove the lid and cook a few minutes more before draining well in a colander. Press it down with a wooden spoon or saucer to get rid of as much wateriness as possible, then chop it. Melt a knob of butter in the pan, return the spinach and turn it over and over to coat evenly. Season with a little nutmeg or mace and perhaps a squeeze of lemon or orange juice or a sprinkling of grated cheese. Perhaps nicest of all, eat it as a lunch or supper dish topped with a couple of poached eggs.

Spinach soup

Smooth and creamy, this olive-green soup subtly flavoured with lemon is delicious served cold or, if the weather is chilly, serve it hot with fried chopped bacon and sippets

50 g (2 oz) butter	1 bay leaf
1 onion, chopped	freshly grated nutmeg
450 g (1 lb) fresh or frozen spinach	juice of $\frac{1}{2}$ lemon
225 g (8 oz) potatoes, quartered	salt
1 litre ($1\frac{3}{4}$ pints) stock	freshly milled black pepper
sprig of parsley	2 tablespoons single cream
	1–2 tablespoons snipped chives

Melt the butter in a saucepan and fry the onion gently for several minutes. Add the spinach and potatoes, cover and leave to sweat over a low heat for 5 minutes. Pour in the stock and add the parsley, bay leaf, grated nutmeg and lemon juice. Season with salt and pepper. Bring to the boil and simmer for 30 minutes. Purée in a food processor or liquidizer. Put into a soup tureen or serving bowl, cover and leave to cool. Refrigerate until ready to serve. If the soup seems too thick, stir in a little more stock or water. Check the seasonings – cold food can often be more bland than when it is heated. Stir in the cream, creating a marbled effect, and scatter with the chives.

WATERCRESS

Watercress, with its distinctive bitter flavour, used to be gathered wild in the spring from streams and brooks. Not as idyllic as it sounds, as the water was often polluted and typhoid was rife. Nowadays it is grown commercially in special beds, rooted in clean gravel over which water drawn from underground chalk streams is constantly flowing, and because the temperature of the water remains at a constant 11°C even in winter, it is available all the year round.

Follow the custom of the nineteenth-century workmen, who ate watercress sandwiches for breakfast, although you might prefer it a little later in the day with the addition of a handful of prawns and a spread of mayonnaise. Use it as a garnish, either whole to accompany grills, roast poultry or game, or chopped in place of parsley. It gives a distinctive bittersweet flavour to salads and looks especially pretty mixed with sliced orange, a sprinkling of grated carrot and moistened with a little oil.

Perhaps most famously of all it makes interesting soups, which are equally good chilled in summer or hot in winter.

Watercress and leek soup

In this recipe watercress combines with leek and potato and is flavoured at the end with a sprinkling of either chopped parsley, coriander leaves or chervil.

25 g (1 oz) butter	salt
2 tablespoons oil	freshly milled black pepper
2 leeks, chopped	2–3 tablespoons single cream or
1 large potato, chopped	thick yoghurt
1 bunch watercress, chopped	2–3 tablespoons chopped
1 litre (1¾ pints) chicken stock	parsley, coriander or chervil

Heat the butter with the oil in a large saucepan. Add the chopped leeks and potato followed by the watercress. Mix, put on the lid and sweat the vegetables over a low heat for 5–10 minutes. Pour in the stock and season with salt and pepper. Simmer, covered, for 30–40 minutes. Purée in a blender until smooth.

If serving cold, allow to cool and refrigerate. Once cold, if the soup seems too thick, stir in a little cold water. Just before serving, check the seasoning and if necessary add a little more salt and pepper. Stir in the cream or yoghurt and garnish with the parsley, coriander or chervil.

If serving hot, stir in the cream or yoghurt and add the herb garnish straight away.

Samphire

In spring and early summer, marsh samphire or salicorne can be found growing wild around the coast, especially in Norfolk. Just as the word sparrowgrass is a corruption of sparagus so samphire is a corruption of the French name, *herbe de St Pierre*. In England it is also known as glasswort because glassmakers used to burn it and use the ashes for their craft. Bright green and fleshy, it is delicious eaten like asparagus with plenty of melted butter.

Rinse it well to remove the sand and cut off the roots if this has not already been done. Either boil or steam the samphire until tender, allowing about 10 minutes for boiling or 15–20 for steaming.

Serve with melted butter seasoned with a little lemon juice, salt and pepper and a sprinkling of chervil or parsley. Dip the sprigs in the buttery sauce and strip the flesh from the stems with your teeth.

Hop tops

For a land of beer lovers, we are surprisingly ignorant about hop tops. These are the shoots of the hop plant which appear from around March to the end of May. If you live where beer is produced perhaps you are lucky and have access to them. If you do, you probably don't need to be told how delicious they are.

Wash well under the tap, tie in bundles like asparagus and cooked in salted water with the juice of a lemon until tender. Eat with melted butter flavoured as in the above recipe or with the cream and lemon sauce on page 103.

Summer and Autumn Fruits

When the hedgerows and commons are laced with elderflowers, the first of the little, hard gooseberries arrive; tart but full of flavour they make the perfect English fool or can be turned into sauces and stuffings for mackerel and pork. Later, if you are lucky, you will come across cherries from Kent and the first of our strawberry crop. Ripe and juicy and brimming with juice, with that first bite it is hard to realize how we managed to enjoy flavourless, imported strawberries at Christmas. But best of all, perhaps, is the brief spell when raspberries appear, along with gleaming red, black, white and pink currants. This is the moment for indulgent puddings and no holding back on the cream.

And when summer turns to autumn is the time for thinking ahead and making preserves. Just the smell of jams and pickles takes me back to one of my favourite rooms in my grandmother's house: the walk-in larder with its stone floor on which she stood the milk in a jug covered with one of those muslin cloths with coloured beads sewn all along the edge. The room was cool and dimly lit from a window which looked into the passageway leading into the garden, so it shone with a sort of green reflected light. The larder had shelves on all four walls, a broad one all round for storing everyday foods and then above were narrow shelves for putting her home-made preserves. They gleamed all colours from pale gold to deep red and made this greedy little girl dream of the lovely treats that were still to come.

At the end of summer the new season's crop of apples begins to appear in the shops, to be made not just into delicious tarts and crumbles but to give added interest and flavour to soups, celery, chutney, pheasant and pigeon as well as bangers and mash. Cider, too, comes into its own, in dishes or pies made with mussels and eels, fish, game, guinea fowl, chicken and pork.

Berries and soft fruits

Mackerel with gooseberry stuffing

Pork chops with gooseberry sauce

Gooseberry fool

Gooseberry charlotte

Cherry pudding

Cherry brandy and others

Strawberries and redcurrants

Strawberry fool

Strawberries and burnt cream

Strawberry shortbread

Strawberry tartlets

Summer fruit salad

Raspberries

Summer pudding

Raspberry and redcurrant shortcake

Raspberry vinegar

Mackerel with gooseberry stuffing

Gooseberries like northern climates, so it is not surprising that they flourish here, getting better and better the further north we go. In the nineteenth century, gooseberry shows were all the rage in the Midlands and further north. It is said the best are grown in Scotland.

It is very much an English idea, invented in the sixteenth century, to match their acidic flavour against the oiliness of mackerel. This recipe, in which the fish are stuffed with a gooseberry stuffing flavoured with ginger, is a variation on the more familiar dish in which the fish is served with a sauce made from the fruit.

Mackerel must be spanking fresh. Judge them by their bright eyes, stiff spine and sparkling skin. Ask the fishmonger to bone them for you, or do it yourself. Slit the fish along the belly and open them up as much as possible before laying them belly-side down on to a board. Press all along the backbone with your thumbs until you feel it yielding away from the flesh and the fish flattens. Turn the fish over and ease out the spine and attached bones with the help of a pointed knife. Remove any stray bones either with your fingers or by using tweezers.

225 g (8 oz) gooseberries	salt
1 teaspoon grated fresh or	freshly milled black pepper
$\frac{1}{2}$ teaspoon powdered ginger	4 mackerel
50 g (2 oz) butter	300 ml ($\frac{1}{2}$ pint) strong dry cider
50 g (2 oz) breadcrumbs	

Heat the oven to Gas 5/375°F/190°C.

Make the stuffing by putting the gooseberries into a saucepan with the ginger and half the butter. Simmer them gently until tender. Purée them by putting them through a sieve or mouli-légumes. Mix in the breadcrumbs and season with salt and pepper. Stuff the mackerel. Lay them in a buttered dish, pour over the cider and dot with the remaining butter. Bake for 25 minutes.

Pork chops with gooseberry sauce

This pale green sauce with its bittersweet flavour of gooseberries and cider is delicious not only with pork but with duck and goose too, and, as just about everybody knows, it also goes well with mackerel and other oily fish. This recipe, in which it is served with grilled pork chops, is perfect for a summer's evening, when the chops can perhaps be cooked over a barbecue.

4 pork chops	225 g (8 oz) gooseberries
juice of $\frac{1}{2}$ lemon	2 tablespoons sugar
sprigs of rosemary	$\frac{1}{4}$ teaspoon mace
freshly milled black pepper	25 g (1 oz) butter
5 tablespoons strong dry cider	

Marinate the chops in the lemon juice with the sprigs of rosemary and freshly milled black pepper for at least 30 minutes.

Meanwhile make the gooseberry sauce. Put the cider, gooseberries, sugar, mace and butter into a saucepan and simmer until the gooseberries are soft. Sieve or put through a mouli-légumes, return to the pan and set aside until ready to eat.

Heat the grill for 4–5 minutes and grill the chops for 3–4 minutes on either side. Reheat the sauce. If it seems too runny, boil it hard to reduce, stirring all the time. Put the chops on to a warm serving dish and pour the sauce all round.

Gooseberry fool

Gooseberry fool has a beautiful sweet yet refreshing flavour, but it can look very unenticing if it is so well mixed that it takes on an overall beige-green appearance. The secret is to mix it lightly so that it is streaked with green and cream. The same recipe can be used for rhubarb or apricots – dried apricots especially make a delicious fool. Use raspberries or strawberries in the same way; there is no need to cook them, and leave out the cinnamon. When elderflowers are in season, it's a nice touch to dip two or three heads into the cooked gooseberries; they give a lovely muscat flavour to the fool. In the absence of the flowers, stir in a tablespoon or two of elderflower cordial.

450 g (l lb) gooseberries
$\frac{1}{4}$ teaspoon cinnamon
75 –100 g (3–4 oz) caster sugar

300 ml ($\frac{1}{2}$ pint) whipped cream
finely grated peel of 1 lemon

Put the gooseberries into a saucepan with very little water and the cinnamon and simmer for 10–15 minutes until they are soft. Sieve or put through a mouli-légumes to make a purée and get rid of the pips, tops and tails. Add sugar to taste leaving a hint of tartness. When completely cold, lightly fold in the whipped cream to achieve a marbled effect. Spoon into individual pots or glasses and chill. Sprinkle each with a little grated lemon peel just before serving.

Gooseberry charlotte

This essentially English pudding, often made with apples, is linked in culinary myth with Charlotte, the wife of George III, who is supposed to have taken an interest in fruit growing. It is a sort of cooked summer pudding, slices of bread being used to line a mould and enclose a purée of sweetened fruit. This recipe uses gooseberries but the fruit could just as well be apples, rhubarb, plums, apricots or greengages. It comes out of the oven crisp and golden, to be eaten hot or warm with lashings of cream. For best results, use good bread, not soggy, ready sliced.

450 g (l lb) gooseberries
75 –100 g (3–4 oz) soft brown
   sugar
$\frac{1}{4}$ teaspoon cinnamon
1 tablespoon water
1 egg yolk

100 g (4 oz) melted butter
sufficient thin crustless slices
   white bread to line and cover
   your dish
caster sugar
single cream

Heat the oven to Gas 6/400°F/200°C.

Put the gooseberries, soft brown sugar and cinnamon into a saucepan with the water and simmer, uncovered, for 10–15 minutes until the fruit is soft. Put through a sieve or mouli-légumes to form a purée and get rid of the pips. Mix in the egg yolk. Melt the butter in a saucepan and brush a little over the base and sides of a deep metal pie dish, cake tin or charlotte mould of about 1 litre (1$\frac{3}{4}$ pint) capacity. Dip both sides of the bread slices into the melted butter and line the base and sides of your container with them, patching any gaps with small pieces. Pour in the fruit purée, cover the top with more slices of buttered bread and sprinkle with a little caster sugar.

Bake for 30–40 minutes until golden brown. Loosen the sides of the charlotte by running the blade of a knife all round the tin and carefully invert on to a warm serving plate. Add a sprinkling of caster sugar and serve hot or warm with cream.

CHERRIES

The cherry probably came to England from Persia in the first century AD, brought here by the Romans. It flourished especially in Kent but also in Buckinghamshire, Berkshire, Herefordshire and Gloucestershire. There are basically two kinds: sour cherries, which are ideal for cooking, pickling or preserving in brandy, and sweet cherries, which can be eaten just as they are. The best of the cooking cherries are morellos.

Cherry pudding

In Kent they make a pudding similar to a *clafoutis*, which is simply a batter pudding poured over the cherries and steamed or baked for an hour. I prefer this variation, which is more like bread and butter pudding. Make it with those gleaming black morello cherries. Out of season, or for cooks in a hurry, use the canned, stoned variety, in which case the fruit needs no cooking and the amount of sugar in the recipe should be reduced by half.

When cherries are out of season, use other kinds of fruit such as pears, peaches or plums, cutting them into even-sized slices and discarding cores or stones.

450 g (1 lb) black cherries
1 tablespoon water
100 g (4 oz) caster or vanilla
  sugar (see Etceteras)

50 g (2 oz) butter
6 thin slices of day-old white
  bread

Put the cherries into a pan with the water, and half the sugar. Stew them over a low heat until they are soft. Allow to cool and, if you prefer them unpitted, remove their stones, reserving the juice.

Heat the oven to Gas 6/400°F/200°C.

Use about three-quarters of the butter to butter the bread. Lay half the bread slices, butter side down, over the base of a shallow ovenproof dish. Spread the cherries on top and pour over 150 ml ($\frac{1}{4}$ pint) of their juice (or the syrup from the can). Put the remaining bread slices on top, again butter side down. Sprinkle with the remaining sugar and dot with the rest of the butter cut in small pieces. Bake for 25–30 minutes until the top is golden brown and crisp and the sugar has begun to caramelize. Delicious eaten piping hot, warm or cold.

Cherry brandy and others

Tart morello cherries steeped for several months in sugar and brandy make a wonderful liqueur which used to be widely made in Kent, and the marinated cherries themselves are delicious to eat. You don't need to limit yourself to cherries but can use all kinds of other soft fruits such as strawberries, raspberries, blackberries, mulberries and grapes. If brandy is too expensive use gin or vodka instead. These soft fruits go mushy and because the alcohol bleaches their colour tend to look unappealing, so it is better to strain the liqueur into a bottle. The fruits themselves can be mixed with whipped cream and sugar and made into ice cream. Drunk as liqueurs or used to give interest to plain ice creams, these alcoholic drinks are a cheerful reminder of summer during the winter months.

450 g (1 lb) morello cherries   2 cloves
225 g (8 oz) granulated sugar   sufficient brandy to cover

Remove the stalks from the fruit and prick each one with a darning needle. Put them into a 1 litre ($1\frac{3}{4}$ pint) preserving jar and sprinkle in the sugar. Add the cloves and pour in sufficient brandy to cover. Seal and leave for at least 3 months before using. Serve by putting two or three cherries into small cups or glasses and topping up with the now crimson brandy. The cherries can be eaten with the fingers or with a small teaspoon.

STRAWBERRIES AND REDCURRANTS

The cultivated strawberry was unheard of anywhere until a wild variety was brought to France in the eighteenth century by a French naval officer called Freziers. It came from Chile and had large yellow berries and a flavour like pineapple. It didn't actually do very well and didn't taste half as good as our native wild strawberries. Then someone had the idea of crossing the Chilean strawberry with wild ones from Virginia. The result: the first of the modern strawberry, so delicious dipped in sugar and cream.

Red and black currants were introduced from northern Europe in the sixteenth century. It was thought they must be the fruits which became dried currants (in reality black grapes from Corinth) so they were giving their erroneous name. They are actually part of the gooseberry family. White and pink are simply varieties of red. They appear in the shops for a few brief weeks to add a sharp flavour to puddings and fruit salads or to be made into jams or jellies. So when you get tired of strawberries and cream, try putting them in a bowl with a handful or two of redcurrants. Not only do they look pretty, glistening like beads, but add a sharp contrast to the strawberries' sweetness. An easy wasy to strip currants from their stalks is by running them through the prongs of a fork.

Strawberry fool

Nothing can be simpler. It's just a question of mashing the fruit, mixing with sugar and folding the mixture into whipped cream. Allow 300 ml ($\frac{1}{2}$ pint) cream to every 225 g (8 oz) of fruit.

Strawberries and burnt cream

Forget today's low-fat desserts and follow the example of Trinity College, Cambridge, which enthusiastically adopted *crème brulée* as its own and served the creamy mixture with its brittle caramel topping during May week accompanied by piles of strawberries.

Prepare the burnt cream a day ahead. Incidentally, the vanilla pod can be one used to flavour caster sugar (see Etceteras). After you have used it, simply rinse it under the tap, leave it to dry and return it to the sugar jar.

4 egg yolks   caster sugar
600 ml (1 pint) double cream   450 g (1 lb) strawberries in a
1 vanilla pod   bowl

Beat the egg yolks until frothy in a heatproof bowl large enough to hold the cream. Heat the cream with the vanilla pod in a saucepan until just below boiling point. Remove the vanilla pod and pour the cream over the egg yolks, stirring constantly. Stand the bowl in a saucepan of hot water, heat gently and stir constantly, until the custard thickens, taking care it does not boil or the mixture will curdle. If this should happen, immediately put the bowl into a basin of cold water, which will lower the heat and prevent further curdling. Pour the custard into a shallow heatproof dish and leave overnight.

Two or three hours before serving, heat the grill until red hot. Sprinkle the surface of the custard with sufficient caster sugar to cover it completely. Put under the hot grill until the top caramelizes and turns a golden brown. Put in a cool place for the top to glaze and harden, but not in the fridge where it would simply turn limp.

Strawberry shortbread

When strawberries are expensive, which they usually are, this shortbread recipe is a perfect way to turn quite a small quantity into a luxurious dessert for four.

100 g (4 oz) butter
50 g (2 oz) caster sugar
100 g (4 oz) plain flour
50 g (2 oz) ground almonds

300 ml ($\frac{1}{2}$ pint) double cream, whipped
225 g (8 oz) strawberries, hulled

Heat the oven to Gas 4/350°F/180°C.

Rub the butter and sugar together and gradually mix in the flour and ground almonds until you have a thick dough. (This can be done speedily in a food processor.) Roll the dough into a ball, flatten it and put into the centre of a buttered 20 cm (8 in) flan tin with a removable base. Spread it out evenly over the base using your fingers. Prick all over with a fork and bake for 20–25 minutes until the surface is pale gold. Allow to cool in the tin.

Just before serving, remove the outer ring from the flan tin, spread the cream over the surface of the shortbread and decorate with the strawberries.

Strawberry tartlets

Use deepish tart tins to make these little tartlets, modestly described by Eliza Acton in her *Modern Cookery for Private Families* as 'good'.

225 g (8 oz) shortcrust or sweet
  pastry
225 g (8 oz) strawberries, hulled

50 g (2 oz) caster sugar
4 eggs, beaten

Line the tart tins with the pastry. Crush the strawberries and mix them with the caster sugar. Stir in the eggs and whisk until frothy. Fill the pastry tarts two-thirds full and bake for 12–15 minutes until the mixture is puffed and golden.

Summer fruit salad

Nothing can be simpler than making a summer fruit salad. It can be flavoured with wine or cider or the juice of a lemon but for a change try using jasmine or rosehip tea or one of the flower or fruit herbal varieties. The quantity of fruit will depend on the size of your bowl and the number who are eating. Allow 150–225 g (6–8 oz) per head.

300 ml (½ pint) strong jasmine,
  rosehip, or flower or fruit
  herbal tea
mixture of summer fruits i.e.
  black cherries, seedless grapes,

raspberries, strawberries, red
or white currants,
loganberries, tayberries etc.
2 tablespoons caster sugar

Make the tea and set aside to cool. Put the fruit into a bowl and sprinkle with the sugar. When the tea is quite cold, pour it over the fruit. Mix gently and put into a cool place until ready to serve.

RASPBERRIES

My favourite fruit are as transitory and elusive as summer itself. Grow them if you can and have the pleasure of picking them just when you want to eat them instead of having to buy them, already going slightly mouldy, in punnets in the supermarket or greengrocer. Although raspberries have probably always grown wild in Britain, it took France to cultivate them and send them to us. They took immediately to our more northern climate and, like gooseberries, flourish the further north you go, especially in Scotland.

They are delicious eaten quite simply with a sprinkling of sugar and a big dollop of clotted or whipped cream. Or turn them into a fool, following the recipe for strawberries on page 120 and adding a little lemon juice.

Summer pudding

A pudding for the height of summer when all the summer berries appear in the shops together. Make it with a base of raspberries with a mixture of white, red or blackcurrants. This type of pudding can be adapted for all seasons. In autumn, use blackberries and apples and in winter, cranberries and frozen raspberries. (Detailed recipes for both of these are in my book, *Kitchen Suppers*.)

Because the bread must absorb the juice from the fruits, this pudding is made at least one day ahead. Eat it with single cream.

700 g (1½ lb) raspberries and a mixture of white, red or blackcurrants
150 g (6 oz) caster sugar

5 mm (¼ in) thick slices stale bread, crusts removed
scented geranium or vine leaves (optional)

Put the raspberries and currants into a saucepan with the sugar. Bring slowly to the boil, stirring occasionally. When the sugar has completely dissolved, simmer for 2–3 minutes until the fruit yields its juices.

Line a pudding basin with slices of bread, plugging any gaps with small pieces. Pour in the fruit and the juices. Cover the top with more slices of bread, trimming it to fit. Cover with a flat-bottomed plate or saucer and weight this down with something heavy like an iron or a couple of tins. Put in the fridge and leave until the next day.

To serve, run a knife round the edge of the pudding and invert on to a serving plate. Decorate with scented geranium or vine leaves if available.

Raspberry and redcurrant shortcake

On a chilly summer evening, serve this dessert with its crumbly topping. Although it can be made with almost any combination of soft summer fruits, here it is made with raspberries, whose slight mustiness contrasts agreeably with the acidity of redcurrants.

150 g (6 oz) self-raising flour   350 g (12 oz) raspberries
50 g (2 oz) butter   100 g (4 oz) redcurrants
75 g (3 oz) caster sugar

Heat the oven to Gas 5/375°F/190°C.

Put the flour into a bowl, rub in the butter until the mixture resembles fine crumbs. Mix with the caster sugar. (This can be speedily done in a food processor.) Lay the fruit over the base of a shallow ovenproof dish and sprinkle with the crumble mixture. Spread it evenly over the surface. Bake for 30–35 minutes. Eat warm with cream.

Raspberry vinegar

Nowadays most of us think of raspberry vinegar as a rather passé relic of nouvelle cuisine, but sweetened fruit vinegars laced with honey or olive oil were the classic remedy for a sore throat. They also make cool summer drinks when diluted with water or soda water and cubes of ice.

450 g (l lb) raspberries   600 ml (1 pint) wine or cider
sugar   vinegar

Put the raspberries in a bowl and pour over the vinegar. Cover and set aside in a cool place for 5 days, stirring once a day. Strain the liquid into a measuring jug and pour into a heavy-based pan. Add 450 g (l lb) sugar for every 600 ml (1 pint) juice. Bring slowly to the boil, stirring occasionally. When all the sugar has completely dissolved, boil for 10 minutes. Pour into bottles, seal and set aside for 2 weeks before using.

Pickled pears to hodgkin

Pickle making

Pickled pears

Pickled damsons

Spiced crab apples

Pickled walnuts

Spiced vinegar

Pickled mushrooms

Jam making and ideas for jams

Jelly making and ideas for jellies

Fruit cheeses

Damson or sloe gin

Hodgkin (fruits in alcohol)

Pickle making

All sorts of fruit and vegetables can be spiced or pickled and I have detailed several in this chapter. There are a few simple rules to follow.

- Don't use pans made of copper, brass or iron because the vinegar will cause a chemical reaction. Only use ones made of stainless steel or which are enamelled.
- Use wooden utensils to stir.
- Don't use jars with unlined metal lids because of the chemical reaction.
- Malt vinegar is normally used although you can use wine or cider vinegars but they are more expensive. Brown malt vinegar has a stronger flavour but white allows the colour and variety of fruit to show through. The choice is yours.

Pickled pears

These pickled pears are perfect accompaniments to cold meats, especially ham or turkey. Use small, hard pears and pickle them several weeks ahead of time so that they are impregnated with the flavour of the spices and mature to pale amber.

350 g (12 oz) granulated sugar
600 ml (1 pint) malt vinegar
sliver of root ginger
$\frac{1}{2}$ stick cinnamon
finely pared peel of $\frac{1}{2}$ lemon

2 teaspoons whole allspice
900 g (2 lb) pears, peeled,
   quartered and halved
whole cloves

Put the sugar and vinegar into a saucepan and heat gently until the sugar has dissolved. Add the ginger, cinnamon, lemon peel and the allspice. Stud each pear half with a whole clove and add to the pan. Simmer until the pear halves are soft enough to be pierced with a toothpick but still hold their shape. Use a slotted spoon to transfer them to warmed preserving jars. Bring the liquid back to the boil and simmer until it turns into a thick syrup. Strain the syrup over the fruit and discard the spices. If it does not completely cover the pears, top up with a little extra vinegar. Seal and keep for 6–8 weeks before eating.

Pickled damsons

Tart little damsons, which sport the grand Latin name of *Prunus domestica damascena*, the prune from Damascus, have adapted with gusto to our sharper, northern climate. They have thick skins and grow profusely in the Lake District, where they are made into damson cheese and damson gin or, as in this recipe, into a pickle which goes well with cold meats like ham or chicken.

900 g (2 lb) damsons   1 stick cinnamon
150 ml ($\frac{1}{4}$ pint) malt vinegar   2 cloves
450 g (1 lb) preserving sugar

Prick each damson with a darning needle. Put them with the vinegar into a saucepan and bring slowly to the boil. Simmer for 5 minutes. Remove the damsons, using a slotted spoon, and divide among three 450 g (1 lb) jars which have been warmed in a low oven. Add the sugar and spices to the liquid in the saucepan and bring slowly to the boil. Once the sugar has dissolved, boil briskly for 15–20 minutes until thick and syrupy. Strain over the fruit and leave to get cold. Seal the jars and leave at least 1 week before eating.

Spiced crab apples

In the Middle Ages crab apples were used to make *verjuice*, a kind of rustic vinegar which was gradually replaced by the more sophisticated version made from grapes. As an alternative to making them into jelly, crab apples naturally lend themselves to spicing and make a piquant accompaniment to cold meats. They are spiced whole and need only be washed, picked over to see there are no blemished fruits and the stalks removed. Prick each one with the prongs of a fork to allow the flavours to penetrate.

450 ml ($\frac{3}{4}$ pint) malt vinegar   piece of ginger, bruised
700 g ($1\frac{1}{2}$ lb) soft brown sugar   thinly pared peel of $\frac{1}{2}$ lemon
2 teaspoons ground cinnamon   900 g (2 lb) crab apples
2 teaspoons allspice

Put the vinegar and sugar into a stainless steel or enamelled saucepan and heat slowly, stirring from time to time, until the sugar dissolves. Add all the remaining ingredients and simmer until the crab apples are just tender. Using a slotted spoon, carefully remove them and pack into warm, sterilized jars.

Boil the liquid over a steady heat for about 30 minutes until it reduces by half and becomes syrupy. Allow to cool for 15 minutes before carefully pouring over the crab apples until the jars are completely filled. Seal and store for 2 months before eating.

Pickled walnuts

If you are lucky enough to have a walnut tree, once common in many farmyards and gardens in southern England, consider pickling them to eat with cold meats or as a traditional accompaniment to steak and kidney pie. The nuts must be gathered while they are still green, some time between Midsummer's Day and mid July, because they must be pickled when the inner husk is still soft (test this by piercing with a skewer). Handle them with rubber gloves, as walnut juice will stain your hands an almost indelible brown.

Prick the walnuts all over with a darning needle and put them into a preserving jar. Cover them with water and add salt, allowing 150 g (6 oz) to every 1½ litres (2½ pints) of water. Leave for a week. Drain them and cover them with fresh water and add salt in the same proportions. Leave for a further week. Drain them, spread them out on a tray and put them in a sunny place until they turn black.

When they are black, pack them into jars and cover them with spiced vinegar (see below).

Spiced vinegar

malt vinegar	allspice
peppercorns	slice of root ginger

Put the vinegar into a saucepan, basing the amount you use on how much water was needed to cover the walnuts. For every 1½ litres (2½ pints) add 1 tablespoon each of peppercorns and allspice and a slice of root ginger, all lightly crushed. Boil for 10 minutes. Allow to cool and strain over the walnuts.

Pickled mushrooms

In the days when mushrooms were purely seasonal it was normal to
pickle them. Recipes go way back and it is only when we get to the
Victorians that garlic disappears from them. Garlic, in fact, has a long
pedigree in English cooking, but as time went by it was regarded with
loathing, perhaps due to the fact that it was so often kept in damp
conditions, and dried garlic thrives on gentle warmth. Although we
can always get mushrooms, this is one way to deal with them if there
happens to be a surplus hanging around. They can be eaten with cold
meats or added to stews and meat dishes.

450 g (1 lb) very fresh button mushrooms	slice of ginger root
salt	2 cloves
300 ml ($\frac{1}{2}$ pint) white wine vinegar	$\frac{1}{2}$ a whole nutmeg
	2 shreds mace
1 teaspoon white peppercorns	1–2 cloves garlic, left whole
	oil

Wash the mushrooms in a colander under running cold water. Half fill
a saucepan with water, add a pinch of salt and bring it to the boil. Add
the mushrooms and simmer them for 3 minutes. Drain well and lay
them to dry between double sheets of kitchen paper.

Put the vinegar, peppercorns, ginger, cloves, nutmeg, mace, garlic
cloves and a teaspoon of salt into the pan and bring to the boil.
Remove from the heat and set aside to cool. Spoon the mushrooms
into clean, dry jars, and strain the spiced vinegar over them. Top up
with oil. Cover and store in a cool, dry place.

Jam making

If you are lucky and have a glut of fruit – perhaps you grow your
own or have found a farm where you can pick and buy – there comes
the question of what to do with it. One solution is to make jam. Easy
to make and even easier to eat, full of the flavours of fruit and sun,
jams are a great antidote to winter blues. They can be successfully
made from most kinds of fruit provided you follow a few simple
rules.

● It is the pectin in the fruit which aids setting and as unripe fruit is
higher in pectin than ripe fruit, go for slightly unripe fruit in perfect

condition. Whenever possible wipe rather than wash the fruit, as it should be dry.

• Jams made from low-pectin fruits, such as strawberries, cherries and marrow, need the addition of extra pectin. This can be added in the form of lemon juice, commercially prepared pectin or a proportion of high-pectin fruit such as gooseberries, black or redcurrants, plums or apples.

• As a rough guideline, add equal weights of fruit and sugar, more or less of the latter depending on the sweetness or sourness of the fruit.

• Use a wide-mouthed pan, preferably a preserving pan. Don't use enamelled cast iron because the high temperature needed ruins the enamelling. Bring the fruit slowly to the boil and let it soften gently before adding the sugar.

• Use preserving or granulated sugar and warm it in a cool oven, Gas $\frac{1}{4}$/225°F/110°C for 10–15 minutes, stirring once or twice and checking it does not burn. Warming the sugar will mean that, when added to the softened fruit, the temperature is not drastically lowered, thus speeding up setting time and reducing the possibility of overcooking and spoiling the fruit.

• The sugar must dissolve completely over a low heat before the jam is brought to boiling point, otherwise it will crystallize. Once the sugar has dissolved, boil the jam vigorously until setting point is reached.

• To test setting point have ready a very cold saucer (you can cool it quickly in the freezer). Remove the pan completely from the heat and drop a small splodge of jam on to the saucer. Let it cool, then push it with your finger. If set, the jam will wrinkle. If not, return the pan to the stove and boil rapidly, testing every few minutes in the same way.

• Only skim the jam if absolutely necessary and then only at the end of cooking time.

• Use clean, warm jars – warm them in the turned-off oven once the sugar has been removed. Fill them very full with the aid of a special jam funnel or an ordinary, plastic funnel with the spout cut off – it saves all kinds of stickiness. Cover and seal immediately or when the jam is quite cold. Use commercial jam covers or jars with screwtop lids.

• While still warm, wipe the jars with a very hot cloth and when they are cold, label them with the name and the date. Store in a cool, dry place.

Ideas for jams

Below are just a few ideas; with each, follow the above procedure.

Apricot Cut in half and remove the stones. Tie these in a piece of muslin and put into the preserving pan with the fruit. Add a little water and cook until the fruit is soft before adding the warmed sugar.

Blackberry and apple Allow 500 g (1 lb) peeled, cored and sliced apples to every 1½ kg (3 lb) blackberries, plus the peel and pips of 2 lemons tied in a muslin. Simmer until soft before adding the juice of the lemons and the warmed sugar.

Blackcurrant Stalk the blackcurrants using the prongs of a fork. Add 600 ml (1 pint) water to every 900 g (2 lb) fruit and simmer for 1 hour before adding the warmed sugar.

Damson Simmer the whole fruit until soft, then add the warmed sugar. Skim off the stones as they rise to the surface.

Gooseberry Allow an extra 125 g (4 oz) sugar to every 500 g (1 lb) fruit.

Greengage As apricot.

Loganberry Let the whole fruit soften with no added water before adding warmed sugar.

Plum As apricot.

Raspberry As loganberry.

Strawberry To every 1 kg (2 lb) fruit) allow 600 g (1¼ lb) sugar and the juice of 1 lemon. Add the juice at the same time as the warmed sugar.

Jelly making

All kinds of home-grown summer and autumn fruits can be turned into gleaming jellies, ranging in colour from deep amber to crimson. They are eaten either spread on bread, in puddings or as accompaniments to certain meats like lamb or game. All these jellies are made to the same basic rules.

• Use slightly under-ripe fruit and simmer with enough water barely to cover until soft.

• Allow the contents of the pan to cool, then strain through a jelly bag suspended for several hours over a bowl to extract the juice. (The bag, which can be improvised using a square of muslin or net curtaining, must not be squeezed as this causes the jelly to be cloudy.)

• Measure the juice and for every 500 ml (1 pint) juice, allow 500 g (1 lb) of sugar, although sour fruits like red or blackcurrants need 100 g (4 oz) more.

• Warm the sugar, which should be granulated or preserving, in a cool oven while the juice is being reheated.

• Additional flavouring such as lemon peel or mint can be tied in a piece of muslin for easy removal.

• Keeping the heat low, gradually add the sugar to the juice in the pan and stir until it has all completely dissolved.

• Raise the heat and boil the liquid hard until setting point is reached. Begin testing after 5 minutes, removing the pan from the heat during this process.

• Test by putting a small amount of the liquid jelly on a cold saucer. As the jelly cools, it will wrinkle when pushed with a finger. If not, then it must be brought back to the boil and tested again after a few minutes.

• Only skim the jelly if absolutely necessary and then only at the end of cooking time.

• Once setting point is reached, remove the flavourings and pour the jelly into warm, clean jars. Seal and cover.

Ideas for jellies

The following fruits make interesting jellies. Make them according to the list of principles above, washing the fruit and cutting large ones like apples or quinces into pieces. There is no need to peel, core or stem them as the debris is left behind in the jelly bag.

Apple Flavour with either 2–3 strips of lemon peel, a handful of chopped mint, 3–4 scented geranium leaves or several lemon verbena leaves.

Black and redcurrants These can be cooked in preserving jars or an earthenware casserole in the oven at Gas 2/300°F/150°C without any added water. Cook until the fruit is soft and releases its juice before proceeding as usual.

Bramble Allow equal quantities of blackberries and apples and add 1 teaspoon mixed spice to every 600 ml (1 pint) juice.

Crab apple Wash but leave the fruit whole. Flavour with lemon peel or scented geranium leaves.

Damson Add a stick of cinnamon and 1 or 2 whole cloves.
Elderberry and apple Allow twice as many berries as apples.
Flavour with strips of orange peel and a stick of cinnamon.
Gooseberry Flavour with 3–4 heads of elderflower.
Medlar Flavour with lemon peel and add the juice of 1 lemon to
every 600 ml (1 pint) of liquid.
Quince Flavour with lemon peel or scented geranium leaves.
Rosehip and blackberry Allow equal quantities of rosehips and
blackberries and add the juice of 1 lemon for every combined 500 g
(1 lb).
Rowan and apple Allow twice as many berries as apples.

Fruit cheeses

Fruit cheeses, so called because they are made in a mould and turned
out to be eaten, were the thrifty housewife's answer to what to do with
the pulp left over from making fruit jellies. The most famous are
damson and quince, the former to be eaten with roast lamb as they do
in Cumbria, and the latter a perfect accompaniment to pork or
venison. Plums and apples also make good cheeses. Any of them can
be eaten with bread and butter or scones, or sliced and served with
cream and chopped nuts as a dessert. Cut in squares and rolled in
caster sugar fruit cheese can be eaten as a sweetmeat. Don't sample the
cheeses for at least 2 months after making.

Weigh the fruit pulp remaining in the jelly bag (if the fruit contains
stones, you will need to sieve it first) and add an equal weight of sugar.
Heat over a low heat until the sugar is dissolved, stirring all the time.
Continue to cook very gently for 45–60 minutes, stirring from time to
time to prevent the pulp scorching. It is ready to pot when it is so thick
that it leaves the sides of the pan. Turn into small, warm, straight-sided
jars and seal immediately. If you grease the jars with glycerine, the
cheeses can be turned out easily.

Damson or sloe gin

Wherever there is a profusion of sloes or damsons, country people add
them to gin to make warm, satisfying winter liqueurs. Sloes can be
found in hedgerows all over England. As for the damson, it comes into
its own in Cheshire (the purple dye from the fruit was used in the

cotton industry), and particularly in Cumbria, where the fruit is known locally as witherslack. Here, old orchards cling to the sides of the hills around the farms and houses in the valleys.

The same recipe is used for either damsons or sloes. If using the latter, wait for the first frost before picking the fruit, this is said to soften the skins. Patience is called for. The fruit must be left soaking in the gin for at least 6 months before being strained and bottled. It should then be left to mature for a further 6 months before the richly stained liqueur is ready to sample.

450 g (1 lb) damsons or sloes   sufficient gin to cover
225 g (8 oz) granulated sugar

Prick each fruit with a darning needle and put them into a 1 litre (1¾ pint) jar. Sprinkle in the sugar and top up completely with gin. Seal and leave for 6 months. After this time, strain and bottle. Leave for a further 6 months.

Hodgkin

This is the Kentish version of the German *Rumtopf* or the French *confiture de vieux garçon*. Soft summer fruits, sprinkled in sugar, are steeped in brandy from early June right through until autumn and are then left to mature until Christmas. The fruits add an alcoholic lift to the end of the meal, either eaten on their own or used to jazz up plain ice creams, and the brandy can be drunk as a liqueur or used as a sauce for desserts.

The quantities of the different fruits are a matter of choice, but you should allow 225 g (8 oz) granulated sugar to every 450 g (l lb) of fruit and you will need a bottle of brandy, although you could equally well use vodka or white rum. Choose from the soft summer fruits such as strawberries, raspberries, red, black and white currants, cherries, apricots, peaches, loganberries, tayberries etc., but don't include citrus fruits. The larger fruits, such as apricots or peaches, should be halved or sliced.

Use a large stone, glazed earthenware or glass jar. Add fruits as they come into season and sprinkle each layer with sugar, adding sufficient brandy to cover. Continue until September before covering securely and setting aside in a cool, dry place.

Apples

Courgette and apple soup

Pigeons in beer

Roast pheasant

Apple and onion sauce

Bangers and apples

Jugged celery

Apple pie

Apple dumplings

Apple pasties

Bramble crumble

Apples fried in butter

Apple and tomato chutney

West Country wassail

Grown for at least 3000 years, the cultivated apple was developed from the European crab apple and thrives in our northern climate. Easily cross-fertilized, there are thousands of different varieties of which only a few are grown on a commercial scale. These are divided into dessert and cooking. Cooking apples include varieties such as Bramley, Newton Wonder, Lord Derby, McIntosh and Grenadier, they are usually too sour to eat raw and they cook to a pulp. However, this is not always desirable and for many dishes, I much prefer to use a dessert apple which holds its shape and doesn't need loads of sugar to make it palatable. The sort of dessert apples which cook well include Cox's Orange Pippins, Blenheims, Reinettes, Granny Smiths and Red Delicious.

If you are lucky and live in an apple-growing area you may be able to get local varieties which are not produced in the vast quantities demanded by the supermarkets. Seek them out and learn all your can from their grower. You'll be in for a treat.

Courgette and apple soup

Marrows, introduced into England in the nineteenth century from the Americas, where they are known as summer squash, are simply overgrown courgettes. For some reason it took us until the mid-twentieth century before we realized how much tastier they are when eaten small than when they are allowed to grow into big brother. Marrows may win prizes at horticultural shows but with their woody skin and pallid flavour, they don't do a lot for the kitchen. So, although you can use a small marrow, I prefer to make this soup using courgettes. Coloured a refreshing green, flavoured with apples and lemon juice, it can be served chilled while the weather is still warm or hot with fried sippets when it turns chilly. Don't be surprised at the small amount of stock in the recipe – courgettes and marrows are watery and yield plenty of liquid to thin the soup.

450 g (1 lb) courgettes or a small   grated nutmeg
  marrow   300 ml ($\frac{1}{2}$ pint) chicken stock
1 tablespoon oil   juice of $\frac{1}{2}$ lemon
50 g (2 oz) butter   salt
1 large green apple, cored and   freshly milled black pepper
  cut in cubes   2–3 tablespoons chopped parsley
1 bay leaf

Wash but don't peel the courgettes, then slice them. (If using a marrow, cut it in half and, using a spoon, scoop out and discard the seeds. Cut the flesh into cubes.) Heat the oil and butter in a large pan and add the courgettes (or marrow) and the apple. Cover and leave to sweat over a low heat for 10 minutes. Add the bay leaf, nutmeg, stock and lemon juice. Season with salt and pepper. Simmer, covered, for 35–40 minutes. Blend to a purée. Garnish with the chopped parsley.

Pigeons in beer

A simplified version of an eighteenth-century recipe, pigeon are stewed in ale, the bitterness of which is offset by the sweetness of apples and prunes. Pigeons can be tough, so need long, slow cooking to make them tender. You can use any kind of beer, ale or stout, although I think a light ale is best because the flavour is not too pervasive.

4 pigeons   8 prunes
2 tablespoons oil   sprigs of marjoram and thyme
25 g (1 oz) butter   1 bay leaf
1 onion, sliced   salt
4 eating apples, quartered, peeled   freshly milled black pepper
  and cored   watercress, to garnish
300 ml ($\frac{1}{2}$ pint) pale ale

Heat the oven to Gas 3/325°F/160°C.

Split each pigeon in half down the breast bone. Heat the oil and butter in a heavy-based pan and brown the pigeon halves all over, skin side down first. Put them into an earthenware casserole as you go. Fry the onion and apples until beginning to soften. Pour over the ale and bring to the boil. Pour this mixture over the pigeons. Tuck the prunes around them together with the herbs and bay leaf. Season with salt and pepper. Cover the casserole with a sheet of foil and then with the lid. Put into the oven for $2\frac{1}{2}$–3 hours until the pigeons are tender. Arrange them on a serving dish surrounded by the apples, prunes and onions, pour over some of the liquid from the casserole and garnish with watercress.

Roast pheasant

A young pheasant is delicious simply roasted wrapped in fatty bacon and basted several times to ensure the bird is moist. The hen, although smaller, is meatier than the cock. Although traditionally served with bread sauce, try it is accompanied by an apple sauce flavoured with onions (see below). Other accompaniments could be forcemeat balls and game chips.

If the pheasant giblets are available, make the gravy by simmering them for $1\frac{1}{2}$–2 hours in water flavoured with herbs, onion, a bay leaf and $\frac{1}{2}$ teaspoon whole peppercorns. Discard most of the cooking juices from the roasting tin, stir in the drained stock and let it bubble and reduce, stirring well to mix thoroughly. If you have no giblets, make the gravy by stirring wine or strong dry cider into the cooking juices instead.

1 pheasant	50 g (2 oz) butter, softened
4 rashers streaky bacon	

Heat the oven to Gas 7/425°F/220°C.

Wrap the pheasant in the streaky bacon and secure with string. Spread the butter over the top. Put the bird in a roasting tin and roast, allowing 20 minutes per 450 g (l lb) and 10 minutes over, basting two or three times.

Apple and onion sauce

This sauce goes wonderfully well not only with pheasant, but with pork, duck or goose.

25 g (1 oz) butter	generous pinch of cinnamon
225 g (8 oz) onions, sliced	1 tablespoon water
225 g (8 oz) firm eating apples, peeled, cored and sliced	

Melt the butter in a small saucepan and gently fry the onions for a few minutes until beginning to soften. Add the apples, cinnamon and the water. Cook over a low heat, stirring from time to time until the onions and apples have reduced to a jammy consistency.

Bangers and apples

Nothing could be simpler than bangers and mash but this recipe, in which the browned sausages are cooked with rosy-skinned apples flavoured with cinnamon, turns a basic dish into something special. Choose good spicy or herb-flavoured sausages and an apple like a Cox, which melts to a golden yellow.

1 tablespoon oil	450 g (1 lb) Cox's apples,
700 g (1½ lb) sausages	quartered and cored
mashed potatoes	½ teaspoon cinnamon

Heat the oil in a frying pan, add the sausages and brown them all over. Tuck the quartered, unpeeled apples around them and sprinkle them with the cinnamon. Cover the pan with a lid or a sheet of foil and put over a low heat to cook gently for about 20 minutes. Serve the apples and sausages on top of a mound of mashed potatoes.

Jugged celery

In this Devonshire recipe, celery, flavoured with bacon and onion surrounded by a purée of apples, was cooked in a tall earthenware pot standing in a pan of boiling water. Nowadays it is simpler to cook the dish in the oven. Ideally you should use a deep earthenware casserole in which the stalks can stand firmly upright, but failing that cut the stalks into lengths which can be stood in your chosen pot.

25 g (1 oz) butter	1 head celery
450 g (1 lb) cooking apples,	1 onion, chopped
peeled, cored and sliced	1 clove
2 tablespoons water	sprig of rosemary
1 heaped teaspoon brown sugar	salt
4 rashers streaky bacon, cut in	freshly milled black pepper
half	

Heat the oven to Gas 4/350°F/180°C.

Put the butter, apples and sugar into the base of a deep earthenware casserole with the water. Lay four half-rashers of bacon on top.

Remove any stringy fibres from the stalks of celery and trim them to the height of the pot. Stand them in it upright, adding the leafy trimmings from the stalks. Sprinkle in the chopped onion and add the clove, rosemary, salt and pepper. Lay the remaining half-rashers of bacon on top. Cover and bake for $1\frac{1}{2}$–2 hours until the celery is meltingly tender.

Apple pie

What could be more English than an apple pie? We have been making them since the sixteenth century. In Marldon in Devon, they even have an apple pie fair. They were so popular in the north of England in the eighteenth century that apples from Kent were sent there on the returning coal barges.

Everyone has their special recipe and this is just one of them. You could add 225 g (8 oz) or so of blackberries or copy the Kent custom and top the fruit with a layer of thinly sliced cheese before putting on the pastry lid.

Apples discolour quickly so put them as you prepare them in a bowl of water with a little salt or lemon juice. They also give out a lot of juice when cooked, so it is better to make this pie with just a top layer of pastry, as a bottom layer just becomes soggy. Serve the pie with lots of single cream or with a home-made custard (see Etceteras).

450 g (1 lb) cooking apples, cored, peeled and sliced
225 g (8 oz) crisp eating apples
6 tablespoons soft brown sugar
$\frac{1}{2}$ teaspoon cinnamon

thinly grated peel of $\frac{1}{2}$ lemon
1 tablespoon water
225 g (8 oz) puff or shortcrust pastry
1 tablespoon caster sugar
300 ml ($\frac{1}{2}$ pint) single cream

Put a pie funnel or egg cup into the centre of a deep, metal pie dish. Layer the apples and sugar in the dish, making sure the top layer is of apples. Sprinkle over the cinnamon, lemon peel and the water.

Roll out the pastry to a piece large enough to cover the pie dish and allowing sufficient to make a thin strip which will go all round the rim of the dish. Dampen the edge of the dish and lay the strip all round. Dampen the strip and put the pastry cover on top, pressing the two layers of pastry together. Mark the edge all round, with the tip of a knife if using puff or the prongs of a fork if using shortcrust. Cut two slits in the top of the crust and brush it all over with water. Sprinkle the surface lightly with the caster sugar. Set the pie aside for 30 minutes.

Heat the oven to Gas 6/400°F/200°C. Bake the pie for 20 minutes before lowering the heat to Gas 5/375°F/190°C and baking it for a further 20 minutes. Just before serving, pour some of the cream into the pie through the slits. Serve the remainder separately.

Apple dumplings

Wherever people grow apples, cooks wrap them in pastry and turn them into dumplings. Once it was common to steam them in suet crust, but I prefer to bake them in thinly rolled shortcrust or puff pastry. Eat them in the traditional way by cutting a slit in the top of each cooked dumpling and pouring in a little thick cream.

350 g (12 oz) puff or shortcrust pastry
4 sharp eating apples, peeled and cored

4 cloves
cinnamon
4 tablespoons brown sugar
1 egg yolk, beaten

Heat the oven to Gas 6/400°F/200°C.

Divide the pastry into four and roll each piece into a square large enough to wrap an apple. Brush all round the edge of the pastry with water. Put an apple in the centre of each and fill it with a clove, a sprinkling of cinnamon and 1 tablespoon of sugar. Bring up the four sides of the square to form a parcel and press the edges well together. Lay them smooth side uppermost on a baking sheet. Brush all over with the egg and bake for 30–35 minutes until golden brown.

Apple pasties

The only difference between these and dumplings is that the apple is not cooked whole but diced. Use the same ingredients and proceed as in the previous recipe, but peel, core and cut the apples into smallish dice, piling them into the centres of the pastry squares and flavouring them with the sugar and spices. If you want them to melt into a purée, use a cooking rather than a dessert variety. Brush all round the rim with beaten egg and fold the pastry over to form a rectangle. Press well together to seal and either twist the edges into a crenellated pattern or mark all round with the prongs of a fork. Brush all over with the

remaining beaten egg and bake for 30–35 minutes at Gas 6/400°F/
200°C.

Bramble crumble

Occasionally, just occasionally, at the beginning of autumn, there
might be an opportunity to pick ripe blackberries from our fast
disappearing hedgerows. Otherwise you can buy, somewhat expen-
sively, a punnet from the greengrocer or supermarket. Black and juicy,
they add their purple stain and sharp flavour to the apples in this
simple recipe for crumble. Of course when the blackberry season is
over, you can just use apples or perhaps a mixture of apples and
bananas. To add a touch of luxury to the topping, substitute 50 g (2
oz) ground almonds for some of the flour.

150 g (6 oz) plain flour
75 g (3 oz) softened butter, cut in
  small pieces
75 g (3 oz) soft brown sugar

450 g (1 lb) crisp eating apples,
  peeled, cored and sliced
225 g (8 oz) blackberries

Heat the oven to Gas 5/375°F/190°C.

Put the flour into a bowl and rub in the butter until the mixture is
like fine crumbs. Mix in the sugar. (Alternatively, put the flour, butter
and sugar into a food processor and process for 10 seconds.)

Put the sliced apples and blackberries into a pie dish. Spread the
crumble topping over the fruit and put into the oven for 25–30
minutes until the top is golden brown. Serve with clotted, double or
soured cream.

Apples fried in butter

A quick dessert for children and adults that can be made with any
good crisp apples. It is even better if you stir a tablespoon or two of
strong dry cider or brandy into the frying pan before adding the
cream. The same recipe can be used with pears.

50 g (2 oz) butter
4 apples, peeled, cored and sliced
3–4 tablespoons soft brown sugar

$\frac{1}{4}$ teaspoon cinnamon
single cream

Melt the butter in a frying pan and when it is foaming, add the slices of apple. Fry gently until the apples are soft. Turn them over and over, sprinkle in the sugar and cinnamon and continue cooking until they are surrounded by a syrupy sauce. Transfer the apples slices to a warm plate. Pour the cream into the frying pan and stir quickly so that it heats and absorbs the buttery juices but does not boil or it will curdle. Pour over the apple slices.

Apple and tomato chutney

Chutneys came to us via India in the eighteenth century and can be made with all kinds of fruit and vegetables, from pears and apricots to green tomatoes, rhubarb and gooseberries, plums, peppers and marrow. They are a perfect accompaniment to cold meats. If there is a surfeit of fruit, it really is worth making your own chutneys, especially if you find commercial brands are far too sweet. Apple and tomato chutney is my favourite, perhaps because the sweet, spice-laden smell pervading the house transports me back to my grandmother's kitchen in Devon with its pine, cream-painted dresser and cool scullery. Her recipe has not survived, if it was ever written down, so this is an approximation based on nostalgia.

Chutneys, like pickles, should be made in a heavy-based stainless steel or enamelled saucepan, never metals like copper, iron or brass which react unfavourably with vinegar. The fruit need not be in prime condition, so it is an ideal way of using up windfall apples or bruised tomatoes, but make sure you cut away any discoloured or damaged bits. Store the chutney in small glass jars, preferably with a plastic lid rather than metal, which will taint the contents.

900 g (2 lb) apples, peeled, cored and sliced
900 g (2 lb) tomatoes, peeled and sliced
450 g (1 lb) sultanas
450 g (1 lb) onions, chopped
6 cloves garlic, chopped

1 litre ($1\frac{3}{4}$ pints) malt vinegar
1 tablespoon mustard seeds
1 tablespoon coriander seeds
1 teaspoon white peppercorns
2 teaspoons ground ginger
900 g (2 lb) soft brown sugar

Put all the ingredients into a large china bowl, mix well with a wooden spoon, cover and leave overnight.

The next day, transfer everything to a large saucepan, bring slowly to the boil, stirring from time to time. Simmer for $1\frac{1}{2}$–2 hours, continuing to stir from time to time, until the liquid has reduced by about half, the chutney has a soft, jammy consistency and has darkened to a rich brown.

Put into warm, clean jars and seal. Leave at least 2 months before eating but much longer is better as chutneys mature with ageing.

West Country wassail

It used to be the custom to wassail or toast the apple trees to guarantee the coming harvest. Depending where you lived this ceremony might be carried out on Christmas Eve or on Twelfth Night. The name derives from the Norse words *ves heill*, equivalent to our 'good health'. A large bowl containing the hot, spicy drink would be passed round for everyone to sample. In the absence of trees to wassail, it makes a cheering drink to welcome friends or carol singers on a winter's evening. The Somerset version known as lamb's wool is similar but they add the pulp of the apples rather than floating them in the wassail.

3–4 large red-skinned apples
1 litre (1¾ pints) brown ale
6 tablespoons soft brown sugar
300 ml (½ pint) dry sherry or
   white wine

2–3 strips lemon peel
¼ teaspoon each of cinnamon,
   nutmeg and ginger

First bake the apples by heating the oven to Gas 4/350°F/180°C and putting them into a casserole with 3–4 tablespoons of the ale and the brown sugar. Cover and bake for 20–30 minutes until the apples are tender but still holding their shape. Remove apples to a plate.

Put the remaining ale, sherry or wine, lemon peel and spices into a large pan, bring slowly to just below boiling point and leave over the heat, keeping it just below simmering point for 5 minutes. Transfer to a wide serving bowl, float the apples in it and serve by ladling into warmed wine glasses.

Cider

Roman mussels

Eels and elvers

Eel pie

Jellied eels

Mackerel with rhubarb sauce

Fish pie

Quail braised with apples

Chicken in cider

Guinea fowl with mushrooms

Rabbit with cider and prunes

Rabbit pie

Honeyed pork chops with apples

Farmer's wife pork

Squab (lamb) pie

Ham glazed with honey

Cider cake

Although the first cider apples could have been introduced to us by the Romans, it is likely that our skill in making cider didn't really take off until after the Norman conquest – the very name comes from the Old French word, *sidre*. Orchards were planted in Kent and Sussex and it wasn't long before they spread across southern England into the West Country. By the seventeenth century there were more than 300 different varieties of cider apples grown, with wonderful names like Foxwhelp, Slack-my-girdle, Brown Snout and Handsome Maud's, and cider-making had become a cottage industry in Devon, Dorset, Herefordshire and Somerset. East Anglia produces cider, too, made with a mix of cooking and eating apples. The best cider is fine and dry and the roughest is known as scrumpy. Rough and ready, it is the sort they delight in plying you with in West Country pubs, to see you reel over after half a glass.

As the Normans knew, cider was not just for drinking but also for cooking and many of these recipes in which it is used have a strong French connection. When cooking with cider, it is important to use a good quality, strong dry cider – sweet ciders are just too cloying.

Roman mussels

If the Romans gave us our first lesson in cider-making, they also devised and passed on ideas for cooking the fish and shellfish which were so abundant around our shores. Mussels have an ancient lineage. Around rocky shores and estuaries, Stone Age man (and woman) ate them raw or roasted them on stones in the hot ashes of a bonfire, feasting on this welcome change from the dried fish and meat which formed their winter diet. Mussels remained popular throughout the centuries. The Romans had a passion for them and shells are found wherever they settled, as far north as Hadrian's Wall. They cooked them in *passum*, a kind of fortified wine made from dried grapes, flavoured with leeks, cumin, savory and *garum*. Their taste buds must have been stronger than ours, because *garum* was a sort of sauce made from dried and salted small fish mixed with the entrails of larger ones like tuna.

This recipe is a modern version using white wine or cider instead of *passum* and salted anchovies instead of *garum*. Savory can be grown in the garden or in pots. There are two kinds, summer and winter, but the first is considered to be superior in flavour. It is a pungent herb not dissimilar to thyme but more bitter. It dries well.

1 kg (2 lb or pints) mussels	2–3 sprigs of savory or thyme,
1 tablespoon flour	tied in a bunch, or 1 teaspoon
1 teaspoon sea salt	dried
2 tablespoons oil	4 tablespoons strong dry cider or
½ teaspoon crushed cumin	white wine
4 anchovy fillets, chopped	freshly milled black pepper
1 leek, finely chopped	

Wash the mussels well under running cold water and pull off their beards. Discard any which are open or broken. Put them in a bucket with the flour and salt and leave for 2–3 hours, during which time they will open to feed and release any sand in their shells.

Heat the oil in a large saucepan and add the cumin, stir for a couple of minutes, then add the chopped anchovies and leek. Mix well, cover and leave to sweat for 10 minutes. Add all the other ingredients. (Check that all the mussels shells are firmly closed. Tap any that remain open with a wooden spoon; if they fail to close, discard them.) Cover the pan and leave it over a medium heat for a further 5 minutes until all the mussels have opened. Serve in soup bowls with plenty of crusty bread.

Eels and elvers

In the spring, elvers, tiny immature eels, arrive *en masse* in the estuaries of rivers such as the Severn or those in East Anglia. They come from the Sargasso Sea, where the mature eels go to spawn, and are washed across the Atlantic by the warmth of the Gulf Stream, their journey taking up to three years. Once highly prized here, we now export most of the catch to Spain, where they are fried with garlic and served with plenty of cayenne pepper and chopped parsley. Those that avoid being caught spend their lives in our inland waterways before they too make the return journey to their spawning grounds.

Eels once were very cheap and plentiful and were popular food in the East End of London, the area of the city where the poor lived. They were sold from barrows and in eel shops, either in pies, jellied or as eel and mash. A few of these shops still survive and eels and jellied eels are sold by some fishmongers. Perhaps because they were considered poor food they went out of fashion. Not so on the continent, where they are much appreciated, especially in Scandinavia, Holland, Belgium and France.

Eels are sold live and must be stunned and skinned before they can be cooked – a fairly gruesome task so ask the fishmonger to do it for you and to cut it into small chunks. Cook the eel the same day.

If you are lucky enough to come across smoked eel, eat it just like smoked salmon with plenty of lemon juice, a little cayenne pepper and lots of brown bread and butter.

Eel pie

On an island on the Thames near Richmond there was an inn which was famous for its eel pies and people would come from miles around to enjoy a day on the river and feast themselves when they got hungry. So famous did it become that the island was known as Eel Pie Island and although the inn and pies are no more, the name remains. The succulent flesh of eels makes wonderful pies which can be eaten hot or cold. Cold is perhaps best, because then the pieces of eel are surrounded by a rich jelly. A superb pie for a picnic.

3 eggs
900 g (2 lb) eels, skinned and cut in chunks
2 tablespoons flour
1 onion, sliced
salt
freshly milled black pepper
1 tablespoon chopped fresh thyme, parsley and rosemary
$\frac{1}{4}$ teaspoon grated nutmeg
juice of $\frac{1}{2}$ lemon
300 ml ($\frac{1}{2}$ pint) mixture strong dry cider and water
225 g (8 oz) puff pastry

Hard boil 2 of the eggs by putting them in a pan of cold water, bringing to the boil and boiling for 9 minutes. Put them under running cold water and when they are cool enough to handle, crack the shells, peel and chop.

Put a pie funnel or upturned egg cup in the centre of a pie dish. Roll the pieces of eel in the flour and put them in the pie dish with the chopped egg, onion, salt, pepper, herbs and nutmeg. Sprinkle with the lemon juice and pour over the cider and water.

Roll out the pastry to cover the top, allowing sufficient margin to cut strips to line the rim of the dish. Brush the rim of the dish with water and lay the pastry strips all round the pie dish. Brush them with water and set the lid of pastry on top. Trim the edge and press the two layers of pastry together. Mark all round with the point of a knife and cut a slit in the centre. Beat the remaining egg and brush all over the top. Set aside for 30 minutes in a cool place.

Heat the oven to Gas 6/400°F/200°C. Bake the pie for 30–40 minutes until the pastry is risen and golden.

Jellied eels

Rich and filling, jellied eels are an acquired taste to those who haven't grown up with them, so buy some ready-prepared and if you like them, next time make your own.

1 eel, skinned and cut in chunks	2–3 sprigs of parsley
1 onion, chopped	salt
1 carrot, chopped	freshly milled black pepper
1 stick celery, chopped	strong dry cider, water or white
1 bay leaf	wine, just to cover

Put the pieces of eel into a saucepan with the onion, carrot, celery, plus the bay leaf and sprigs of parsley. Season with salt and pepper. Just cover with the cider, water or white wine. Bring slowly to the boil and simmer, covered, for 1 hour.

Transfer the pieces of eel to small pots. Boil the cooking liquid until it reduces by about one quarter. Strain the liquid over the pieces of eel, discarding the herbs and vegetables. Cover and set aside to cool, when the liquid will turn into a rich jelly. Eat with a squeeze of lemon and plenty of buttered toast.

Mackerel with rhubarb sauce

Mackerel are oily and rich and benefit from something just a little tart to accompany them. Gooseberry sauce is one idea (there's a recipe on page 116), but in Bristol they bake their mackerel in cider and serve them with a rhubarb sauce flavoured with lemon juice and mace.

8 bay leaves

8 mackerel fillets

½ teaspoon whole peppercorns

150 ml (¼ pint) strong dry cider

225 g (8 oz) rhubarb, chopped
  into 2–3 cm (1 in) pieces

1 teaspoon lemon juice

50 g (2 oz) dark brown sugar

½ teaspoon mace

Heat the oven to Gas 4/350°F/180°C.

Lay a bay leaf on each of the mackerel fillets, roll them up and lay them in a single layer in a buttered ovenproof dish. Add the peppercorns and sprinkle over all but 1 tablespoon of the cider. Bake for 20–25 minutes.

Meanwhile, make the sauce. Put the chopped rhubarb, lemon juice, sugar, mace and remaining tablespoon of cider into a saucepan and bring slowly to the boil. Simmer gently for about 15 minutes until the rhubarb has melted into a sauce, stirring from time to time so that it does not burn. Mash with a fork and serve in a sauce boat.

Fish pie

A well-made fish pie is a sophisticated dish far removed from the often bland ready-prepared variety. It is simple enough but needs time and patience, involving as it does several stages. Make it with two or three kinds of white fish, choosing from species like cod, coley, haddock, hake, whiting and dogfish, which is usually sold as rock salmon or huss. Of course, everyone has their own version. In this one fish fillets are first gently poached with a generous handful or two of mussels which add greatly to the flavour. The pie is topped either with puff pastry or, if you prefer, a layer of freshly cooked potatoes mashed with plenty of butter. You can ring the changes as you will, adding perhaps a few prawns and a spoonful or two of cream, or substituting smoked fish for the fresh.

700 g (1½ lb) two or three kinds
  of fillets of white fish (see
  above)
600 ml (1 pint) mussels
1 bay leaf
sprigs of parsley, plus 2
  tablespoons chopped parsley
½ teaspoon black peppercorns
450 ml (¾ pint) fish stock
150 ml (¼ pint) strong dry cider

50 g (2 oz) butter
50 g (2 oz) flour
1 tablespoon capers, rinsed and
  chopped
salt
cayenne pepper
mashed potato from 700 g (1½ lb)
  potatoes, plus 25 g (1 oz)
  butter, or 225 g (8 oz) puff
  pastry, plus 1 egg yolk, beaten

Put the fish and mussels into a saucepan and pour over sufficient water just to cover. Add the bay leaf, sprigs of parsley and the peppercorns. Bring to the boil, cover and simmer very gently for 5 minutes. Set aside until the fish is cool enough to handle and then remove it and the mussels to a colander.

Strain 450 ml (¾ pint) of the liquid into a measuring jug and add the cider. Pour this liquid into a small saucepan, add the butter and the flour and heat over a medium heat, beating constantly with a wire whisk. As soon as the sauce begins to thicken, lower the heat and continue beating until it comes to the boil. Let the sauce simmer for 2 minutes to cook the flour, stirring all the time. Add the capers, chopped parsley, salt and cayenne pepper.

Carefully remove all skin and bones from the fish, flake it and lay it in a pie dish, setting a pie funnel in the centre. Shell the mussels and scatter them on top. Pour over the sauce

Either cover with the mashed potato, marking the top with the prongs of a fork and dotting it with small pieces of butter, or set aside to cool and then cover with a layer of puff pastry, using the pastry trimmings to make decorative leaves. Brush the pastry with beaten egg yolk and leave the pie to rest for 30 minutes to prevent the pastry shrinking when put into the hot oven.

Heat the oven to Gas 6/400°F/200°C and bake the pie for 30–35 minutes until the topping is golden brown.

Quail braised with apples

This recipe, in which quails are braised with apples and cider and flavoured with sage and mace, comes from the West Country. Quails, though tiny, are quite meaty, but you may prefer to allow two per person.

8 sage leaves
4 quails
8 rashers streaky bacon
2 tablespoons oil
25 g (1 oz) butter

4 Cox's apples, quartered, cored
    and peeled
$\frac{1}{4}$ teaspoon mace
salt
freshly milled black pepper
4 tablespoons strong dry cider

Put 2 sage leaves on either side of the breast bone on each quail, wrap each bird in 2 rashers of bacon and secure with string. Heat the oil and butter in a flameproof casserole, add the quails and brown them all over on a medium heat. Add the apples, mace and a seasoning of salt and pepper. Pour over the cider and let it bubble fiercely for a moment or two. Lower the heat, cover and simmer for 25–30 minutes.

Transfer the quails to a warm serving dish, remove the string, surround by the apples and pour over the cidery juices from the casserole.

Chicken in cider

The Normandy combination of chicken, apples, cider and cream is a particularly delicious mixture so I was pleased when I came across a similar idea from Kent. The recipe I was given called for quite a lot of milk or single cream but I prefer to use a small amount of double cream because it is not likely to curdle.

50 g (2 oz) butter
1 free range or corn-fed chicken
1 onion, chopped
2 carrots, sliced
450 g (1 lb) Cox's apples,
    quartered, peeled and cored
$\frac{1}{2}$ teaspoon powdered cinnamon

300 ml ($\frac{1}{2}$ pint) strong, dry cider
2 tablespoons oil
sprigs of fresh thyme or $\frac{1}{2}$
    teaspoon dried
salt
freshly milled black pepper
4 tablespoons double cream

Melt half the butter in a heavy-based casserole in which the chicken will fit comfortably. Brown the chicken all over and transfer it to a plate. Melt the remaining butter and fry the chopped onion, carrots and apples until they begin to turn golden. Sprinkle over the cinnamon, pour in the cider, raise the heat and let it boil fiercely until reduced by about a half. Lower the heat and put the chicken, breast side down, on top of the onions, carrot and apples. Add the thyme and season with salt and pepper, put the lid on the pan and let it simmer for 1 hour. Turn the chicken breast side up and add the cream. Continue to simmer for a further 20 minutes, uncovered.

Transfer the chicken, apples, carrot and onion to a serving dish. Boil the sauce down hard until it reduces and thickens. Pour over the chicken and serve.

Guinea fowl with mushrooms

Guinea fowl may look small but there is a high proportion of meat to carcase and one comfortably feeds four. In this no-nonsense recipe the bird is pot-roasted with herbs, mushrooms and cider. Eat it with new potatoes flavoured with mint and fresh garden peas.

2 onions, sliced	2 tablespoons oil
sprigs of thyme, marjoram and parsley	salt
	freshly milled black pepper
2 carrots, chopped	150 ml ($\frac{1}{4}$ pint) strong dry cider
1 guinea fowl	225 g (8 oz) mushrooms, sliced

Heat the oven to Gas 4/350°F/180°C.

Lay the onion slices, herbs and chopped carrots in the base of a flameproof casserole in which the guinea fowl will sit snugly. Put the bird on top. Sprinkle over the oil and season with salt and pepper. Pour over the cider. Put into the oven, covered, for $1\frac{1}{4}$ hours. After this time, remove the lid and add the mushrooms, tucking them around the bird. Raise the temperature to Gas 6/400°F/200°C and return the casserole to the oven for a further 25–30 minutes to allow the mushrooms to cook and the bird to brown.

Transfer the bird and vegetables to a warm dish, discard the herbs, and return it to the turned-off oven for 10–15 minutes to allow the meat to compact and be easier to carve.

Rabbit with cider and prunes

Wild rabbit can be bought very cheaply in country game dealers and some supermarkets sell it already jointed for half the price of the tame variety. It has a stronger flavour than one raised in captivity and benefits from being marinated, in this case in strong dry cider with spices and herbs. It needs to be complemented by something sweet and in this Devon recipe it is cooked with prunes and shallots. (Incidentally, if you have difficulty peeling shallots, steep them for a few minutes first in boiling water.) If you buy a whole rabbit, ask your supplier to joint it and to give you the liver which, if added right at the end of the cooking time, almost melts in the mouth. This rabbit casserole is delicious with stump (see Roots).

1 rabbit, cut into 8–10 joints	600 ml (1 pint) strong dry cider
1 blade mace or $\frac{1}{2}$ teaspoon powdered	2 tablespoons flour
	50 g (2 oz) butter
sliver of root ginger or $\frac{1}{2}$ teaspoon powdered	1 tablespoon oil
	4 shallots
1 clove	salt
1 teaspoon coriander seeds, crushed	freshly milled black pepper
	12 prunes
sprigs of rosemary, sage and thyme	

Put the rabbit into a glass or china dish with the mace, ginger, clove, coriander seeds and some sprigs of rosemary, sage and thyme. Pour over the cider and leave to marinate overnight.

The next day, heat the oven to Gas 4/350°F/180°C.

Take the rabbit pieces out of the marinade and pat them dry with kitchen paper. Roll them in the flour to coat them evenly all over. Melt the butter and oil in a frying pan and fry the pieces of rabbit until golden brown, transferring them as you go into a deep earthenware casserole. Peel the shallots and fry them for a few minutes without browning and add them with the strained marinade to the rabbit. Bring to the boil. Skim away and discard any scum that forms with a slotted spoon. Add fresh sprigs of herbs, season with salt and pepper and put the casserole into the oven for $1\frac{1}{2}$ –2 hours until the rabbit is tender.

Meanwhile pour boiling water over the prunes and leave to swell.

When the rabbit is tender, add the drained prunes and continue cooking for a further 30 minutes. Remove from the oven and add the liver, if available, cut into 3–4 pieces. Cover and set aside for 5 minutes to allow the liver to cook before serving.

Rabbit pie

Rabbit pie was a childhood treat and in trying to rediscover my grandmother's recipe I have come across ideas dating back to the Elizabethans. In some recipes, the rabbit is put raw into the pie dish before being covered with the pastry, but if it is on the tough side, the result is not always satisfactory. It is better to cook the rabbit first, as in this version, in which it is first browned in butter before being simmered with bacon and onions, herbs and spices in cider. If you like, you could do this the day before, adding the pastry and cooking the pie an hour or so before you plan to eat it.

2 tablespoons flour
1 rabbit, jointed, or 700 g ($1\frac{1}{2}$ lb) rabbit pieces
50 g (2 oz) butter
2 onions, chopped
100 g (4 oz) streaky bacon, chopped
300 ml ($\frac{1}{2}$ pint) strong dry cider, stock or water

salt
freshly milled black pepper
pinch of mace
1 clove
sprigs of thyme, sage and parsley tied in a bunch
225 g (8 oz) puff pastry
1 egg yolk, beaten

Put the flour on to a plate and roll the rabbit pieces in it to coat evenly. Heat the butter in a heavy-based casserole and fry the rabbit pieces all over until golden, in two or three batches as necessary. Remove them to a plate. Add the chopped onion and bacon to the pan and fry for a few minutes. Return the rabbit pieces and pour over the cider, stock or water. Season with salt and pepper and add the mace, clove and the bunch of herbs. Bring to the boil, cover and simmer for about $1–1\frac{1}{2}$ hours until the rabbit is tender.

Remove the bones from the rabbit and put the meat with the onions and bacon into a pie dish, discarding the herbs. Pour over enough liquid to come about three-quarters of the way up the meat. Set aside to cool.

Brush the rim of the pie dish with water. Roll out the pastry large enough to form a lid plus an extra amount which is cut into strips to line the rim of the dish. Lay the strips in place, brush them with water and set the pastry lid on top, pressing the edges together. Trim the pastry and mark all round with the tip of a knife. Cut a slit in the centre and brush the lid all over with beaten egg yolk. Use any remaining scraps of pastry to cut out decorative leaves (mark the veins with the blunt side of a knife). Lay the leaves on the lid and brush them with egg. Set the pie aside for 30 minutes before putting it into the oven.

Heat the oven to Gas 7/425°F/220°C.

Bake the pie for 20 minutes, then lower the heat to Gas 5/375°F/ 190°C and bake a further 20 minutes, covering the top with a piece of foil to prevent it burning.

Honeyed pork chops with apples

This quick and simple dish of pork chops cooked in cider with apples and glazed with honey is another West Country inspiration. For a change try it using blueberries, cranberries, cherries or prunes instead of the apples. These chops go beautifully with a dish like scalloped potatoes or perhaps potatoes mashed with celeriac.

4 pork chops	salt
freshly milled black pepper	4 crisp apples, peeled, quartered
juice of $\frac{1}{2}$ lemon	and cored
2 tablespoons oil	2 tablespoons clear honey
150 ml ($\frac{1}{4}$ pint) strong, dry cider	cinnamon

Lay the chops in a china or glass dish, season with pepper, sprinkle with the lemon juice and leave to marinate for about 1 hour. Heat the oil in a large frying pan and brown the chops on both sides. Pour in the cider, season with salt and pepper and lay the apple quarters on top. Dribble over the honey and sprinkle with cinnamon. Cover with a lid or piece of kitchen foil and simmer for 20–25 minutes. Transfer the chops to a warm serving dish and boil the cooking liquid hard until it reduces by about half. Pour over the chops and serve.

Farmer's wife pork

This dish of pork chops, onions, potatoes and apples, which comes from the Shires, was left to stew for several hours while the farmer's wife went to market. It is a perfect answer to those days when you plan to be away from home and want to return to a house filled with appetizing smells and the knowledge that supper is ready. It has many permutations, such as adding a few chopped tomatoes, or sage instead

of rosemary; the cider and stock can be replaced by all of one or the
other and the addition of four or five whole garlic cloves doesn't come
amiss. The kidneys do add something to the flavour but the dish is still
presentable without, especially if you top it with a few rashers of
streaky bacon.

700 g (1½ lb) potatoes, sliced
2 onions, sliced
salt
freshly milled black pepper
4 lean pork chops or escalopes
2 pig's kidneys, skinned and
  sliced

1 sprig of rosemary
4 apples, peeled, cored and sliced
½ teaspoon cinnamon
150 ml (¼ pint) strong dry cider
150 ml (¼ pint) stock
25 g (1 oz) butter

Heat the oven to Gas 4/350°F/180°C.

Lay half the potatoes and onions over the base of a large
earthenware casserole and season with salt and pepper. Put the chops
on top, together with the sliced kidneys. Tuck in the sprig of rosemary.
Cover with the remaining potatoes and onions, then the apples.
Season again with salt and pepper and sprinkle over the cinnamon.
Pour over the cider and stock and dot with the butter. Cover and put
into the oven. (If the lid of your casserole is not a good fit, either seal it
by smearing a little flour and water paste all round the inner rim of the
lid or cover the casserole with a double layer of foil and put the lid on
top.)

After 30 minutes lower the heat to Gas 2/300°F/150°C and cook for
at least another 2½–3 hours. Longer won't hurt.

Squab pie

The name of this robust pie is a puzzle because there's not a hint of a
squab, a young pigeon, in it. On the other hand, a squab is also a
well-stuffed bolster or cushion, so perhaps the pie gets its name
because it is filled not only with lamb but puffed up with a generous
amount of apples, prunes and onions flavoured with cider, cinnamon
and allspice.

Squab pie has its origins in the West Country though there are
variations countrywide. It can be made with pork chops instead of the
lamb, in which case it is known as Dartmouth pie. Traditionally it is
served with a bowl of clotted cream but you could use single cream

instead, warming it in a saucepan just before serving and seasoning it with a little lemon juice.

8 lean lamb cutlets	12 prunes, stoned and halved
6–8 Cox's apples, peeled, cored and sliced	150 ml ($\frac{1}{4}$ pint) strong dry cider
grated nutmeg	salt
$\frac{1}{2}$ teaspoon cinnamon	freshly milled black pepper
2–3 whole allspice crushed or	225 g (8 oz) shortcrust or puff
$\frac{1}{2}$ teaspoon powdered	pastry
2 onions, sliced	1 egg yolk, beaten
	150 ml ($\frac{1}{4}$ pint) clotted cream

Put a pie funnel in the centre of a deep pie dish. Lay half the lamb chops around it and cover with half the apple slices. Season with nutmeg and half the spices. Lay half the onions and prunes on top. Repeat with the remaining chops, apples, spices, onions and prunes. Pour over the cider and season with salt and pepper.

Roll out the pastry to fit and cut the trimmings into strips long enough to go all round the edge of the dish. Brush the rim of the dish with water and lay the strips all round. Brush the strips with water and set the pastry lid on top, pressing the edges together and marking, with the prongs of a fork if using shortcrust or the tip of a knife for puff pastry. Cut a slit in the top for the steam to escape. Brush the surface of the pastry with the beaten egg yolk and, if you like, decorate the pie with leaves cut out of the pastry trimmings. Set aside for 30 minutes to allow the pastry to rest and prevent it shrinking when baked.

Heat the oven to Gas 6/400°F/200°C. and bake the pie for 20 minutes. Lower the heat to Gas 3/325°F/160°C and bake for a further 45 minutes. If the pastry appears to be getting too brown, cover it with a piece of foil. Hand round the cream separately.

Ham glazed with honey

In our household, Christmas wouldn't be complete without a glazed ham. We eat it hot on Christmas Eve with baked jacket potatoes and carrots cooked in their own juice (see Buttered carrots, page 225). The rest of the cold joint is then produced throughout the remaining days of the festivities as part of a cold table, served with pickled fruits like damsons or pears.

Today's hams are nothing like as salty as those of the past, so there is no need to pre-soak your joint. Use the stock in which the ham is cooked to make a flavoursome soup. Although this recipe uses honey with which to glaze the ham, you could just as happily use brown sugar, marmalade, cranberry jelly or redcurrant jelly. In this West Country recipe, the ham is cooked in cider which imparts a delicious sweet flavour to the finished dish.

1 ham joint weighing at least 2 kg (4½ lb)	½ teaspoon dried thyme
	½ teaspoon dried marjoram
1 onion	approx. 1 litre (1¾ pints) strong
1 carrot	dry cider
1 turnip	whole cloves
1 leek	1 tablespoon mild mustard
sprigs of parsley	2–3 tablespoons honey

Put the ham into a large saucepan with the onion, carrot, turnip, leek and the herbs and add sufficient cider to cover (top up with water if necessary). Bring to the boil, cover, and simmer the joint, allowing 30 minutes per 450 g (1 lb) plus 30 minutes, but if the joint is over 2½ kg (5 lb) reduce the cooking time to 20 minutes per 450 g (1 lb) plus 20 minutes.

Half an hour before the end of the cooking time, remove the ham from the saucepan and set it aside until it is cool enough to handle.

Set the oven to Gas 5/375°F/190°C.

Peel away the rind of the ham, using a sharp knife to ease it off. Score the fat all over in a diagonal, criss-cross pattern. Stud the ham fat with whole cloves at each intersection. Mix together the mustard and honey and smear all over the fat. Put into the oven for 30 minutes, basting after 15 minutes.

Cider cake

Spicy and sometimes fruity, cakes mixed with cider come from the
West Country – in other areas they might use cold tea instead. This
cake is nicest eaten with apples cooked to a purée with a little
cinnamon and thick cream.

100 g (4 oz) butter or margarine

100 g (4 oz) soft brown sugar

juice and finely grated peel of 1
  orange

2 eggs

225 g (8 oz) self-raising flour,
  sifted

$\frac{1}{2}$ teaspoon powdered allspice

$\frac{1}{2}$ teaspoon cinnamon

200 ml (7 fl oz cider)

100 g (4 oz) mixed dried fruit

caster sugar

Grease a 22 cm (8 in) cake tin and heat the oven to Gas 4/350°F/
180°C.

Cream the butter and sugar together with the orange peel until pale
and fluffy. Beat in the eggs one at a time. Lightly fold in half the flour,
the allspice and cinnamon. Fold in the cider and orange juice followed
by the remaining flour and the dried fruit. Turn into the tin, smooth
over the top and bake for 35–40 minutes until risen and golden. Test
with a skewer. If it comes out clean it is done; if not, leave for a few
minutes longer. Allow to cool a little and remove from the tin. When
cold, sprinkle with a little caster sugar.

Autumn and Winter
Matters

Outside the weather is bleak. Snow lies in frozen patches over the grass, outlines the branches of the trees and blankets the roof of the garden shed which is dotted with cat prints. As the afternoon darkens and the fading light tinges everything blue, so the lit up windows of the surrounding houses glow with ever-deepening orange. What better time to be in the kitchen cooking with almonds and dried fruits, making things for Christmas as well as indulging in a few puddings and cakes? Cake-making is, or was, one of our favourite things, and even those who say they can't cook nearly always have a favourite recipe up their sleeve.

Then there are bittersweet oranges and lemons, which not only give zest to all sorts of game and fish dishes but are also used to flavour puddings and cakes. In winter, too, we can make the most of all those northern British vegetables, from cabbages to potatoes. As we enjoy that special sweet flavour of roast parsnips or the slight bitterness of turnip soup, we can pity our European neighbours who think of them as nothing better than cattle food.

Of course this is the season for game, for which Britain is famous. Throughout our history hunting rights were very much the province of the wealthy and poaching became a capital offence in the eighteenth century. Fortunately times have changed and nowadays all kinds of game is sold in supermarkets as well as through specialist game dealers. The main season opens on 12 August, when the first grouse are shot (although it's not the moment to eat one; they need to be hung for a few days) and closes at the end of January, at least for most feathered game. Wood pigeon and rabbit are available all the year round, as is hare, although these last are protected on Sundays and Christmas Day and cannot be sold between March and July. The sale of venison is governed by different dates according to their species.

Almonds and dried fruits

Almond soup

Trout with almonds

Hindle wakes (cold chicken with prune and almond stuffing)

Simnel cake

Easter biscuits

Mincemeat

Godcakes (mincemeat pastries)

Plum or Christmas cake

Marzipan or almond paste

Royal icing

Plum or Christmas pudding

Jessie Jackson's plum pudding

Rum and brandy butters

Newmarket (bread and butter) pudding

Bakewell pudding

Madeleine's chocolate cake

Maids of honour

Rock cakes

Salted almonds and raisins

Almond trees flourish in the warmth and sun of Mediterranean countries and the delicate flavour of sweet almonds has been prized in English cooking since medieval times. One of the principal ways in which they were used was ground to a powder and mixed with water, this almond milk being used as a curious alternative to the real thing. The use of bitter almonds is restricted to making almond essence, which can be added to give flavour to certain sweet dishes, and to the production of an oil used in confectionery. A similar flavour occurs in the kernels of certain other fruits, such as apricots, cherries, plums and peaches.

Fruits have been dried for thousands of years. The process probably began in the Middle East with sun-dried dates, apricots and figs and it was a perfect way of preservation. The shrivelled fruit accumulating a natural sweetness and intensity of flavour that was miraculously released when soaked in water, and swollen again to their original size, the fruits would have provided a sweet and welcome relief to an otherwise stark autumn and winter diet.

In English cooking, we think of dried fruits mainly to mean currants, sultanas, raisins and prunes. The first three are all grapes. Currants, which arrived here in the fourteenth century, are dried seedless grapes originally from Corinth. Sultanas are dried white grapes whose name – sultan's wife – refers to their Turkish origins. Raisins, the finest of them all, are dried muscatel grapes from Spain. And prunes? They are of course dried plums. It is a pity so many English people associate them with dreary English breakfasts. Prunes deserve better than that, as was recognized not so many centuries ago – so many of our rich and wonderful festive puddings and cakes using dried fruits were suffixed with the word 'plum'.

Almond soup

This sweet-tasting, elegant soup can trace its history back to the Norman conquest. It calls for a home-made chicken stock to which is added the pieces of meat picked from the bone, chopped celery and ground almonds, flavoured with nutmeg, coriander and lemon. If you make the stock the day before, the soup itself is assembled in minutes and only needs to be simmered for a further half an hour before being puréed and served with sippets of fried bread.

1 chicken carcase	white pepper
1 stick celery, finely chopped	1 bay leaf
50 g (2 oz) ground almonds	finely grated peel of 1 lemon
freshly grated nutmeg	2 tablespoons breadcrumbs
½ teaspoon crushed coriander seeds	150 ml (¼ pint) single cream
salt	(optional)

Make a stock from the chicken carcase (see Etceteras). Strain the contents into a saucepan and remove as much of the meat from the bones as possible. Add the pieces of meat to the stock in the pan, together with the celery, ground almonds, nutmeg, coriander, salt and pepper, bay leaf and lemon peel. Simmer for 30 minutes. Remove the bay leaf, stir in the breadcrumbs and put the soup through a food processor or liquidizer. Return to the pan and heat gently. Stir in the cream, if using, but do not let the soup boil. Check the seasoning. Serve in hot bowls.

Trout with almonds

Oxbridge lays claim to many recipes and Magdalen College, Oxford, is rather proud of this one, though if the truth were told, trout with almonds crops up all over the place.

2–3 tablespoons flour	3–4 tablespoons oil
salt	50 g (2 oz) butter
freshly milled black pepper	50 g (2 oz) slivered almonds
4 trout, gutted and cleaned	juice of 1 lemon

Put the flour on to a plate and season it with salt and pepper. Roll the trout in it until they are coated all over. Heat the oil in a frying pan and when it is hot add the trout. Fry them for 3–5 minutes on each side. Remove them to a warm serving dish.

Discard most of the oil, add the butter to the pan and when it melts throw in the almonds. Put the pan on a medium heat and turn the almonds over and over using a spatula, until they just turn golden – on no account let them get burnt. Squeeze over the juice of the lemon and pile the mixture on top of the fish.

Hindle wakes

This Lancastrian dish of cold chicken with its prune and almond stuffing needs to be prepared a day ahead. No one seems to know quite how it got its name. There are various theories, one being that it derives from a play of the same name, written early this century by Stanley Houghton which is set in an imaginary town in Lancashire. On the other hand, perhaps the play was called after the dish. Another theory suggests that the name is a corruption of a mixture of French and English, *hen de la wake* and that the recipe was brought over by Flemish weavers in the fourteenth century; wake being the local name for the eve of the village fête which celebrated the parish's saint's day.

Whatever the name, there is no doubt that this dish, with its rich stuffing, makes a colourful centrepiece for a cold spread. In the days before factory farming, a boiling fowl, a hen grown too old to produce any more eggs and therefore destined for the pot, would be used. It needed long, slow cooking to make it tender but the flavour was much more robust than that of a young bird. You may be lucky and be able to order one from your butcher. If you can you will need to boil it for 3–4 hours, not $1\frac{1}{2}$ hours as in this recipe.

900 g (2 lb) pitted prunes	salt
225 g (8 oz) breadcrumbs	freshly milled black pepper
50 g (2 oz) chopped almonds	1 large free-range chicken,
2 tablespoons chopped mixed	weighing about 2 kg ($4\frac{1}{2}$ lb)
fresh herbs comprising parsley,	2 tablespoons soft brown sugar
sage, marjoram and thyme	25 g (1 oz) butter
50 g (2 oz) beef or vegetarian	25 g (1 oz) flour
suet	300 ml ($\frac{1}{2}$ pint) chicken stock
150 ml ($\frac{1}{4}$ pint) white malt	2 eggs
vinegar	3 lemons
	sprigs of parsley

Cover the prunes in boiling water and soak for 30 minutes. Set 6 aside and chop the rest. Mix the chopped prunes with the breadcrumbs, almonds, herbs, suet, 1 tablespoon of the vinegar and season with salt and pepper. Use this mixture to stuff the chicken. Secure with string or with a toothpick.

Put the chicken in a large pot, cover it with water and add the remaining vinegar and the sugar. Bring to the boil, cover and simmer for $1\frac{1}{2}$–2 hours or until tender.

Half an hour before the chicken is cooked make a sauce by melting the butter in a small saucepan and stirring in the flour. Let it cook, still stirring, for 2 minutes. Stir in 300 ml ($\frac{1}{2}$ pint) of the stock in which the chicken is cooking and bring to the boil, lower the heat and let the sauce simmer for 10–15 minutes. Break the eggs into a bowl, beat lightly and stir in a tablespoon or two of the sauce. Pour the eggs into the sauce in the pan, taking care it does not boil and curdle. Once it is thick and creamy, remove from the heat, season with salt and pepper and stir in the peel and juice of 2 of the lemons. Set aside to cool.

When the chicken is cooked, leave it to cool in the stock. When cool remove from the stock and put in the fridge until the next day (the stock can be used for a soup).

The next day, skin the chicken, put on to a dish and coat with the sauce which has been gently reheated just sufficiently to make it pliable. Use a palette knife dipped in hot water to spread it evenly. Garnish with the remaining prunes cut in half, the third lemon, sliced and the sprigs of parsley.

Simnel cake

In *The Art of British Cooking*, Theodora Fitzgibbon relates how the name of this cake derives from the Roman *siminellus*, a kind of fine bread eaten during spring fertility rites. Much later the name attached itself to a fruit cake enriched with marzipan which young girls in service were allowed to take home to their mothers on the fourth Sunday in Lent, Mothering Sunday. It is a cake that keeps well, so perhaps this is why it eventually became associated with Easter, when it is traditionally decorated with marzipan balls representing the eleven faithful apostles.

350 g (12 oz) bought or home-
    made marzipan (see page 180)
100 g (4 oz) butter or margarine
100 g (4 oz) soft brown sugar
3 large eggs, beaten
150 g (6 oz) plain flour, sifted

$\frac{1}{2}$ teaspoon mixed spice
350 g (12 oz) mixed dried fruit
50 g (2 oz) chopped mixed peel
grated peel and juice of 1 lemon
apricot jam, warmed
1 egg white

Heat the oven to Gas 3/325°F/160°C. Grease and line an 18 cm (7 in) cake tin.

Take one third of the marzipan, knead it well and roll it into a ball.

Roll out on a board dusted with icing sugar into a circle the same diameter as the cake tin.

Cream the butter and sugar together and when the mixture is light and fluffy, beat in the eggs one at a time. Fold in the sifted flour, mixed spice, dried fruit, mixed peel and the grated peel and juice of the lemon. Turn half the mixture into the cake tin. Cover with the circle of marzipan and add the rest of the cake mix, smoothing the top. Bake for 1 hour, lower the heat to Gas 2/300°F/150°C and bake for a further hour. Allow the cake to cool, turning it on to a rack after 10 minutes.

When cold, roll out the remaining piece of marzipan into a circle large enough to cover the top of the cake. Brush the cake with apricot jam and lay the marzipan on top. (Decorate the cake if you wish with 11 marzipan balls made from the trimmings.) Brush with the egg white and return to the oven, heated to Gas 4/350°F/190°C, for 10–15 minutes until the top is lightly browned.

Easter biscuits

At Easter time, instead of hot cross buns, I prefer to make Easter biscuits, which are just as spicy and far less trouble. In any case hot cross buns are on sale from just after Christmas until Easter and are no sort of novelty – in my childhood, the excitement of their appeal was they only appeared on Good Fridays. I now learn from John Ayto's *A Gourmet's Guide* that this was a custom dating back to Tudor times, when a law was passed forbidding the sale of crossed buns except at funerals, Christmas and Easter, when the cross could be seen to symbolize the Crucifixion. This seems very curious until it emerges that bakers always used to put a cross on their dough, not only because they thought it helped it to rise but also as a guard against the devil. This sort of papist superstition was too much for the Protestant faction, hence the ban.

This recipe makes approximately 30 biscuits.

100 g (4 oz) caster sugar, plus
   some for sprinkling
100 g (4 oz) butter or margarine
1 egg, separated
225 g (8 oz) plain flour, sifted

½ teaspoon mixed spice
50 g (2 oz) currants
25 g (1 oz) chopped candied peel
approx. 3 tablespoons milk

Cream the sugar and butter or margarine until light and fluffy. Beat in

the egg yolk. Fold in the flour, mixed spice, currants and candied peel.
Gradually stir in sufficient milk to make a stiff dough. Heat the oven to
Gas 3/325°F/160°C.

Roll the dough out on a floured board until about 3 mm (1/8 in)
thick. Cut into 5 cm (2 in) rounds with a fluted pastry cutter and lay
them on greased baking sheets. Bake for 10 minutes. Remove from the
oven, brush each biscuit with the egg white and sprinkle with a little
caster sugar. Return to the oven for 5–10 minutes until they are a pale
gold. Remove from the baking sheets with the aid of a palette knife
and cool on wire trays.

Mincemeat

As almost everyone knows, mincemeat used to contain finely chopped
beef or mutton and little pies based on this original idea are still made
in the south of France, introduced there by Lord Clive of India.
Mincemeat is very easy to make but must be done at least 2 weeks
ahead of time, to allow the dried fruit with its flavourings of almonds,
spices, sherry and brandy to mature. It will keep much longer than
this, at least several months. This recipe is only one of the dozens of
variations to be found and can be changed and adapted to suit your
taste.

25 g (1 oz) almonds, chopped
25 g (1 oz) glacé cherries,
  chopped
100 g (4 oz) raisins
100 g (4 oz) currants
100 g (4 oz) candied peel
100 g (4 oz) dark brown sugar
100 g (4 oz) beef or vegetarian
  suet

1 apple, peeled, cored and finely
  chopped
1 teaspoon mixed spice
grated peel and juice of 1 lemon
grated peel and juice of 1 orange
3–4 tablespoons sweet sherry
3–4 tablespoons brandy

Mix all the ingredients together, put into jars, cover and store for at
least 2 weeks before using. Use to make mince pies or, as a variation,
make the godcakes in the recipe below.

Godcakes

These triangular pastries filled with mincemeat were given to the children of Warwickshire by their godparents on birthdays, at New Year and on confirmation. The three points represented the Holy Trinity. People judged your wealth by the size of the godcakes you gave, so they would be anything up to 45 cm (18 in) across – and so presumably shared by the family. However, in the following recipe I have gone for very much smaller ones which look more appealing and can be eaten with the fingers. Having said that, they are also delicious if eaten with thick cream or with a brandy or rum butter. In any event, they should be eaten either straight from the oven or warm. The following quantities make 24 godcakes.

225 g (8 oz) puff pastry   1 egg white
mincemeat   granulated sugar

Roll the pastry into a rectangle 45 x 30 cm (18 x 12 in). Divide this into 24 squares each measuring 7.5 cm (3 in). Put a teaspoon of mincemeat into the centre of each square, dampen the edges of the pastry with water and fold the square over to form a triangle. Pinch the edges together and mark them with the prongs of a fork. Cut three slits in the top of each godcake and lay them on to dampened baking sheets. Set them aside while you heat the oven to Gas 7/425°F/220°C.

Brush the godcakes all over with the egg white and sprinkle generously with granulated sugar. Bake for 12–15 minutes until puffed and golden.

Plum or Christmas cake

From Elizabethan times, 'plum' was used as a name for rich cakes and puddings containing any sort of dried fruits, whether or not they included dried plums – prunes – and along with the rest of the world this is the name that my grandmother used to describe her Christmas cakes and puddings. A good Christmas cake is packed with dried fruit and nuts and is flavoured with spices. In this recipe it is further enriched by cider and brandy. It is easy to make and keeps for weeks in an airtight tin. Make it at least a month before it is to be eaten.

450 g (l lb) currants
350 g (12 oz) raisins
50 g (2 oz) glacé cherries,
    chopped
50 g (2 oz) chopped mixed peel
scant 300 ml ($\frac{1}{2}$ pint) cider
100 g (4 oz) almonds, chopped
100 g (4 oz) walnuts, chopped
4 tablespoons brandy
225 g (8 oz) butter

225 g (8 oz) soft brown sugar
2 tablespoons black treacle
juice and grated peel of 1 lemon
4 eggs
350 g (12 oz) self-raising flour
$\frac{1}{2}$ teaspoon cinnamon
$\frac{1}{2}$ teaspoon ginger
$\frac{1}{2}$ teaspoon nutmeg
$\frac{1}{2}$ teaspoon mace
$\frac{1}{2}$ teaspoon mixed spice

The day before you intend to make the cake put the currants, raisins, cherries and mixed peel into a bowl and cover with the cider. Leave overnight.

The next day prepare a 23 cm (9 in) cake tin by lining it with a double layer of waxed baking paper. Cut a double circle for the top. Preheat the oven to Gas 3/325°F/160°C.

Add the almonds, walnuts and 2 tablespoons of the brandy to the fruit mixture.

In a large mixing bowl, beat the butter and sugar until soft and creamy. Beat in the black treacle and the grated peel and juice of the lemon. Beat in the eggs, one at a time, adding a little flour if the mixture appears to curdle. Sift the flour with the cinnamon, ginger, nutmeg, mace and mixed spice and gradually fold it into the mixture. Lastly, gradually stir in the fruit.

Transfer the mixture to the prepared cake tin, lay the paper circles on top and bake for 2 hours. Lower the heat to Gas 2/300°F/150°C for a further 1$\frac{1}{2}$ hours. Test it is cooked by plunging a skewer in the centre; it should come out clean. Leave in the tin to cool.

Once cold, remove from the tin. Turn the cake upside down and pierce with a skewer in several places, pouring a little brandy into each hole. Repeat this process every week for four weeks. Keep the cake wrapped in foil in an airtight container.

Marzipan or almond paste

Plum cake can be eaten just as it is or iced with marzipan and royal icing. Home-made marzipan is a mixture of ground almonds, icing sugar, lemon juice and raw egg yolk. If you are concerned about eating raw egg, use ready-made marzipan instead. Cover the cake with the marzipan a week ahead of eating, and leave for two days before icing.

350 g (12 oz) ground almonds   juice of 1 lemon
225 g (8 oz) icing sugar, sifted   apricot jam
3 egg yolks

Mix the ground almonds with the sugar. Beat the egg yolks with the lemon juice and mix into the almond mixture. Use your hands to knead the mixture to a paste and roll into a ball (or do the whole operation in a food processor).

To cover the cake, stand it upside down on a board. Heat some apricot jam with a very little water, sieve it and brush it all over the cake while still warm.

Divide the marzipan into two pieces, one twice the size of the other. Use this larger piece for the top of the cake, rolling it into a circle on a board sprinkled with icing sugar. Fold it in half and lift it carefully on to the cake, flipping it over so that it fits the top. Press it gently down. Brush the sides of the cake with more apricot glaze and roll out the remaining marzipan into a strip large enough to cover the sides. Press it into position, patching it as necessary with any bits left over.

Royal icing

Glycerine will prevent royal icing from setting rock hard and can be bought at the chemist. One bottle will last for years but can be used in between times, mixed with rose water, as a very good hand lotion.

450 g (l lb) icing sugar, sifted $\frac{1}{2}$ teaspoon glycerine
2 egg whites

Put the icing sugar into a large bowl (a mixer comes in very handy here). Beat the egg whites until stiff and beat them, with the glycerine, into the sugar. If using a mixer, start at a very low speed (and if you have an open bowl, put a clean tea towel over the bowl to prevent clouds of icing sugar covering the kitchen). As the eggs begin to be incorporated increase the speed. Beat until you have a gleaming white mixture. Set aside for 1 hour before using.

Using a palette knife dipped in very hot water, cover the top and sides of the cake with about half of the mixture. Pile the rest on top and complete the effect of a snowy landscape by raising it in peaks with the knife. Decorate, if you wish, with artificial holly or a miniature snowman.

Plum or Christmas pudding

There was a time when everyone had their favourite recipe for our national Christmas pudding. My grandmother used to make three: one for the great day itself and the others to be stored and eaten on my and my brother's birthdays. Nowadays a huge variety is sold in supermarkets and shops and the idea of making one, especially if you never have, may seem like a needless chore. In fact, it is very easy and extremely enjoyable and, once the scents of fruits and spices begin to mingle with the zest of lemons and oranges, the whole house is permeated with a feeling of anticipation. Traditionally everyone must have a stir!

The pudding needs 7 hours' steaming but it can be mixed one day and cooked the next. Make it at least six weeks before Christmas, longer is better, so that the pudding is able to slowly mature and darken.

The following is just one version of the dozens of variations and the ratios of the differents fruits can be altered to suit your own taste buds. This quantity is enough to make a 1 litre (1¾ pint) pudding plus another half that size.

100 g (4 oz) self-raising flour	1 teaspoon mixed spice
100 g (4 oz) fresh white breadcrumbs	½ teaspoon salt
	1 carrot, grated
100 g (4 oz) beef or vegetarian suet	1 eating apple, peeled and grated
100 g (4 oz) soft brown sugar	juice and finely grated peel of 1 orange
100 g (4 oz) sultanas	juice and finely grated peel of 1 lemon
100 g (4 oz) currants	
100 g (4 oz) dried apricots, chopped	3 eggs, beaten
100 g (4 oz) raisins	2–3 tablespoons brandy
50 g (2 oz) chopped mixed peel	approx. 150 ml (¼ pint) stout, brown ale or milk

Brush the basins with oil. In a large bowl, adding each ingredient one at a time, mix the flour, breadcrumbs, suet, sugar, sultanas, currants, dried apricots, raisins, mixed peel, mixed spice, salt, grated carrot and apple. Stir in the grated peel and juice of the orange and lemon followed by the eggs and brandy. Add sufficient stout, ale or milk to make a dropping consistency. Put into the basins, leaving a 5 cm (2 in) gap at the top for the puddings to expand. Cover each with a piece of foil, pleated in the centre, to allow for expansion, and secure either with string or with a thick rubber band.

Put each pudding into a saucepan with a tight-fitting lid. Pour boiling water to reach half-way up the bowls and put over a low heat for the puddings to steam. Allow 7 hours for the larger one, 5 for the smaller. The water must bubble continuously without spilling over. Check every hour or so and if the water is diminishing, top up with more boiling water.

Once the puddings are cooked, set aside to cool and cover them with fresh foil. Store in a cool, dark, airy place for at least six weeks.

On the day itself, steam the larger one for a further 3 hours, the smaller for 2 hours. Turn out on to a warm plate and bring to the table flaming. This is achieved by heating 2–3 tablespoons of brandy in a metal soup ladle or a small saucepan. When it bubbles set it alight, pour over the pudding and rush to the table. Serve with brandy or rum butter (see below) or real custard (see Etceteras).

Jessie Jackson's plum pudding

This is a real family recipe. It was given to me by Kate Hobson, who unearthed my first book, *The Student's Cookbook*, from the slush pile at Faber. It was her grandmother's recipe and, as Kate explained, 'it is the most simple, basic recipe you could possibly imagine. I use brown sugar, and have varied the dried fruit. I use a very large carrot indeed and vegetarian suet. It is a moist pudding which tends to fall apart when it is turned out. I just mould it back together again and it doesn't worry me, but it may worry some people. Alcohol is optional. We usually eat it at my grandmother's large oak dining table with lots of rum sauce!'

I have listed the ingredients exactly as Kate gave them to me. You will see the flour and sugar are measured in cups, which is how her grandmother measured them. Kate uses an ordinary English teacup. If you want to add some alcohol, stir in some stout or ale, or something stronger like brandy, rum or whisky instead of the milk.

2 cups self-raising flour
2 cups sugar
1 teaspoon salt
1 large carrot, grated
25 g (1 oz) mixed peel
450 g (1 lb) currants

450 g (1 lb) raisins (large preferred)
225 g (8 oz) beef or vegetarian suet
2 eggs, beaten
milk or stout to mix

In a large bowl, mix all the dry ingredients together in the order given. Stir in the beaten eggs and sufficient milk or stout to hold everything together. Put into basins, cover and steam for 5 hours.

On the day, steam for 1 hour.

Rum and brandy butters

Either rum butter, also known as Cumberland butter on account of the smugglers all along that coast, or brandy butter, whose origins can perhaps be traced to Cornwall, is an essential accompaniment to Christmas pudding. Make it days or even weeks in advance and store in the fridge. Remember to take it out an hour or so before you want to use it so that it softens a little and the flavour has time to develop.

225 g (8 oz) butter
100 g (4 oz) soft brown sugar
grated nutmeg

2–3 tablespoons rum or brandy
a little grated lemon or orange peel

Cream the butter and sugar with the grated nutmeg until light and creamy. Beat in the rum or brandy, a little at a time to prevent it curdling. Lastly, add the grated peel: lemon for rum butter, orange for brandy butter. Pile into a jar. Cover tightly with foil and refrigerate until ready for use.

Newmarket pudding

More familiar as bread and butter or nursery pudding, this perennial favourite dates back at least to the eighteenth century. Assemble it a couple of hours ahead, so that the bread soaks up the milk and absorbs the flavours of the dried fruits, spices and brandy. This last is optional but turns the pudding from a childish affair into something rather more sophisticated.

butter

6 thin slices stale white bread, crusts removed

4 tablespoons raisins

4 tablespoons currants

2 tablespoons dried apricots, chopped

2 eggs, plus 1 yolk

300 ml ($\frac{1}{2}$ pint) creamy milk

2 tablespoons brandy or apple brandy

grated peel of $\frac{1}{2}$ lemon

$\frac{1}{2}$ teaspoon ground ginger

$\frac{1}{2}$ teaspoon grated nutmeg

$\frac{1}{2}$ teaspoon cinnamon

1–2 tablespoons caster sugar

Butter the bread on one side. Grease a shallow ovenproof dish with more butter and sprinkle in half the raisins, currants and apricots. Cover with half the bread slices. Sprinkle over the remaining dried fruit and top with the rest of the bread. Beat the eggs, including the extra yolk, in a bowl and whisk in the milk, brandy or apple brandy, grated lemon peel, ginger, nutmeg and cinnamon. Pour over the bread and set aside for a couple of hours.

Heat the oven to Gas 4/350°F/180°C.

Sprinkle the sugar over the pudding and bake for 30–40 minutes until puffed and golden.

Bakewell pudding

Like many gourmet delights, Bakewell pudding was a happy accident, or so legend tells us. Apparently a novice cook at the Rutland Arms in Bakewell, Derbyshire, misunderstood the instructions on making a simple jam tart; the result was sensational and Bakewell was put on the culinary map. This recipe, with its emphasis on eggs, ground almonds and butter, bears no relation to those stodgy, mass-produced tarts with which most people are familiar.

225 g (8 oz) puff or shortcrust pastry

5–6 tablespoons strawberry or raspberry jam

3 eggs, beaten

100 g (4 oz) caster sugar

100 g (4 oz) butter, melted

50 g (2 oz) ground almonds

Heat the oven to Gas 6/400s°F/200°C.

Line a 20 cm (8 in) flan tin or pie dish with the pastry and trim the edges. Spread the jam thickly over the base. Beat the eggs with the sugar until frothy and stir in the melted butter and the almonds. Pour the mixture over the pastry. Stand the tin on a baking sheet and bake for 25–30 minutes until the filling is set and golden. Serve warm or cold, with or without cream.

Madeleine's chocolate cake

Rich and gooey, made with ground almonds instead of flour, and flavoured with marmalade, this is just one of the many versions of chocolate cake that we so glory in. It is based on a recipe given to me by my daughter, who in turn was given it by a friend.

It was the Aztecs who discovered that the seeds of the cacao tree could be ground and made into a delicious drink and when the idea was brought to Europe by the Spanish in the seventeenth century it became all the rage. Later we discovered how the ground and roasted seeds could be hardened and used in confectionery – slab chocolate, which is used in this recipe, was born. There are different grades of plain cooking chocolate, the higher the amount of cacao, the better the chocolate. Inferior varieties are usually sweetened and contain large amounts of cocoa butter.

225 g (8 oz) plain cooking chocolate	4 eggs, separated
170 g (6 oz) butter or margarine	200 g (7 oz) ground almonds
100 g (4 oz) caster sugar	4 tablespoons Seville orange marmalade
	1 tablespoon water

Heat the oven to Gas 4/350°F/180°C and grease a 20 cm (8 in) loose-bottomed cake tin.

Put three-quarters of the chocolate into a heatproof bowl and stand it in a cool oven until melted (or use a microwave). Meanwhile cream two-thirds of the butter or margarine with the sugar until pale and fluffy. Remove the melted chocolate from the oven and beat in the egg yolks one by one. Stir into the creamed mixture and fold in the ground almonds. Beat the egg whites until they are firm and fold into the cake mixture. Turn it into the tin and smooth the surface. Bake for 45–50 minutes. Remove from the oven and allow to cool for a few minutes before turning on to a wire rack.

When the cake is cool, melt the remaining chocolate and butter in the same way as previously. Put the marmalade into a small saucepan with the water. Heat it gently and when it has melted put it through a sieve. Brush all over the top of the cake with this marmalade glaze.

Beat the melted chocolate and butter together and spread over the top of the cake, letting it run down the sides. As the chocolate and butter harden, so does the icing.

Maids of honour

On the way to Richmond-upon-Thames one wet and windy afternoon we went to the Maids of Honour tea rooms, just opposite the wall of Kew Gardens, where they serve these little cakes, puff pastry tarts filled with a creamy custard flavoured with lemon juice and almonds. They are made to a special recipe said to have been handed down from the court of Henry VIII; they are reputed to have been the invention of Catherine of Aragon's pastry cook. Perhaps he was French, because they are so similar to the little almond tarts of Normandy known as *mirlitons*. On the other hand, another story says that Anne Boleyn invented them when she was one of Catherine's maids of honour and Henry was so impressed by her and the cakes that he called them after her. Perhaps she was the original knave of hearts. Like all secret recipes, there are numerous variations on the theme, all claiming to be the authentic version. This is just one. Eat them warm or cold. These quantities are sufficient for 24 tarts.

225 g (8 oz) puff pastry
2 eggs, plus 1 yolk
75 g (3 oz) caster sugar
75 g (3 oz) butter, softened
1 tablespoons self-raising flour

75 g (3 oz) ground almonds
juice and finely grated peel of 1
  lemon
6 tablespoons double cream

Roll out the pastry and cut into rounds to line tartlet tins. Set aside in a cool place. Heat the oven to Gas 6/400°F/200°C.

Beat the eggs and the extra yolk with the caster sugar until pale and fluffy. Beat in the softened butter. Fold in the flour and almonds, followed by the lemon juice and grated peel. Lastly, fold in the cream. Spoon the mixture into the lined tins, filling them about two thirds full. Bake for 25 minutes until golden brown.

Rock cakes

Rock cakes, or rock buns as they are also called, were not always regarded as the simple children's treat they have become. In the nineteenth century they were eaten with sherry by city businessmen. They are, however, child's play to prepare, the only proviso is to make sure the mixture is very stiff – too much liquid and the cakes will lose their rocky appearance and flatten out as they cook. This recipe will make 18–20 rock cakes.

200 g (8 oz) self-raising flour,
    sifted
pinch of salt
100 g (4 oz) butter or margarine
75 g (3 oz) caster sugar

100 g (4 oz) currants and
    sultanas, mixed
25 g (1 oz) chopped candied peel
2 eggs, beaten
milk, if necessary

Heat the oven to Gas 7/425°F/220°C.

Put the sifted flour into a mixing bowl with the salt. Add the butter or margarine cut in small pieces and rub in until the mixture resembles fine crumbs. Stir in the sugar, currants and sultanas and the candied peel. Add the eggs and mix with a fork. If the mixture does not quite hold together, stir in a very little milk, no more than 1 teaspoonful at a time.

Grease 2 baking sheets. Using two forks, divide the mixture into pieces the size of an egg and place on the baking sheets. Bake for 15–20 minutes until golden brown. Remove to a wire rack and leave to cool.

Salted almonds and raisins

At Christmas in my grandmother's house there was an abundance of food of all kinds. We just seemed to go on eating all day long, right from the orange at the toe of the stocking to the final mince pie. Just in case we got hungry in between, she made dishes of salted almonds and raisins. You can buy almonds ready-blanched but if you want to save money and benefit from the superior flavour, buy them in their husks and blanch your own by steeping them for a few minutes in boiling water. As they cool, pick them up one by one and rub away the skin between your fingers.

salt
5 tablespoons olive oil

225 g (8 oz) blanched almonds
225 g (8 oz) raisins

Put a piece of greaseproof paper on to a plate and sprinkle it generously with salt. Heat the oil in a frying pan and fry the almonds in batches until golden brown, but don't let them burn. Transfer them to the greaseproof paper as you go. When they are all done, turn them over and over, adding a little more salt. When quite cold mix with the raisins.

Oranges and lemons

Wild duck with orange

Partridges or pigeons with cabbage

Rabbit and orange

Jugged hare

Game and mushroom pie

Orange and watercress salad

Whole fruit marmalade

Marmalade pudding

Spiced oranges

Rhubarb pie

Scallops with bacon

Miller's wife sole

Baked trout with bacon

Spatchcock

Pancakes with lemon

Victoria sponge sandwich

Orange and lemon syrup cake

Madeira cake

Lemon curd

Lemonade

. . . say the bells of St Clements. Everyone knows the old nursery rhyme. Once, the people who lived around Clement's Inn of Court used to be presented with the fruits on the last Thursday in March.

The first orange trees, with their sweet-scented flowers and brilliant, tangy fruits, grew in China. They reached Persia via India and the Persians devised ways of cultivating them using irrigation channels, so that the fruit thrived in the hot climate. Their name is a corruption of the Persian *narang*. Arabs adopted the Persian method of orange growing and spread their culture throughout southern Europe across from Sicily to Spain. Lemons from Persia and Arabia followed the same route and the first oranges and lemons reached England as a present for Eleanor of Castile, the beloved wife of King Edward I, seven hundred years ago. The oranges were bitter, like today's Sevilles, and it is this type of orange which is called for in many of the following recipes. When Sevilles are not around, use instead sweet oranges with a lemon.

Oranges and lemons give a sharp zest to dishes of game and fish as well as to sweet dishes. Their bright colours alone adding a feeling of cheer to the kitchen when outside it is grey and dreary.

Wild duck with orange

Duck with orange is a classic combination and it works particularly well when the duck is a mallard. These are in season between September and February. In this recipe, they are first browned, then simmered in wine or cider and flavoured with orange. You can cook duckling in the same way but they have a high proportion of fat, so if you do so, prick the skin all over with the prongs of a fork before browning, to release some of the fat. Discard most of it from the pan before adding the shallots.

25 g (1 oz) butter
2 tablespoons oil
2 mallards
2 shallots, chopped
150 ml ($\frac{1}{4}$ pint) white wine or
    strong dry cider

2 Seville oranges or 2 sweet
    oranges and $\frac{1}{2}$ lemon
salt
freshly milled black pepper
watercress

Melt the butter with the oil in a large, flameproof casserole in which the birds will fit comfortably, and brown the ducks all over. This process will take 10–15 minutes. Transfer them to a warm plate. Add the chopped shallots and let them soften, but not brown which makes them bitter. Return the ducks to the pan. Pour in the wine or cider and add the peel and juice of one of the oranges. (If using sweet oranges, also add at this stage the grated peel and juice of the half lemon.) Season with salt and pepper, cover and simmer for 30–40 minutes.

Transfer the ducks to a serving dish and keep warm. Boil the sauce hard until reduced by half, pour over the birds and garnish with the remaining orange either quartered or cut in slices, pips removed, and the watercress.

Partridges or pigeons with cabbage

Orange, cider and redcurrant jelly all add to the gamy flavour of this Somerset way with partridges. The same recipe can be used for pigeons, which are much cheaper and widely available, but they do take much longer to cook.

2 tablespoons oil
4 partridges or pigeons
4 rashers bacon, chopped
1 onion, sliced
1 carrot, sliced
2–3 sprigs of thyme, tied in a
    bunch
freshly grated nutmeg

salt
freshly milled black pepper
300 ml ($\frac{1}{2}$ pint) strong dry cider
2 tablespoons redcurrant jelly
grated peel and juice of 1 Seville
    orange or 1 sweet orange and $\frac{1}{2}$
    lemon
1 Savoy cabbage, finely sliced

Heat the oil in a flameproof casserole and brown the birds all over. Remove to a plate. Add the bacon, onion and carrot to the pan and fry for a few minutes. Return the birds and add the thyme and nutmeg and season with salt and pepper. Pour over the cider, stir in the redcurrant jelly and add the grated peel and juice of the orange (and the $\frac{1}{2}$ lemon if using a sweet orange). Cover and simmer for 30–45 minutes (2–3 hours if using pigeons). Add the finely sliced cabbage and cook for a further 30 minutes.

Rabbit and orange

Rabbit, especially wild rabbit, is strong and flavoursome, so goes well with the bitter-sweetness of oranges and lemons. In this easy-to-prepare recipe, which is loosely based on one of Hannah Glasse's, I have used Seville orange marmalade, but when they are available you could stir in the zest and juice of 2 Seville oranges. If the quantity of wine seems extravagant, use a strong, dry cider instead. Serve with a vegetable like jugged celery (see Apples) and either rice or steamed potatoes.

700–900 g ($1\frac{1}{2}$–2 lb) rabbit, jointed
300 ml ($\frac{1}{2}$ pint) dry white wine
several sprigs of rosemary and sage
juice and grated peel of 1 lemon
freshly milled black pepper

2 tablespoons flour
2 tablespoons oil
2 tablespoons Seville orange marmalade
225 g (8 oz) mushrooms, sliced
salt

Marinate the rabbit pieces overnight in the wine with sprigs of rosemary and sage, the lemon peel and juice and a sprinkling of black pepper.

The next day, heat the oven to Gas 4/350°F/180°C.

Take the rabbit pieces out of the marinade, pat them dry with kitchen paper and roll them in the flour. Heat the oil in a heavy-based pan and fry the rabbit all over until golden, in two or three batches as necessary, transferring them to an earthenware casserole as you go. When the casserole is half full, put in fresh sprigs of rosemary and sage, the marmalade and top with the remaining rabbit. Fry the sliced mushrooms in the pan for a few minutes and transfer them to the casserole. Season with salt and pepper.

Heat the liquid from the marinade and when it boils, strain it over the contents of the casserole. Cover with foil and put on the lid. Put the casserole into the oven and after 30 minutes lower the heat to Gas 2/300°F/150°C. Continue to cook for $1\frac{1}{2}$–2 hours until tender.

Jugged hare

On Boxing Day in Somerset, jugged hare or even badger, was the poor man's feast. Flavoured with onions, spices and herbs it was cooked in a deep earthenware pot which stood in a pan of boiling water suspended over the fire. Quick and easy to prepare, nowadays it is cooked in the oven. Traditionally the sauce was thickened with the animal's blood which was stirred in at the last moment, care being taken not to let the mixture boil or it would curdle. If you buy your hare from a game dealer ask him to joint it for you and to give you the blood. If you buy pieces from a supermarket, the sauce can be thickened with cornflour. Serve the hare with steamed or boiled potatoes dusted with chopped parsley and a green vegetable. Redcurrant, rowan, crab apple or quince jelly is a pleasing accompaniment, as are forcemeat balls (see Sweet Herbs).

4 rashers bacon, chopped
2 onions, chopped
4 shallots, chopped
1 hare, jointed or 6–8 pieces of hare
2 cloves garlic
grated peel and juice of a Seville orange or of 1 sweet orange and ½ lemon
sprigs of parsley, marjoram and thyme tied in a bunch

2 cloves
pinch of mace
pinch of nutmeg
freshly milled black pepper
300 ml (½ pint) red wine
salt
blood of the hare or 1 tablespoon cornflour mixed to a paste with cold water
1 lemon, quartered

The day before, put half the bacon, onions and shallots in a deep earthenware casserole, lay the hare pieces on top, cover with the remaining bacon, onions and shallots. Put the garlic on top. Add the orange juice, herbs, cloves, mace, nutmeg and black pepper. Pour in the red wine. Leave to marinate overnight.

The next day, heat the oven to Gas 4/350°F/180°C.

Season the contents of the casserole with salt, cover it and put into the oven for 30 minutes. Lower the heat to Gas 2/300°F/150°C and leave for a further 3–3½ hours.

Put the hare on to a serving dish. Transfer the liquid to a saucepan, bring to the boil and boil hard until reduced by about half. Off the boil, stir in the blood (or cornflour paste) and when it thickens pour over the hare and garnish the dish with the lemon quarters.

Game and mushroom pie

Game pie makes an ideal focus to a winter supper or picnic. It can be made from almost any kind of game, including venison, hare, pigeon or pheasant. Whatever you use, you can have just one variety, or mix two or three different kinds together, and if you feel you haven't quite enough, augment it with a piece of rump steak cut in cubes. Bacon can be added to give additional flavour, while some recipes call for two or three hard-boiled eggs quartered. If the pie is to be eaten hot, puff pastry can be used but if to be eaten cold, it is better to choose shortcrust.

2 tablespoons oil
700 g (1½ lb) boned game such as
   venison, hare, pigeon or
   pheasant, cut in 2–3 cm (1 in)
   cubes
1 onion, chopped
225 g (8 oz) mushrooms, sliced
1 tablespoon flour
150 ml (¼ pint) red wine
150 ml (¼ pint) stock

2 tablespoons Seville orange
   marmalade
sprigs of thyme and sage, tied in
   a bunch
1 bay leaf
½ teaspoon mace
salt
freshly milled black pepper
225 g (8 oz) puff or shortcrust
   pastry
1 egg yolk, beaten

Heat oven to Gas 3/325°F/160°C.

Heat the oil in a flameproof casserole and brown the pieces of game all over, in two or three batches, transferring them to a plate as you go. Add the onion to the pan and stir for a few minutes before adding the sliced mushrooms. Let these cook until soft, stirring occasionally. Sprinkle in the flour, mix well and pour in the red wine and stock. When it boils, add the marmalade, the herbs and mace. Season with salt and pepper. Cover and put into the oven for 1½ hours. Empty into a pie dish and set aside to cool.

Roll out the pastry to make a lid, allowing sufficient over to make strips to line the rim of the dish. Brush the rim with water, lay the strips all round the edge and brush again with water. Put the lid on top and press the pastry edges together to seal. Mark all round with a knife or the prongs of a fork. Brush the top with the beaten egg, make leaves with the trimmings and put in place, brushing them with the egg glaze.

Set aside for 30 minutes. When ready to cook the pie, preheat the oven to Gas 7/425°F/220°C if using puff pastry, or Gas 5/375°F/190°C if using shortcrust.

Bake the pie for 35–40 minutes. If the lid is puff pastry, after 20 minutes lower the heat to Gas 5/375°F/190°C. Check to see the pastry is not getting too brown and if it is cover it with a piece of foil.

Orange and watercress salad

Arrange watercress in a shallow bowl. Slice two oranges thinly – use if possible seedless ones like navels, and place them on top, together with thin slices of red onion. Sprinkle with olive oil and a little wine vinegar, and season with salt and pepper.

Whole fruit marmalade

There is nothing more cheering on a bleak January day than the smell of Seville oranges simmering in the kitchen, and nothing nicer in the weeks that follow than home-made marmalade for breakfast. This recipe in which the oranges are cooked whole before being cut up is one of the simplest.

Follow the rules for jam making on page 130–31.

1 kg (2 lb) Seville oranges
2 litres (3½ pints) water

2 kg (4 lb) granulated or
preserving sugar

Wash the oranges, put them into a large saucepan with the water, bring to the boil and simmer, covered, for 1½ –2 hours until the skins can easily be pierced with the head of a pin. Set the pan aside to cool.

Warm the sugar by putting it into a baking tin in a cool oven, Gas ¼/225°F/110°C for 10–15 minutes. Put a saucer into the freezer to get really cold.

As soon as the oranges are cool enough to handle, remove them from the pan and quarter each one on a plate. Use a fork and a pointed knife to scoop out the pips; return these to the liquid in the saucepan. Once all the pips have been extracted, boil the liquid hard for 5 minutes to release their pectin. Cut the oranges into thin strips, either using the knife and fork, or by putting them into a food processor. Put the cut fruit into a heavy, wide-mouthed large pan and strain over the liquid from the other saucepan. Discard the pips.

Empty the warm sugar on to the fruit and put the pan over a

low heat, stirring occasionally until all the sugar has dissolved.

Once the sugar has completely dissolved, raise the heat and bring to a rapid boil, stirring constantly to prevent the marmalade sticking and burning. If you are using preserving sugar, setting point can be reached within a few minutes, so start testing after 5 minutes. Put a dab of marmalade on to the cold saucer: when cool it should wrinkle when pushed with your finger. If not, continue to boil fiercely and test every few minutes in the same way, remembering to remove the pan from the heat each time. Be careful not to prolong the cooking time longer than is necessary or the marmalade will be dark and too bitter.

Once setting point is reached let the marmalade rest in the pan for 5 minutes (this prevents the fruit rising in the jars), before stirring well and filling the jars right to the top. Cover each jar with a circle of waxed paper and use a really hot, wet sponge to wipe away any stickiness. Put on the lids, leave to cool, then label each jar and store in a cool, dry place.

Marmalade pudding

This is a very nursery pudding to be eaten on a cold winter's day. It is so good natured that longer cooking won't hurt. Golden syrup can be used instead of marmalade, in which case it becomes treacle pudding, or of course you can use any sort of jam. Whatever you use, it is traditionally served with real custard (see Etceteras), although many people prefer it with cream.

225 g (8 oz) marmalade   100 g (4 oz) caster sugar
225 g (8 oz) self-raising flour   2 eggs, beaten
pinch of salt   milk
100 g (4 oz) butter

Spoon the marmalade into a 1 litre ($1\frac{3}{4}$ pint) pudding basin and tip it from side to side so it coats the whole surface. Sift the flour into a bowl and add the salt. Cut the butter into small cubes and rub it into the flour until it looks like fine breadcrumbs. Stir in the sugar, followed by the beaten eggs. Use sufficient milk to form a soft dough which drops easily from a spoon. Tip the mixture into the basin and cover the top with a circle of waxed or greaseproof paper. Use a double layer of foil to make a lid which covers the sides of the basin by about 2–3 cm (1 in). Stand the basin on a rack or saucer in a large saucepan and pour in enough boiling water to come half way up the basin. Put on the lid and steam the pudding over a low heat for $1\frac{1}{2}$ hours, checking the water level once or twice to make sure it has not boiled dry. Turn out on to a serving plate when ready to eat.

Spiced oranges

Wonderful with duck, pork or ham, either hot or cold. If you fancy serving these glistening spiced oranges at Christmas, make them in the autumn because they need to mature for a couple of months before using. If navel oranges are available, use them because they are seedless, but any other kind of good quality orange will do.

6 oranges	2 sticks cinnamon
600 ml (1 pint) white wine	6 blades mace
vinegar	1 teaspoon whole cloves
1 kg ($2\frac{1}{4}$ lb) granulated sugar	

Slice the oranges about 5 mm ($\frac{1}{4}$ in) thick and remove any pips. Put them in a pan, just cover with water, bring to the boil and simmer, covered, for about 30 minutes until the peel is soft.

Put the vinegar and sugar into a large, wide pan and heat gently until the sugar dissolves, then add the spices. Using a slotted spoon, remove the orange slices from their cooking water and put them in the pan with the vinegar, sugar and spices. Cover and simmer gently for about 40 minutes until the oranges are translucent. Remove the pan from the heat and set aside for 24 hours before carefully transferring the slices of orange to preserving jars. Strain over the syrup and seal the jars. Leave for two months before using.

Rhubarb pie

Rhubarb came to England from Russia in the late sixteenth century but it was not until the beginning of the nineteenth that it became popular, especially the pale, pink stalks of winter rhubarb, forced in darkened greenhouses. (Summer rhubarb grown outdoors is darker, coarser and far more acidic in flavour.)

Winter rhubarb is delicious gently stewed until just soft, flavoured with brown sugar and perhaps ginger and angelica or with orange. It can either be served as it is or made into a fool by mixing with thick cream or home-made custard (see Etceteras).

The following recipe for a simple plate pie is also good with a spoonful or two of beer instead of orange juice and both versions are even nicer served with a little pouring cream.

450 g (l lb) rhubarb
2–3 tablespoons caster or vanilla
   sugar (see Etceteras)
freshly grated nutmeg

juice and finely grated peel of 1
   orange
150 g (6 oz) sweet or plain
   shortcrust pastry

Wash and cut the rhubarb into 2–3 cm (1 in) pieces (summer rhubarb may need to be peeled). Lay the pieces in a pie plate or dish, piling the fruit high as it shrinks when cooked. Sprinkle with the sugar, nutmeg, orange juice and grated peel.

Roll out the pastry to make a lid. With the pastry remnants roll out strips to fit the rim of the plate. Brush the rim with water, lay the strips all along the rim and brush again with water. Settle the pastry lid on top, pressing the outer edges so that they adhere to the pastry rim and this in turn adheres to the plate. Trim all round with a sharp knife and mark all round the edge with the prongs of a fork. Cut a slit in the centre for the steam to escape. Set aside for 30 minutes to allow the pastry to settle (otherwise it will shrink when it goes into the oven). Heat the oven to Gas 5/375°F/190°C.

Brush the pastry all over with a little water and sprinkle with caster sugar. Bake for 25–30 minutes until golden. Eat hot, warm or cold.

Scallops with bacon

In Yorkshire when scallops are plentiful they serve them for high tea, a substantial meal served in the early evening in which fish or meat is eaten with plenty of bread and butter, followed by pies and cakes.

8 scallops
flour
1 egg, beaten

breadcrumbs
8 rashers smoked bacon
juice of $\frac{1}{2}$ lemon

Separate and set aside the coral from the white part of each scallop. Coat the white parts first in flour, then in beaten egg and finally in breadcrumbs. Fry the bacon rashers in a large frying pan until all the fat runs. Remove and transfer to a plate in a warm oven. Add the scallops to the pan and fry them gently in the hot bacon fat for a minute or two. Add the corals and continue frying until the fish is cooked through and the breadcrumbs are crisp and brown. Squeeze over the lemon juice. Serve the scallops surrounded by the bacon rashers and with plenty of brown bread and butter.

Miller's wife sole

The name of this recipe derives from the fact that the fish is coated in flour before being fried in butter and served sprinkled with lemon and dusted with parsley. It is a perfect way of cooking either lemon sole or Dover sole. Dover sole, so called because it was from there that most of London's supplies were sent, are much dearer than lemon sole, but they are far superior. A large one will feed two, or alternatively buy small ones weighing around 225 g (8 oz) each. Get the fishmonger to remove the tough dark skin for you.

The quantities below are for two. If preparing for four, double the amounts and use two frying pans.

1–2 sole, depending on size	25 g (1 oz) unsalted butter
1–2 tablespoons flour	juice of $\frac{1}{2}$ lemon
50 g (2 oz) concentrated or	2–3 tablespoons chopped parsley
clarified butter (see Etceteras)	lemon wedges for garnish

Coat the fish evenly all over in the flour. Melt the concentrated or clarified butter in a large frying pan and when it sizzles add the fish. Fry over a medium heat, turning the fish over when the underside is golden. Fry the other side and transfer to a warm plate in a low oven.

Discard all the butter and wipe out the pan with kitchen paper. Melt the unsalted butter, when it foams squeeze in the lemon juice, stir and pour over the fish. Serve at once sprinkled with the parsley and lemon wedges.

Baked trout with bacon

The saltiness of bacon goes beautifully with the delicate flavour of trout in this dish which came to England via the Welsh.

8 rashers streaky bacon	freshly milled black pepper
4 trout	2 lemons
salt	2 tablespoons chopped parsley

Heat the oven to Gas 4/350°F/180°C.

Line the base of a shallow ovenproof dish with the rashers of streaky bacon. Lay the trout on top. Season with salt and pepper and squeeze over the juice of 1 lemon. Scatter the parsley over the top. Bake for 20–25 minutes. Serve garnished with the other lemon cut in quarters.

Spatchcock

Spatchcocking is an ideal way of cooking little birds like small chickens, usually sold as poussins, and quails. The name actually stems from the words 'dispatched cock', the bird in question having been split, flattened and put over the fire minutes after its neck was wrung! Grilling is fine if you are using a barbecue, but at other times of the year I prefer to roast them in the oven. In this recipe, the birds are sprinkled with grated cheese but some recipes use breadcrumbs instead. Allow one quail or half a poussin per head, unless appetites are keen in which case allow two quails or one poussin each.

2 poussins or 4 quails
2–3 teaspoons ready-made whole-seed mustard
freshly milled black pepper
sprigs of thyme or $\frac{1}{2}$ teaspoon dried

2 lemons
2–3 tablespoons oil
2–3 tablespoons hard cheese like mature Cheddar, grated
3–4 tablespoons strong dry cider or white wine

Split the poussins completely in half. The quails should simply be opened out by splitting down the backbone. Lay them on a board, cut side down and flatten them by pressing on them with the blade of a heavy knife. Put them skin side up in a single layer in an ovenproof dish (this could be enamelled cast iron but not plain metal as this causes a toxic reaction with the lemon juice) and spread them with the mustard. Season with pepper and lay the sprigs of thyme on top (or sprinkle with the dried thyme) and the juice of 1 lemon. Set aside for 30 minutes.

Heat the oven to Gas 6/400°F/200°C.

Sprinkle the oil over the birds. Roast the poussins for 40 minutes, the quails for 30 minutes. Half way through the cooking time, scatter over the cheese and baste the birds well. Take the dish out of the oven, pour round the cider or wine and return to the oven for a further 5 minutes. Serve the birds in their sauce, garnished with the remaining lemon cut in quarters.

Pancakes with lemon

In the eighteenth century very thin, crisp pancakes made with eggs and cream were piled in a stack and were nicknamed 'a quire of paper' but for the *hoi polloi* it was a simpler version which became associated with Shrove Tuesday. The day before Ash Wednesday, this was the last chance to indulge in an egg or two before the 40-day Lenten fast began. These pancakes are usually served sprinkled with sugar and lemon juice but they are also delicious spread with jam or honey, or thick cream or yoghurt. Try them, too, with a filling of apples which have been stewed in butter with brown sugar and a flavouring of cinnamon.

Traditionally, of course, the half-cooked pancake is tossed to turn it over and cook the underside. This takes practice and needs confidence and a slick twist of the wrist, so either practise in secret or turn the pancake with a spatula instead. Whatever you do, use a small, heavy frying pan and only sufficient oil to grease it. The following quantities will make 10–12 pancakes.

100 g (4 oz) flour, sifted	150 ml ($\frac{1}{4}$ pint) water
salt	oil
1 egg, plus 1 yolk	caster sugar
150 ml ($\frac{1}{4}$ pint) milk	1–2 lemons, cut in wedges

If you have a food processor put the flour, salt, egg and yolk, milk and water into it and process until well blended and frothy. Otherwise, sieve the flour and salt into a bowl, make a well in the centre, add the egg and yolk and half the milk. Mix thoroughly before gradually mixing in the rest of the milk and the water. Beat until light and frothy. Set aside for 1 hour before using.

If you plan to serve all the pancakes at once instead of one at a time as they are cooked, heat the oven to Gas 3/325°F/160°C, butter an ovenproof dish and put it into the oven to warm.

Before cooking beat in 1 tablespoon of oil into the batter. Put a little oil into a saucer, screw a piece of kitchen paper into a wodge and dip it in the oil and use this to grease a small heavy frying pan. Heat it and when it begins to smoke, pour in just enough batter to coat the base, tilting the pan from side to side so that it is completely covered. Let the pancake cook for about 1 minute over a medium heat until the surface becomes opaque and blisters begin to form. Turn it over and cook the other side for about 30 seconds, by which time it will be brown and slide easily out of the pan.

Repeat the process for each pancake, either serving them immediately sprinkled with sugar and lemon juice or putting each pancake as it is cooked into the buttered dish. Sprinkle each pancake with sugar and return the dish to the oven as you cook each successive pancake. Once all the pancakes are cooked, roll them up and serve them with the lemon wedges.

Victoria sponge sandwich

When Prince Albert died, Victoria took refuge every year on the Isle of Wight and it was here that in time she formed the habit of giving afternoon tea parties in which invariably a sponge of this kind featured, hence its name. It is one of the easiest cakes to make and, unlike a sponge made with no fat, it will keep for several days. The filling can be varied to suit whatever you have on hand, from a simple spread of jam to fresh fruit, with or without a layer of whipped cream. Raspberry or apricot jam gives a good flavour, or try freshly made lemon curd (see page 207) or take advantage of soft fruit such as raspberries or strawberries when they are in season.

150 g (6 oz) margarine or butter
150 g (6 oz) caster sugar
3 eggs
150 g (6 oz) self-raising flour,
  sifted

grated peel of 1 lemon
150 ml ($\frac{1}{4}$ pint) double cream,
  whipped (optional)
jam or fruit for filling
icing sugar, sifted

Grease 2 sandwich tins 20 cm (8 in) in diameter. Heat the oven to Gas 5/375°F/190°C.

Cream the butter and sugar together until pale and fluffy. Beat in the eggs one at a time, adding 2 teaspoons of flour with each. Fold in the remaining flour and the grated lemon peel. Spoon the mixture into the sandwich tins, spreading it evenly. Bake for 25–30 minutes until risen and golden. Remove from the oven and after 5 minutes turn out to cool on a rack.

Spread the cream over one half, if using, and top with a layer of jam, lemon curd or fruit. Sandwich the two halves together and dust the top with sifted icing sugar.

Orange and lemon syrup cake

Glistening with a tangy citrus-flavoured syrup, this cake is made using the basic Victoria sponge sandwich recipe above but in a single layer. Once cooked the cake is brushed with the syrup which it absorbs as it cools.

Victoria sponge mix (see   125 g (4–5 oz) caster sugar
  previous recipe)   juice of 1 orange and 1 lemon

Heat the oven to Gas 4/350°F/180°C.

Make the sponge mixture as in the previous recipe and spoon it into a greased 20 cm (8 in) cake tin. Bake for 35–40 minutes until it is cooked. (Test with a skewer: it should come out clean; if not, continue baking for a little longer.) Meanwhile, make the syrup by putting the sugar and strained fruit juice into a small saucepan. Heat them gently until all the sugar has melted and mingled with the juices.

Take the cake from the oven and cool for a few minutes in the tin before turning out and transferring it to a shallow bowl or dish. Spoon the syrup over the cake, spreading it evenly with the back of the spoon so that as much of the syrup as possible covers the top of the cake. Leave the cake to cool and absorb the syrup. When it is cold transfer to a plate.

Madeira cake

A plain and simple cake despite its rather grand name, which it was given because in the nineteenth century it was eaten with a glass of madeira. If you like the flavour of caraway seeds, you can add a few and make a seed cake, which was extremely popular in Victorian times, although the unexpected taste of the sharp pungent seeds does not impress everyone – especially children! Orange flower water is sold in chemists and some supermarkets.

150 g (6 oz) butter   250 g (9 oz) self-raising flour
150 g (6 oz) caster or vanilla   grated peel of 1 lemon or 1
  sugar (see Etceteras)   teaspoon orange flower water
4 eggs

Lightly grease and line an 18 cm (7 in) cake tin with waxed paper. Heat the oven to Gas 4/350°F/180°C.

Cream the butter and sugar together until fluffy. Beat in the eggs one by one. Sieve the flour and fold it into the mixture, together with the grated peel of the lemon or the orange flower water. Turn the mixture into the tin, make a slight hollow in the centre and bake for $1\frac{1}{4}$ hours. Test with a skewer, which should come out clean. If not, continue the baking for a little longer. Take the cake from the oven and leave in the tin for 10 minutes or so until it begins to shrink from the sides. Turn on to a wire tray to cool.

Lemon curd

Lemon curd has its roots in the cheesecakes made in the seventeenth century, and turns toast or plain bread and butter into a treat. It is lovely, too, as a filling for cakes and tarts. It doesn't have a long shelf life but will keep in the fridge for a month. Make it if you can with unwaxed lemons that are sometimes on sale. Orange curd can be made in just the same way but if using sweet oranges, only use 2, plus the sharp flavour of a lemon.

juice and finely grated peel of 3 lemons
150 g (6 oz) caster sugar

100 g (4 oz) butter
3 eggs, beaten

Put the peel and lemon juice into a heatproof bowl with the sugar and butter. Stand it in a pan of simmering water. Stir until the butter has melted and the sugar dissolved. Remove from the heat and strain the beaten eggs into it. Return the bowl to the pan of simmering water and stir until the curd thickens and coats the back of the spoon. Do not let it boil or it will separate and curdle. Put into clean warm jars and seal.

Lemonade

Old-fashioned English lemonade first appeared in the seventeenth century and makes a cool, refreshing drink for summer, far superior to commercial lemon squash. Citric and tartaric acids can be bought from chemists.

4 lemons	2 teaspoons citric acid
l litre ($1\frac{3}{4}$ pints) water	2 teaspoons tartaric acid
700 g ($1\frac{1}{2}$ lb) granulated sugar	

Peel the lemons using a swivel-bladed peeler, taking care not to remove any of the pith. Put the peel into a saucepan with the water, bring to the boil and simmer for 2 minutes. Squeeze the juice from the lemons into a large basin, add the sugar, citric and tartaric acids. Strain the water containing the lemon peel over the contents of the bowl and stir until all the sugar has dissolved. Strain and funnel into a clean bottle. Cap and store.

It will keep for several weeks in a cool place. Dilute to taste with water.

Cabbages to Brussels sprouts

Cabbage or greens with nutmeg

Cabbage with juniper

Red cabbage with apples

Pork with red cabbage

Cauliflower cheese

Calabrese and broccoli

Brussels sprouts with butter

Sprouts with chestnuts

The poor cabbage has a rotten reputation. Over-boiled until it collapsed with exhaustion into a sodden heap, it became synonymous with the worst of English cooking. The only rule to follow when cooking this vegetable is to give it the minimum time in boiling, salted water or, better still, steam it. As soon as the leaves turn limp but haven't lost their bite, it is done.

Wild cabbage flourished in England in Celtic times but it was the Romans who introduced the first cultivated cabbages. There are several different kinds. The best is Savoy, with its crinkly deep green outer and golden yellow inner leaves; it has a sweet delicious flavour. When buying cabbages or greens avoid any that look limp and dull.

Cabbage or greens with nutmeg

This most simple of recipes can be used not just for cabbage but also for all kinds of leafy vegetables such as spring and winter greens, curly kale and Brussels and turnip tops.

1 Savoy or other kind of cabbage   freshly grated nutmeg
salt   freshly milled black pepper
25–50 g (1–2 oz) butter

Discard any tough outer leaves. Divide the cabbage into four and cut out the woody stalk. Wash well and slice. Either boil it in salted water for 5–8 minutes or steam it with added salt for 8–12 minutes. Drain well. Melt the butter in the saucepan and add the cabbage. Turn it over and over to coat it evenly. Season with the nutmeg, a little salt and freshly milled black pepper. Eat at once.

Cabbage with juniper

In this recipe from East Anglia, Savoy cabbage is cooked in cider and butter with a flavouring of onion, garlic and juniper berries.

25 g (1 oz) butter
1 small onion, chopped
1 clove garlic, chopped
6 juniper berries, crushed
450 g (1 lb) Savoy cabbage,
　shredded

2–3 tablespoons strong dry cider
　or water
salt
freshly milled black pepper

Melt the butter in a large saucepan and fry the onion, garlic and juniper berries for about 5 minutes until the onions are golden, taking care the garlic does not burn and become bitter. Add the cabbage and the cider or water and mix well. Put over a low heat, covered, for about 10 minutes until the cabbage is tender but still a little crisp. Season with salt and pepper and serve.

Red cabbage with apples

Red cabbage, which is satisfyingly tasty and crunchy eaten raw in salads, was once invariably pickled in vinegar. It breaks all the rules for cooking cabbage, because it needs a long, slow process. It goes beautifully with the flavour of apples, onions and spices and with dishes of game, pork or ham. Recipes always include a tablespoon or two of vinegar which preserves its colour, otherwise it would turn quite blue.

25 g (1 oz) butter
4 rashers streaky bacon, chopped
1 onion, chopped
1 carrot, chopped
450 g (l lb) tart eating apples,
　peeled, cored and sliced
1 red cabbage, finely sliced
1 clove garlic, crushed

freshly grated nutmeg
1 bay leaf
2 cloves
2 tablespoons red wine
2 tablespoons wine or cider
　vinegar
salt
freshly milled black pepper

Heat the oven to Gas 2/300°F/150°C.

　Melt the butter in a large flameproof casserole and add the chopped bacon, onion and carrot. Let them soften for a few minutes. Stir in the sliced apples, cabbage and garlic. Add the nutmeg, bay leaf and cloves and stir in the red wine and vinegar. Season with salt and pepper. Cover and put into the oven for 3 hours.

Pork with red cabbage

This East Anglian recipe is robust country cooking at its best. Boned shoulder of pork is cooked in cider on a bed of red cabbage, apples, sugar and spices. It is quick to prepare but needs long, slow cooking so that the meat is tender and succulent. Ask the butcher to remove the rind.

3 tablespoons red wine vinegar
450 g (1 lb) red cabbage, shredded
900 g (2 lb) boneless pork shoulder
2 tart eating apples, peeled, cored and quartered
1 bay leaf

2 cloves
½ teaspoon nutmeg
1 tablespoon soft brown sugar
salt
freshly milled black pepper
4 tablespoons strong dry cider or water

Heat the oven to Gas 4/350°F/180°C.

Half fill a saucepan with water, add 1 tablespoon of the vinegar and bring to the boil. Add the shredded cabbage, bring back to the boil and drain immediately.

Cut away the thick outer rind from the pork if not already done, and resecure with string. Use an earthenware casserole in which the pork and cabbage will sit comfortably and put in the cabbage and quartered apples. Add the remaining two tablespoons of vinegar, the bay leaf, cloves, nutmeg and sugar and season with salt and pepper. Lay the pork on top and sprinkle over the cider or water. To ensure a good seal, cover the pot with foil before putting on the lid. Transfer to the oven for 30 minutes. Lower the heat to Gas 3/325°F/160°C and continue the cooking for 2 hours. Serve the pork on a warm dish surrounded by the cabbage and apples.

Cauliflower cheese

Cauliflower, that most superior member of the cabbage family, is a relative newcomer, not reaching us from mainland Europe via Asia until the late sixteenth century.

Only buy firm, creamy specimens and avoid those with brown blemishes and ones the greengrocer has trimmed of their outer green leaves in an effort to disguise the fact that they are past their prime.

Although you can cook cauliflower whole, I prefer to divide it into florets. It speeds up the cooking time and makes sure it is cooked evenly. Discard any woody stalk, but the tender parts can be sliced and added to the pot.

Cauliflower can be served quite simply with melted butter and a sprinkling of cheese or turned into this traditional dish which can be eaten as a light supper or lunch dish or as an accompanying vegetable.

1 cauliflower
salt
300 ml (½ pint) milk
65 g (2½ oz) butter
40 g (1½ oz) flour
150 ml (¼ pint) reserved cooking liquid

½ teaspoon ready-made mustard
100 g (4 oz) Cheshire or Cheddar or other good melting cheese, grated
freshly milled white or black pepper

Divide the cauliflower into florets and discard the outer coarse leaves. Slice the tender ones and the tender parts of the stalks and put them with the florets into boiling, salted water or into a steamer. Cook until the vegetable is soft but still firm: 5–10 minutes for boiling, 10–15 for steaming. Drain well but save 150 ml (¼ pint) of the cooking liquid.

While the cauliflower is cooking make a cheese sauce by putting the milk with 40 g (1½ oz) of the butter and all the flour into a saucepan. Put over a medium heat and bring to the boil, whisking all the time. As it thickens, lower the heat. Continue to cook for 2 minutes before removing from the heat. After draining the cauliflower, return the sauce to the heat and stir in the reserved cooking liquid, followed by the mustard and all but 2 tablespoons of the grated cheese. Stir until the cheese melts but do not let the sauce boil. Season with salt and pepper. Put the drained cauliflower into a deep ovenproof dish. Pour over the sauce and sprinkle the surface with the remaining 2 tablespoons of cheese and dot with the remaining butter.

If to be eaten immediately, simply brown the surface by putting under a hot grill. Otherwise, heat the oven to Gas 5/375°F/190°C and put the cauliflower in it for 20–25 minutes until it is bubbling and the top is golden brown.

Calabrese and broccoli

Calabrese is a green, large-headed variety of broccoli and, unlike the purple and white-headed varieties, is available all year round. The other two have a short season and are more expensive but make an interesting change from their more common cousin.

Developed by the Italians, broccoli came to England in the seventeenth century and was eaten with as much appreciation as asparagus. In fact it makes a delicious first course served with melted butter or the cream and lemon sauce on page 103. Cook it like cauliflower cheese or simply boil or steam it like cauliflower and serve it as an accompanying vegetable with a knob of butter or grated cheese.

Brussels sprouts with butter

Eliza Acton describes these as 'delicate little sprouts, or miniature cabbages'. Developed in Belgium, they didn't catch on in England until the mid-eighteenth century. Now we can't live without them. Buy them when fresh and young, which means not too big – large, old sprouts taste rank and bitter. Prepare them by cutting off their stalks and dropping them into salted water for a few minutes to evacuate any insects.

450 g (1 lb) sprouts	freshly grated nutmeg
salt	salt
50 g (2 oz) butter	freshly milled black pepper

Put the cleaned sprouts into a saucepan with very little water and some salt. Bring to the boil and simmer for 5–10 minutes until tender but still with bite. Drain well. Melt the butter in the saucepan, return the sprouts and shake them over a low heat until they are well coated and sizzling, but not browned. Season with nutmeg, salt and pepper and serve.

Sprouts with chestnuts

Delicious with the Christmas bird, pork or game, Brussels sprouts and chestnuts has become a classic combination. Devon takes credit for the original idea.

To peel chestnuts, score each one on its rounded side. Boil for 8–10 minutes in salted water. Use a slotted spoon to remove each chestnut one by one, hold it in a cloth and use a knife to help slip off the outer husk, rub away the inner skin with the cloth.

If this seems a tedious chore, forgo it by buying chestnuts ready-prepared, either in cans or vacuum packed, but make sure you go for the unsweetened variety. Alternatively, you could use dried chestnuts, which need to be soaked for 12 hours or overnight and will need a slightly longer cooking time.

50 g (2 oz) butter	450 g (1 lb) Brussels sprouts
150 g (6 oz) peeled	freshly grated nutmeg
chestnuts	salt
150 ml ($\frac{1}{4}$ pint) chicken stock	freshly milled black pepper

Melt the butter, add the chestnuts and turn them over and over until well coated. Pour in the stock, cover and simmer until tender. (Fresh, canned and dried will take 20–30 minutes; if using vacuum-packed, add the chestnuts as soon as the stock boils.) Prepare the sprouts by trimming the stems and removing any limp leaves. There is no need to cut a cross on the bottom unless they are very large. Add to the chestnuts and season with nutmeg, salt and pepper and simmer for 5–10 minutes until they too are tender but still firm.

Roots

Buttered parsnips

Parsnip soup

Parsnip chips

Mashed parsnips

Roast parsnips

Parsnip cakes

Palestine (Jerusalem artichoke) soup

Turnip soup

Glazed turnips

Buttered turnips

Roast turnips or swedes

Carrot soup

Buttered carrots

Carrots braised with celery

Leg of lamb with caper sauce

Salt beef with dumplings

Pilgrim Fathers' candied sweet potatoes

Baked sweet potatoes

Jacket potatoes

Mash

Mashed potatoes and celeriac

Stump (mashed roots)

Fish cakes

Potato cakes

Roast potatoes

Scalloped potatoes

Chips

Game chips

Matchstick potato cake

Hot pot

Cornish pasties

Once known as parsnep, 'nep' meaning root, the parsnip used to be as widely eaten as potatoes are today. It was the traditional accompaniment to roast beef, but gradually went out of favour when that immigrant from the New World usurped its place. The parsnip was probably brought here by the Romans, which is curious because in Italy today, it is despised as a vegetable and used to fatten the pigs. It is a winter vegetable, the flavour of which is said to be improved after the first hard frost.

Buy firm, creamy roots and avoid any with patches of brown and very big, old parsnips, which are woody. Young parsnips are delicious cooked in their skins but older ones can be peeled before cooking, using a swivel-bladed peeler.

Buttered parsnips

Plainly boiled parsnips cry out for butter and the expression 'fair words butter no parsnips' goes back at least to the seventeenth century.

700 g (1½ lb) parsnips
salt
25 g (1 oz) butter
freshly milled black pepper

1–2 tablespoons chopped parsley
or mixture of parsley, chives
and tarragon

Peel the parsnips and cut into even-sized pieces. Put them in a saucepan and just cover with salted water. Bring to the boil and simmer for about 15 minutes until tender. Drain well and wipe out the pan with kitchen paper. Melt the butter in it, return the parsnips and toss them over a medium heat until glazed all over. Add a generous amount of pepper and sprinkle with the chopped parsley or mixture of herbs.

Parsnip soup

Root vegetables are at their best after the first frosts and parsnips are no exception. In this East Anglian soup their sweet flavour is augmented with that of apples and sage flavoured with a hint of clove. Serve the soup with bread sippets fried until golden brown in butter.

25 g (1 oz) butter
450 g (1 lb) parsnips, peeled and sliced
2 crisp eating apples, unpeeled, cored and sliced
1 litre (1¾ pints) water or stock
salt

freshly milled black pepper
3–4 sage leaves
1 clove
2–3 tablespoons double cream (optional)
2–3 tablespoons chopped parsley

Melt the butter in a heavy-based pan. Add the parsnips and apple and let them sweat, covered, for 10 minutes. Add the water or stock, salt, pepper, sage leaves and the whole clove. Simmer for 25–30 minutes. Purée and stir in the cream, if using. Sprinkle with the parsley and serve.

Parsnip chips

Eliza Acton has a recipe which she calls 'Fried parsneps'. They are made just like potato chips but the parsnips are first boiled in a little salted water for 5–7 minutes until they are half cooked. They are then taken from the pan and drained well before being seasoned with salt and pepper. They can then be fried in deep fat or, perhaps better still, in a frying pan in plenty of butter.

Mashed parsnips

Mashed with plenty of butter and pepper, a little milk or cream and a sprinkling of parsley, parsnips were the proper vegetable to go with Friday's salt cod. This fact perhaps gives no idea of how very pleasant they are.

700 g (1½ lb) parsnips
salt
25 g (1 oz) butter

2–3 tablespoons milk or single
   cream
freshly milled black pepper
1–2 tablespoons chopped parsley

Boil the parsnips in salted water for about 15 minutes until tender.
Drain them well and mash with the butter and milk or cream. Beat until
smooth, season with salt and pepper and sprinkle with the parsley.

Roast parsnips

This is most people's favourite way with parsnips and they go
beautifully with roast beef or chicken, emerging from the oven golden
brown and oozing with sweet succulence. If you are roasting potatoes
at the same time, start the potatoes off first and add the parsnips 15
minutes later.

Peel the parsnips and cut them into even-sized wedges. Put them into
a pan of boiling water, cover and simmer for 5 minutes. Drain well.
Either cook them in the same pan as your joint or put a thin layer of oil
into a roasting tin and put it into an oven heated to around Gas 5–6/
375°–400°F/190°–200°C. Let the oil heat for about 5 minutes before
tipping in the parsnips. Turn them over and over to coat them in the
oil, then roast for 45 minutes, basting once or twice. Put them into a
warm vegetable dish and season with salt and pepper.

Parsnip cakes

Soft and sweet in a crisp, golden crust, these little cakes can be eaten in
place of potatoes, or of course you can use the same recipe using
potatoes instead.

450 g (1 lb) parsnips
salt
freshly milled black pepper
¼ teaspoon mace
25 g (1 oz) flour

50 g (2 oz) melted butter
1 egg, beaten
breadcrumbs
oil for frying

Cook the parsnips in boiling, salted water for about 15 minutes until
tender. Drain them well and mash them. Season with salt, pepper and
mace. Mix in the flour and melted butter. With damp hands, to prevent

the mixture sticking, shape into balls about the size of an egg and flatten them into cakes. Dip the cakes in the beaten egg and then the breadcrumbs. Set aside for 30 minutes to firm up.

Heat sufficient oil in a frying pan to cover the base and fry the cakes, turning them over once, until both sides are crisp and golden brown.

JERUSALEM ARTICHOKES

This knobbly root has nothing to do with Jerusalem and is not related to the globe artichoke. These misnomers stem from the old English habit of turning anything that sounds unfamiliar into something with which we feel more comfortable.

A seventeenth-century emigrant from the New World, the Jerusalem artichoke was first exported to England via Italy where, because its flavour resembled that of globe artichokes and because its flowers turned with the sun, it was called *girasole articiocco*, the sunflower artichoke. It is not hard to see how our name is a corruption of this, or to see why it seemed natural to call a soup made from it, Palestine.

Palestine soup

450 g (1 lb) Jerusalem artichokes
salt
50 g (2 oz) butter
1 tablespoon oil
4 rashers streaky bacon, chopped
1 onion, chopped
1 turnip, sliced
1 litre (1¾ pints) chicken stock
1 bay leaf
freshly milled black pepper
2–3 tablespoons double cream
2–3 tablespoons chopped parsley
and snipped chives

Wash the artichokes and put them into a pan half filled with boiling, salted water. Boil them for 5–10 minutes, drain and cool under running cold water before rubbing off the skins. Slice the artichokes. Wipe out the pan and melt half the butter with the oil. Add the chopped bacon, onion and sliced turnip, cover and set over a medium heat to sweat for 10 minutes. Add the sliced artichokes, stock and bay leaf. Season with salt and pepper. Simmer for 30–40 minutes and purée either in a food processor or using a mouli-légumes. Return the soup to the pan. Stir in the remaining butter and the double cream. Check the seasoning and serve sprinkled with the chopped herbs.

TURNIPS AND SWEDES

Certainly eaten since our Anglo-Saxon days, turnips have often been relegated to the status of cattle food, but although old turnips can be woody and dull, young turnips have a flavour all their own, sweet with a touch of bitterness. In the south of England, the name turnip means the white root of *Brassica rapa*, or rape, the green top of which make a pleasant vegetable. However, in the north and in Scotland, turnip is just as likely to mean swede, *Brassica napobrassica* (known as *rutabaga* in America). The Scottish haggis is invariably served with a dish of neeps – mashed, buttered swedes. The flavour of the two roots is completely different.

Turnip soup

Make this soup when you have some good stock made with the remains of a rabbit or other game. Serve it with fried sippets of bread.

25 g (1 oz) butter
1 tablespoon oil
1 onion, chopped
2 turnips, chopped
1 medium potato, chopped

1 litre (1¾ pints) stock
salt
freshly milled black pepper
2 tablespoons chopped parsley

Melt the butter with the oil in a saucepan and add the chopped onion, turnips and potato. Cover and let them sweat gently for 10 minutes. Pour in the stock, season with salt and pepper, put on the lid and simmer for 30 minutes. Purée the soup and serve it sprinkled with parsley.

Glazed turnips

In this recipe young, white turnips are simmered in water with butter and sugar until almost all the liquid has evaporated and they are sweetly glazed. They make a tasty accompaniment to game or poultry.

450 g (1 lb) white turnips
50 g (2 oz) butter
1 tablespoon caster sugar

salt
freshly milled black pepper
1–2 tablespoons chopped parsley

Cut away any green from the turnips and peel them with a swivel-bladed peeler. Quarter them and put them into a saucepan with the butter and sugar. Barely cover with boiling water and simmer, uncovered, for 25–30 minutes until the turnips are tender and most of the liquid has evaporated. Turn the pieces over from time to time.

At the end of the cooking time, raise the heat to reduce the liquid to 1–2 tablespoons, shaking the pan to prevent the turnips sticking. Season with salt and pepper, sprinkle with parsley and serve.

Buttered turnips

A pleasant accompaniment to chicken.

450 g (1 lb) white turnips, peeled and sliced
50 g (2 oz) butter
salt
freshly milled black pepper
1–2 tablespoons chopped fresh herbs like parsley, chives or tarragon

Put the turnips into a pan and blanch them in salted water for 5 minutes. Drain well. Melt the butter in the pan and fry the slices gently until tender and golden. Serve seasoned with salt and pepper and sprinkled with the herbs.

Roast turnips or swedes

Peel and cut into thick slices and blanch in boiling, salted water for 5 minutes. Drain well. Put a layer of oil into a roasting tin and heat for a few minutes in the oven at Gas 6/400°F/200°C. Add the drained slices to the pan and roast for 40–50 minutes.

CARROTS

Carrots, which appear to us so homely, have quite an exotic past. Although they grow wild in northern Europe, the kind we eat today have been developed from a purple root which grew in Afghanistan around the seventh century. Brought by the Moors to Spain, they spread across Europe and were crossed with other strains until, in Holland, the first bright orange carrots appeared. In Persia they were made into a kind of jam and called it an aphrodisiac, so perhaps that is why they retain their lingering reputation of being good for you!

Like potatoes, most of their goodness lies close to the skin, so ideally they should only be scraped. However, because of the use of insecticides, I prefer to peel them with a swivel-bladed peeler, unless I am able to buy ones which have been organically grown. They add a sweet flavour to all sorts of soups, stews and other dishes and are also delicious grated raw and eaten as a salad with a squeeze of lemon juice, salt, pepper, oil and strewn with chopped herbs such as chives, parsley, fennel or dill.

Carrot soup

This ideal soup for a grey winter's day is subtly flavoured with coriander and marjoram. Coriander is thought to have come to England during the Bronze Age but it was the Romans, with their love of spices and herbs, who introduced both this and marjoram into our cooking habits. Both remained popular until the mid-nineteenth century.

If you can, make this soup with a well-flavoured stock; failing this, use water and add a tablespoon of tomato purée. You can, if you wish, stir in a dollop of double cream just before serving.

50 g (2 oz) butter or 2 tablespoons oil	freshly milled black pepper
2 onions, chopped	1–2 sprigs of marjoram or $\frac{1}{2}$ teaspoon dried
450 g (1 lb) carrots	1 teaspoon coriander seeds, crushed
1 litre (1$\frac{3}{4}$ pints) stock or water	1–2 tablespoon chopped parsley
salt	

Heat the butter or oil in a large pan. Add the onion and carrots, cover and allow to sweat for 10 minutes over a low heat. Pour in the stock or water, season with salt and pepper and add the marjoram and coriander. Simmer for 25–30 minutes until the carrots are tender. Purée the soup and serve sprinkled with the parsley.

Buttered carrots

This recipe is based on Eliza Acton's 'Carrots in their own juice'. The thickly sliced roots are simmered in salted water until, as she puts it, they are tolerably tender, then the water is rapidly boiled until there are just one or two spoonfuls left. She stirs in a mixture of butter and flour before seasoning the carrots with plenty of freshly milled pepper. I don't really think the flour is necessary but I do think it is worth following her advice and adding a sprinkling of chopped parsley, and ringing the changes by sometimes adding a tablespoon or two of thick cream or good gravy. Allow 450 g (1 lb) carrots and 50 g (2 oz) butter to serve four people.

Carrots braised with celery

In this West Country dish flavoured with herbs, the sweetness of carrots and cider contrasts nicely with the slight bitterness of celery.

450 g (1 lb) carrots	½ teaspoon dried thyme
1 head celery	salt
300 ml (½ pint) strong dry cider	freshly milled black pepper
25 g (1 oz) butter	1–2 tablespoons chopped parsley

Heat the oven to Gas 4/350°F/180°C. Cut the carrots and celery into even-sized pieces. Put them into an earthenware casserole and pour over the cider. Add the butter, thyme and a seasoning of salt and pepper. Cook in the oven for about 1½ hours until tender. Serve sprinkled with the parsley.

Leg of lamb with caper sauce

'Mutton and caper' sauce is one of the classics of the English kitchen. Mutton, which has a much stronger flavour than lamb, was once cheap and plentiful, but unfortunately it is now hardly ever available and, if you do order it from your butcher, likely to be expensive. So we must make do with lamb, which may make purists shudder but will produce a wonderfully satisfying dish on a winter's day. Serve it with parsleyed potatoes and a green vegetable like broccoli or mange-tout.

1 leg lamb	bay leaf, sprigs of thyme and
2 onions	parsley, tied in a bunch
2 carrots, quartered	1 teaspoon salt
2 turnips, quartered	1 teaspoon black peppercorns
2 parsnips, quartered	1–2 tablespoons chopped parsley

Caper sauce

25 g (1 oz) butter
25 g (1 oz) flour
salt
freshly milled black pepper

1 tablespoon capers
1 tablespoon chopped parsley
juice of $\frac{1}{2}$ lemon
1–2 tablespoons single cream

Put the lamb with the vegetables and herbs into a saucepan in which they sit comfortably with room to spare. Just cover with cold water and season with the salt and pepper. Bring to the boil and with a slotted spoon skim away all the scum that forms. Simmer gently for 2– 2$\frac{1}{2}$ hours. When the meat is done put it on to a warm serving dish, surrounded by the vegetables and put in a warm place while you make the caper sauce.

To make the sauce, melt the butter in a small saucepan and add the flour. Stir over a low heat for 2 minutes. Take 300 ml ($\frac{1}{2}$ pint) cooking liquid from the lamb and gradually stir it into the flour and butter. When the sauce bubbles and thickens, season with salt and pepper, stir in the capers, lemon juice and single cream.

Bring the lamb to the table sprinkled with parsley and with the end of the bone covered with a paper frill (see below). Serve the caper sauce separately.

To make a paper frill: fold a piece of white A5 paper in half lengthwise. Cut thin strips 5 mm (3/8 in) wide all along the folded edge of the paper, cutting to within about 2.5 cm (1 in) of the base. Roll up, secure with a safety pin and ruffle the frilly edge.

Salt beef with dumplings

Salt beef with dumplings used to be a favourite Sunday lunch but, because there is now no need to salt meat to preserve it, you may find you will have to order your joint in order to enjoy its unique taste. Before the advent of the potato, dumplings were used all over England to add bulk to the broth. Tradition has it that they were invented in Norfolk but most regions have their own recipe.

The meat is cooked with the vegetables with which it is served, so they take on a special flavour from the saltiness of the joint. Potatoes are not normally included because they tend to disintegrate and cloud the broth, so it is better to serve them separately, if at all. The broth in which the meat and vegetables have been cooked can be used as the basis for a soup.

$1\frac{1}{2}$ kg (3 lb) salted brisket or
   silverside of beef
2 onions, each stuck with 2 or 3
   cloves
sprigs of thyme, sage and parsley,
   tied in a bunch

$\frac{1}{2}$ teaspoon black peppercorns
2 carrots, quartered
2 turnips, quartered
2 leeks, quartered

Dumplings

50 g (2 oz) plain flour
50 g (2 oz) beef or vegetarian
   suet
50 g (2 oz) breadcrumbs

$\frac{1}{2}$ teaspoon baking powder
1 tablespoon chopped parsley
salt
freshly milled black pepper

Put the meat into a large saucepan, cover with water and bring to the boil. Boil for 10 minutes, taste the water. If it seems very salty, discard it and cover the meat with fresh water and bring to the boil. Otherwise, continue with the cooking. With a slotted spoon skim off any scum that may have formed. Add the onions, bunch of herbs and the peppercorns. Bring back to the boil, cover and simmer gently, allowing 30 minutes cooking time to every 450 g (1 lb) of meat.

Three-quarter of an hour before the end of the cooking time, add the carrots, turnips and leeks, and prepare the dumplings.

Make the dumplings by mixing the flour, suet, breadcrumbs, baking powder, parsley, salt and pepper together. Add sufficient cold water, 3–4 tablespoons, to form a stiff, sticky dough. Put the dough on to a floured board and, with floured hands, break off small pieces and shape them into balls about the size of a walnut.

At the end of the cooking time, transfer the meat and vegetables to a warm platter and keep warm while the dumplings are cooked. Add the dumplings to the pan and let them poach gently for 10–15 minutes until they swell and rise to the top.

Serve some of the cooking liquid separately in a sauce boat.

SWEET POTATOES

There is no doubt that sweet potatoes, sometimes called Spanish potatoes, reached us via the New World well in advance of our ordinary, unrelated potatoes. They were adopted with enthusiasm and served in many of the ways that we serve potatoes today. Nowadays this vegetable is once again quite widely available and its sweet orange flesh makes a delicious change.

Pilgrim Fathers' candied sweet potatoes

Crystallized slices, surely the forerunners of this dish, were sold in Elizabethan times as a popular aphrodisiac. Soft and sweet, these candied sweet potatoes are pleasant eaten with roast poultry, rather as we eat apple sauce with pork, goose and duck.

450 g (l lb) sweet potato(es)	or 2 tablespoons honey
salt	juice of $\frac{1}{2}$ lemon
4 tablespoons soft brown sugar	25 g (1 oz) butter

Simmer the potatoes for 30–40 minutes in their skins until tender. Drain well and when they are cool enough to handle, remove the skins – they come away easily.

Heat the oven to Gas 6/400°F/200°C.

Cut the potatoes into slices. Lay them in a single layer in a buttered ovenproof dish. Season with salt and sprinkle with the sugar or dribble the honey over them. Squeeze over the juice of the lemon. Dot with the butter and bake for 30–35 minutes, basting once or twice.

Baked sweet potatoes

As a change from ordinary jacket potatoes, try sweet potatoes instead. Allow 1 per person, or half a one if they are very large. Wash them and dry them with kitchen paper, then wipe them all over with olive oil and wrap in foil. Bake in an oven heated to Gas 6/400°F/200°C until tender. Time will depend on their size, but allow 1–1½ hours. Serve them like baked jacket potatoes and hand round salt and pepper, butter and sour cream or yoghurt separately.

POTATOES

It seems likely that this treasure of the Incas reached England via the Spanish although we like to think that it was brought direct to us by Sir Francis Drake. At the time, in fact, we weren't very impressed and potatoes didn't really catch on until almost the end of the eighteenth century and then mainly in the north of England, but eventually they spread right across the country and became an indispensable part of our daily diet.

New potatoes are at their nicest dropped into boiling, salted water with a sprig of mint and then simmered until tender, drained and served with a knob of butter and plenty of chopped parsley, thyme, chives or other summer herbs. There is no need to peel them. Older potatoes when plainly boiled or steamed also benefit from a sprinkling of chopped herbs. It is important to simmer potatoes, rather than boil them fiercely as the latter method makes them break up on the outside before the middle is cooked.

Jacket potatoes

Everyone knows how to bake potatoes in their jackets and we all have our way of doing it. As for me, I cut a cross through the skin, rub oil over them and bake them at Gas 6/400°F/200°C for about 1 hour, depending on their size, with a skewer through their middles to conduct the heat.

Mash

Mashed potatoes are peculiarly our own. No other country can produce anything quite like them and I am convinced the secret is due to our use of that inexpensive kitchen implement, the potato masher. It removes the lumps without turning the mash into a gluey purée, which happens if you use an electric processor and thus destroy the robust character of the potatoes. However, I sometimes finish them off with a hand-held blender because you can control the exact moment to stop.

900 g (2 lb) potatoes, peeled and   50 g (2 oz) butter
   cut in even-sized pieces   4–5 tablespoons milk, warmed
salt   freshly milled black pepper

Just cover the potatoes with boiling water, add a pinch of salt and simmer until tender. Don't let them boil too fast which causes the outsides to crack and collapse before the centre is soft.

Drain the cooked potatoes, return them to the pan and leave for a minute or two for the remaining water to evaporate. Mash them well and add the butter and milk. Using a wooden fork, beat until smooth and season with salt and pepper.

Mashed potatoes and celeriac

Celeriac and potatoes mashed together have a sweet, nutty flavour that goes beautifully with sausages and pork or gamy dishes of rabbit or hare. Make it exactly like mashed potatoes, using half and half quantities of potatoes and celeriac cut in even-sized pieces. You will find celeriac easier to peel if you quarter it first. Celeriac tends to turn brown once peeled, so add a little lemon juice to the cooking water.

Stump

I was introduced to a version of stump years ago by a friend from Yorkshire, only she never called it by this name – she probably thought her London friends would laugh at her. Hers consisted of carrots and swedes mashed together, flavoured with butter and a generous seasoning of black pepper. This recipe includes potatoes.

There are other variations on this theme. At Hallowe'en in some country areas they used to serve 'mash of nine sorts', a warming combination of carrots, potatoes, parsnips, leeks, peas and cream seasoned with salt and pepper. A wedding ring was hidden inside and whoever found it would be the next to be married.

225 g (8 oz) potatoes, peeled and   salt
   quartered   50 g (2 oz) butter
225 g (8 oz) carrots, peeled and   2–3 tablespoons milk
   sliced   freshly milled black pepper
225 g (8 oz) swede, peeled and
   cut into cubes

Put all the vegetables into a saucepan and cover them with boiling water, add a little salt. Simmer them, covered, for about 30 minutes until soft. Drain well. Mash them and beat in the butter followed by the milk. Season generously with freshly milled black pepper and add salt to taste.

Fish cakes

This most nursery of dishes is a perfect way of using up leftover fish like salmon or sea trout. You can also use fish like cod, haddock or coley, and canned salmon or tuna are not to be despised. The cakes should be prepared at least an hour before you want to cook them as the mixture needs time to firm up.

225 g (8 oz) cooked fish, flaked
225 g (8 oz) mashed potato
salt
freshly milled black pepper
squeeze lemon juice
½ teaspoon dried marjoram

1 tablespoon chopped parsley
1 egg, beaten
2–3 tablespoons breadcrumbs or
    fine oatmeal
oil for frying

Discard the skin and bones from the fish. Mix the fish and potato together and stir in the salt, pepper, lemon juice, marjoram, parsley and half the beaten egg. Set aside for 1 hour.

With damp hands, divide the mixture into 4 even-sized balls and then flatten each to form a flat disc. Coat each in the remaining egg and then in the breadcrumbs or oatmeal.

Heat sufficient oil to cover the base of a frying pan and fry the cakes for 5–10 minutes until piping hot and golden brown on both sides.

Potato cakes

Made with mashed potato, cooked on a hot griddle or in a heavy-based frying pan and eaten oozing with butter, this is a children's favourite served for tea, especially after a long, protesting walk on a crisp, winter day.

225 g (8 oz) potatoes
salt
25 g (1 oz) butter
freshly milled black pepper

50 g (2 oz) flour
oil for cooking
butter for spreading

Simmer the potatoes in boiling, salted water until soft. Drain well and mash with the butter. Season with salt and pepper. Mix with enough flour to form a pliable dough. Roll the dough thinly on a lightly floured board and cut into triangles. Heat the griddle greased with a

little oil and fry the cakes, turning once, until they are golden and
blistered on both sides. Serve hot with plenty of butter.

Roast potatoes

The Sunday joint would not be the Sunday joint without roast
potatoes. Cook the potatoes in the same pan as the roast or, if you
like them with a crispy outer skin, in a separate one. At the same
time, for a change, try adding some pieces of chopped pumpkin to the
pan.

900 g (2 lb) potatoes
salt
oil, either olive or a light one like
    sunflower

Heat the oven to Gas 6/400°F/200°C. Peel the potatoes and cut into
even-sized pieces. Put them into a saucepan and just cover with water.
Add a little salt and bring to the boil. Simmer for 5 minutes and drain
well.

Pour sufficient oil into a roasting tin to cover the base generously.
Heat in the oven for 5 minutes, then add the potatoes and turn them
over and over to coat them evenly. Put into the oven and roast for
about 1 hour, basting once or twice during this time.

Scalloped potatoes

This creamy potato gratin is loved by adults and children alike. The
potatoes absorb the milk and buttery juices in which they are cooked
and become meltingly tender and extremely moreish. Don't soak the
potatoes in water before you cook them as they would lose the starch
which contributes to the success of the dish.

50 g (2 oz) butter   salt
700–900 g (1½–2 lb) potatoes,   freshly milled black pepper
    peeled and thinly sliced   300 ml (½ pint) milk

Heat the oven to Gas 5/375°F/190°C.

Generously butter a shallow oven dish and lay the potato slices in it,
seasoning each layer with salt and pepper. Pour over enough milk so
that it almost but not quite covers them, and dot with the remaining

butter cut in pieces. Bake for $1-1\frac{1}{2}$ hours until the top is golden brown and all the liquid has been absorbed.

Chips

Forever linked in our minds with fish, chips were actually a French invention and didn't catch on in England until the late nineteenth century. The Americans acknowledge their source by calling them French fries. It is even probable that the idea of frying fish in batter was brought to England around the same time by immigrant Italians. In Lancashire they took to them both and before long fish and chip shops sprang up all over the country, serving their wares in newspaper with plenty of malt vinegar and salt.

Cut peeled potatoes into strips – the thickness depends on you. Dry them well. Fry them in batches in hot, deep oil until half cooked, putting them in a warm oven as you go. When all the chips are half-fried, raise the heat and return them to the hot oil all together and fry until golden brown and crisp. Drain on absorbent kitchen paper and sprinkle with salt.

Game chips

Game chips, which as their name implies, are traditionally served with game, are very like what we call potato crisps but the Americans would call chips.

Slice the potatoes very thinly (a food processor comes in handy here) and soak them for an hour or two to remove the starch. Dry them thoroughly and fry them in batches in a frying basket, using deep, hot oil and shaking the pan to prevent them sticking. When ready they rise to the top; drain well on crumpled kitchen paper.

Matchstick potato cake

Delicious with chicken or simple dishes, this crisp and golden potato cake turns them into something of a treat. The trick to prevent this or similar cakes from sticking to the pans is not to add salt until the end of the cooking time.

25 g (1 oz) butter   salt
1 tablespoon oil   freshly milled black pepper
450 g (1 lb) potatoes

Melt the butter with the oil over a low heat. Peel the potatoes and cut
them into very fine matchsticks, adding them to the pan as you go.
(They must not be soaked as they would lose all their starch and this is
needed for the dish to work.) When all the potatoes are added, press
them well down in the pan. Cover it with a sheet of foil and a lid. Keep
the heat between low and medium and let the cake fry for 15 minutes.
After this time, turn the cake over – the underside should be brown
and crisp. If it breaks up, don't worry, simply press it well down once
more. Put on the foil and the lid and continue the cooking for a further
15 minutes or until the base is crisp and golden. Season with salt and
pepper and serve from the pan.

Hot pot

A close cousin to Irish stew, this Lancashire mill workers' meal in a pot
was originally cooked in a tall, lidless earthenware container, often in
the bread oven after the last batch of loaves had been baked. Chops,
originally mutton, now more usually lamb, are layered with lamb's
kidneys, sweet herbs, onions, mushrooms and potatoes and allowed to
stew gently until all the flavours mingle into a satisfying winter meal. It
takes minutes to prepare but several hours to cook.

25 g (1 oz) butter   2 bay leaves
900 g (2 lb) potatoes, sliced   sprigs of thyme, parsley and
8 neck of lamb chops, trimmed   marjoram, tied in a bunch
   of most of the fat   salt
4 lamb's kidneys, cut in half   freshly milled black pepper
450 g (1 lb) onions, sliced   300 ml (½ pint) stock or water
100 g (4 oz) mushrooms

Heat the oven to Gas 3/325°F/160°C.
   Butter a deep casserole and lay half the potatoes over the base.
Cover with layers of chops, kidneys, onions and mushrooms, tucking
in a bay leaf and herbs and seasoning each layer as you go. Top with
remaining potatoes, pour in the water or stock and dot with the
remaining butter cut in small pieces. Cover with a piece of buttered

paper and put into the oven for $2\frac{1}{2}$–3 hours. Remove the paper lid during the last 30 minutes to allow the top layer of potatoes to brown.

Cornish pasties

The true Cornish pasty was a complete meal, being the size of a dinner plate with a filling of meat and vegetables at one end and apples at the other. Each pasty was marked in the corner with the initials of the eater, not only so that they could recognize their preferred filling but also, if they had to put them down halfway through demolishing, they could claim ownership.

The savoury filling depended on the affluence or poverty of the family varying from potato, onions and bread to bacon and leeks, lamb or beef and turnips. Pasties can be made with shortcrust or even puff pastry but to be authentic they should be made from a pastry made with self-raising flour. Kept warm wrapped in a cloth or in layers of newspaper, they make the perfect picnic food, especially on a less than ideal summer day.

150 g (6 oz) margarine	100 g (4 oz) turnip or swede,
450 g (l lb) self-raising flour	finely diced
350 g (12 oz) braising steak	salt
1 onion, chopped	freshly milled black pepper
225 g (8 oz) potato, finely diced	2 tablespoons chopped parsley
	1 egg yolk, beaten

Make the pastry by rubbing the margarine into the flour until it resembles fine crumbs. Add sufficient water, 4–5 tablespoons, to make a smooth, firm paste. Flour your hands and roll the pastry into a ball. Set aside in a cool place.

Cut away fat from the meat and either chop it finely or put through a food processor, but don't mince it. Mix the meat with the chopped onion, finely diced potato and the turnip or swede. Season well with salt and pepper and add the parsley. Divide pastry into 4 and roll out on a floured board. Use a side plate as a guide to mark out circles and cut them out.

Heat the oven to Gas 6/400°F/200°C.

Divide the meat and vegetable mixture equally among the pastry circles. Brush all round the edge of each pastry round with beaten egg and bring the edges together up and over the filling. Fold and crimp the edges together. Cut a small slit just below the edge at the top. Put the pasties on a baking sheet and brush all over with the egg. Bake for 20 minutes, lower the heat to Gas 5/375°F/190°C and bake for a further 40 minutes. Check and if the pastry is getting too brown, cover with foil.

Cheese

SOME NOTES ON CHEESE

Cheese-making goes right back to the beginnings of animal husbandry. Ten thousand years ago Mesopotamian shepherds were certainly producing the same sort of simple goat and ewe curd cheeses as are made today and, a couple of millennia later, when the first wild cows were domesticated, their milk was made into cheese. Curd cheeses don't keep very long but over the centuries, methods were invented that allowed the cheese to mature over a period of time; the longer this maturing process the longer the cheese would keep. Not surprisingly many of the cheeses we know today were developed by ever-resourceful monks who had the problem of having to feed large numbers, and also the time to spend experimenting.

Once, every farmhouse in the land produced its own cheese and each one had its own character. Now traditional farmhouse cheeses are rare and only available in specialist shops. These cheeses can't compete in price with supermarkets, most of whose stocks come from the big producers. Much of the process is the same but instead of maturing the cheeses in cylindrical shapes in cloth which allows them to breathe, mass-produced cheeses are pressed in rectangular blocks before being wrapped in plastic film and left to mature, usually for a shorter time than their traditional brothers. The very word plastic speaks for itself. So if you are lucky enough to be able to seek out a supplier of real English cheeses, it's worth spending the extra money. Take the chance, too, to learn from the owner as much as you can about the different cheeses on offer, and before you buy always ask to taste a sliver because in the end it is your own preference that matters.

Despite all sorts of problems with regulations from Brussels which makes it harder and harder for the small producer, there are still many different varieties of cheese on the market, far too many to list in this book, but below are brief notes on some of the most familiar.

Blue Vinney – the name means blue veined, 'vinney' being a corruption of 'vinnid' or 'veiny' – is a Dorset cheese made from semi-skimmed cow's milk. Once produced all over the county, it now comes from just one source: Woodbridge Farm at Stock

Gayland, Sturminster Newton. Stories abound as to how the cheese was once made – the mould was said to have come from that on old boots kept next to the maturing cheeses, or on leather horse tackle dragged through the milk before the cheese-making began. Today's cheese, which takes several months to mature, is a crumblier version of the original.

Caerphilly was developed in Wales during the early part of the nineteenth century. It rapidly became so popular that demand outstripped supply. Over in Somerset, the cheese-makers producing Cheddar soon realized that supplying the Welsh with their own invention would be a profitable business, the great advantage being that Caerphilly matures in five days whereas Cheddar takes at least five months. Welsh production was stopped during the Second World War and since then has barely recovered, so most of today's Caerphilly now comes from Somerset. It is a pale, crumbly cheese, delicious on its own or toasted.

Cheddar seemed to be the only English cheese we could get not so very long ago, and then it wasn't always English. Thanks to mass production and the fact that the name wasn't copyright, Cheddar appeared from as far apart as Scotland to New Zealand. We called it mouse-trap and did our best to ignore it completely, especially as we could get all those exciting imports from France, Italy and elsewhere. This is sad, as anyone who has eaten a piece of traditionally matured farmhouse Cheddar will have discovered. First produced in Somerset in the area around the Cheddar Gorge, its earliest recorded mention is in the fifteenth century but it probably dates back to Henry II. Its production spread to include the neighbouring counties of Devon, Dorset and Wiltshire. Firm, smooth, with a nutty flavour, it is good eaten on its own and is excellent in cooking.

Cheshire is the grandfather of them all, being mentioned in the Domesday book. It is made not only in Cheshire but also by producers in Shropshire and Clwyd. There are two kinds. White Cheshire is a creamy yellow and Red Cheshire is dyed orange red with annatto, which is manufactured from the seeds of a tropical tree, *Bixa orellana*. Nowadays, there is also a blue-veined version produced commercially. Moist with a crumbly texture, it has a salty tang to its flavour and is a good cooking cheese.

Gloucester is at least as old as Cheddar. There are two kinds, double and single. Single Gloucester, which is now only produced by a few individual cheese-makers, is a skimmed milk cheese. It is matured much faster and is smaller than Double Gloucester which is a full-fat cheese. Once dyed orange by carrot juice or saffron, it is nowadays coloured with annatto. It features in cheese-rolling ceremonies at Cooper's Hill, Brockworth in May, traditionally on Whit Monday and at Randwick, just north of Stroud, in Gloucestershire. Here on Rogation Sunday, three cheeses decorated with flowers are taken into the church and afterwards they are rolled, without their decorations, anti-clockwise three times around the church. One is then cut up and distributed to the villagers and the other two are rolled down the hill the following Saturday at the Wap Fair. It is ideal for cooking as it melts well and with its strong, mellow flavour is also delicious on its own.

Lancashire, a close cousin to Cheshire, should be, in the words of Patrick Rance in his *The Great British Cheese Book*, 'a semi-soft, loose-textured, crumbly, buttery cheese' which melts perfectly and is ideal in cooking. Unfortunately commercially produced it has lost much of its character and good farm samples are hard to find.

Red Leicester is a beautiful, nutty cheese with a close, silky texture which was developed around Melton Mowbray well before the eighteenth century. It is deep orange and the traditional cheeses are made in huge cylinders. It can be eaten young but improves on maturing. It is excellent in cooking.

Stilton is the name of a village in Huntingdonshire, but the cheese with whose name it is associated comes from further north. The story goes that it was invented at Quenby Hall in Leicestershire where it was known as Lady Beaumont's cheese. A housekeeper at the Hall, Elisabeth Scarbrow, saw how it was made and later, when she married a local farmer, began to produce similar cheeses herself. When one of her daughters married the innkeeper of The Bell in Stilton, regular supplies were sent there and it wasn't long before travellers began to look forward to their 'Stilton' cheese. The name has been used ever since. Patrick Rance gives two descriptions by Defoe, the first calling it 'our English Parmesan' and the second describing 'the mites and maggots round it so thick, that they bring a spoon for you to eat the mites with . . .' Stilton is the only English cheese whose name is protected by copyright and can only be produced in a specific region, which embraces the Vale of Belvoir in

Leicestershire, parts of south Nottinghamshire and the Dove Valley in Derbyshire.

Stilton at its best has an unbroken outer crust and is creamy coloured with green-blue veins. It is better to buy a piece of Stilton from a large cheese than to buy one of the smaller ones because they mature more rapidly so have not had time to develop their flavour. There is also a cheese called White Stilton, which is not at all like the Blue but has a fresh, pleasant flavour.

Wensleydale has been a cheese-making region since the Norman Conquest. The first cheeses, which were made from ewe's milk, were developed by monks from Cambalou near Roquefort. Apparently the Norman troops stationed at Wensleydale were not impressed with the northern diet and William asked his uncle, the Abbot of Savigny, for help. On their arrival in England the abbot's monks set about producing blue-veined cheeses based on the Roquefort method but ripening them in cellars rather than in natural caves. Cheese-making continued in the region right up to the dissolution of the monasteries, and was carried on after this time but cow's rather than ewe's milk was used.

Commercial productions has not helped this cheese and blue-veined Wensleydale is hard to find but white farmhouse-produced Wensleydale is soft and flaky and delicious eaten on its own or with apple pie.

STORING CHEESE

Except in specialist cheese shops, most of our cheese is sold pre-cut and pre-packed. If you do buy it like this, remove it from its plastic wrapping and store it in foil or greaseproof paper in a cool place rather than the fridge. Don't keep it very long, as cheese begins to deteriorate once cut. Specialist cheese shops are more expensive than supermarkets but usually their cheese is far more interesting. It can be intimidating if you don't quite know what you like or want to buy, so ask for help and ask to taste.

Pan haggerty

Pan haggerty, onions and potatoes topped with cheese, makes a filling and tasty dish for supper. It comes from Northumberland and the name is local dialect for the vegetables with which it is made. It's a dish to be done after roasting a joint of beef because traditionally it is cooked in dripping, but if you prefer use oil or a mixture of butter and oil.

50 g (2 oz) beef dripping or 4 tablespoons oil or butter and oil
450 g (1 lb) potatoes, peeled and thinly sliced

225 g (8 oz) onions, peeled and thinly sliced
100 g (4 oz) grated Cheddar cheese
salt
freshly milled black pepper

Heat the dripping, oil or oil/butter in a heavy-based frying pan and lay the sliced potatoes over the base. Top with the sliced onions and sprinkle with the grated cheese. Season with salt and pepper. Cover with a piece of kitchen foil and put on a lid. Fry over a low heat for about 40 minutes until the vegetables are cooked. Heat the grill until very hot and put the pan under it until the top is golden brown.

Welsh or otherwise rabbit or rarebit

Originally known as Welsh rabbit, versions of this superior kind of cheese on toast, which has been around at least since the early eighteenth century, are found all over England. Is it rabbit or rarebit and where do the Welsh come in? It seems likely the original title was an ironic reference to the fact that there was no rabbit, the word 'welsh' being used in the sense of a failure to fulfil an obligation. Later the rabbit changed to rarebit, it probably sounded nicer, and this simple dish became a popular choice for a late-night snack.

In this recipe, the cheese is flavoured with brown ale, whereas the so-called English version uses red wine and in Yorkshire it is made with stout, flavoured with Worcester sauce and served with a thick slice of bacon and a poached egg. Just with a poached egg on top it is known as buck rabbit.

25 g (1 oz) butter
100 g (4 oz) grated cheese such as Caerphilly or Cheddar
2 tablespoons brown ale

1 teaspoon ready-made mustard
cayenne pepper
buttered toast

Heat the grill. Melt the butter in a small saucepan and stir in the cheese. Stand the pan over a saucepan of boiling water and stir until the cheese melts. It must not melt too fast or it will turn stringy and indigestible. As the cheese melts, stir in the ale, followed by the mustard and season with cayenne pepper. Pile on to slices of buttered toast and put under the grill to bubble and brown.

Double Gloucester cheese and ale

Double Gloucester cheese melts beautifully and, mixed with mustard and ale, combines to make this West Country farmers' snack, a sort of English rabbit or fondue, which was eaten with pickles and mulled ale. It used to be served at inns and posting houses as a savoury after the meat. In the absence of Double Gloucester you can use any good melting cheese such as Cheddar or Cheshire.

225 g (8 oz) Double Gloucester   150 ml ($\frac{1}{4}$ pint) ale
   cheese   4 slices of toast
1 teaspoon ready-made mustard

Heat the oven to Gas 5/375°F/190°C. Slice the cheese thinly and lay the slices in a single layer in a shallow ovenproof dish. Spread over the mustard and pour over the ale. Put into the oven for 5–10 minutes until the cheese has melted. Meanwhile make the toast, put on to plates and when the cheese is ready, spoon over the cheese and ale. The cheese sets to a creamy mass and the ale is absorbed by the toast.

Pastry ramakins

A perfect snack to serve with drinks are these puff pastry ramakins (sic) flavoured with cheese. Popular since the eighteenth century, they used to be served as a savoury at the end of a meal. They can be cut into strips and twisted to form cheese straws or cut into shapes with small pastry cutters and either eaten straight from the oven with pre-dinner drinks or made ahead of time and reheated.

225 g (8 oz) puff pastry   freshly milled black pepper
100 g (4 oz) Cheshire, Stilton or   cayenne pepper
   Cheddar, finely grated   1 egg yolk, beaten

Preheat the oven to Gas 7/425°F/220°C.

Roll the pastry thinly into an oblong. Sprinkle half the grated cheese down the centre of the pastry and season with black and cayenne pepper. Fold one side of the pastry to cover the cheese. Sprinkle this folded side with the rest of the cheese and season again. Fold remaining third over the top and roll lightly into a longer strip and to seal the edges. Brush lightly with the beaten egg yolk. Cut out small shapes using pastry cutters or cut into strips to make cheese straws. Put on to greased baking trays. Bake for 15–20 minutes. Eat at once or cool and store in an airtight tin. Reheat in a hot oven for 5–10 minutes.

Yorkshire cheesecake

Known as sweet pye, this was a country favourite during times of harvesting and sheep-shearing. It comes from a long line of recipes going back to the time of the Crusaders, in which curd cheese tarts were made flavoured with almonds, lemons and dried fruits with a smattering of rose or orange flower water, nutmeg, cinnamon and ginger or sometimes saffron.

225 g (8 oz) sweet or plain
   shortcrust pastry
50 g (2 oz) butter
50 g (2 oz) sugar
225 g (8 oz) curd cheese
2 egg yolks

100 g (4 oz) currants
juice and finely grated peel of 1
   lemon
1 tablespoon brandy (optional)
$\frac{1}{4}$ teaspoon each nutmeg,
   cinnamon and ginger

Roll out the pastry to line a 23 cm (9 in) flan tin with a removable base. Set aside to chill.

Cream the butter with the sugar until pale and fluffy. Beat in the cheese, egg yolks, currants, lemon peel and juice, together with the brandy if using. Heat the oven to Gas 6/400°F/200°C. Spoon the cheese mixture into the pastry case, smooth over the top and sprinkle over the spices. Bake for 30–35 minutes until puffed and golden. Cool, turn out of the tin and serve cold.

Potted cheese

Almost any kind of cheese can be potted and it is a perfect way of using up those ends of pieces which otherwise might never get eaten. You can use just one sort or a mixture of two or more.

100 g (4 oz) hard cheese, grated
25–50 g (1–2 oz) butter, softened
$\frac{1}{4}$ teaspoon mace
cayenne pepper
$\frac{1}{2}$ teaspoon ready-made mustard
1 tablespoon sherry
clarified or concentrated butter,
    melted (see Etceteras)

Mix the grated cheese with enough butter to form a thick paste. Season the mixture with the mace and cayenne pepper and beat in the mustard and sherry. When the mixture is well mixed turn it into a jar or ramekin dish and pour over a thin layer of clarified or concentrated butter. Store in the fridge but remove at least 1 hour beforehand to allow the cheese to soften slightly and the flavour to develop. Eat with buttered toast.

Etceteras: from sippets to clotted cream

Sippets

Stock

Clarified butter

Suet pastry

Shortcrust pastry

Sweet shortcrust pastry

Custard

Vanilla sugar

Dried peel

Lemon or orange sugar

Scones

Clotted cream

Sippets

The French had their *croûtons* and the English their sops and sippets, which might just be the crusts and ends of bread eaten with soup or gravy, or pieces cut into elegant little squares, hearts or diamonds and toasted or fried until crisp and used as a garnish. Sops and sippets went out of fashion and it took our love affair with French food to remind us of the habit. We have remembered the habit but forgotten the name and 'croûton' has become part of the English language. Anyway if you want to make sippets, make them like croûtons, frying small pieces of bread in hot oil or toasting them on a baking sheet at the top of a hot oven.

Stock

The stockpot, constantly added to, suspended over the fire containing a simmering concoction of leftover meat and bones flavoured with herbs and vegetables, was once a feature of every English kitchen. It was a way of preventing food from going off as well as a frugal means of feeding the family. Now we have fridges and stock cubes, the whole idea seems rather archaic. However, there's no doubt that soups enriched with home-made stock have a certain something which is lacking when a stock cube is used instead, and is certainly worth making when you have some leftover bones, either from poultry, game or a joint of ham, beef or lamb. When there is nothing available with which to make stock, don't forget you can always use the water left over from boiling or steaming vegetables and, when you are really pushed, use water with 1 tablespoon of tomato purée added.

Don't add any salt as it is impossible to gauge how much might be needed before the stock has cooked and reduced.

leftover bones	8 peppercorns
1 onion	$\frac{1}{2}$ teaspoon dried thyme
1 carrot	sprigs of parsley
1 bay leaf	water

If using a carcase from poultry or game, cut it up using kitchen shears. Put the bones into a large saucepan. Add the onion, carrot, bay leaf, peppercorns, dried thyme and sprigs of parsley. Cover generously with water. Bring to the boil. If a scum forms on the top, skim it off using a slotted spoon. Simmer, uncovered, for $1\frac{1}{2}$–2 hours. Strain immediately into a bowl and when cool refrigerate. Before using skim off the layer of fat which will have risen to the surface.

Clarified butter

Many supermarkets sell concentrated butter from which much of the water has been removed, which means that it can be fried at a higher temperature than ordinary butter before it burns. If you can't obtain it, it is not difficult to clarify your own.

Heat 100 g (4 oz) butter gently until it separates and a white foam appears on top. Strain the butter into a bowl using a fine nylon sieve or a piece of clean muslin. Use right away or store in the fridge.

Suet pastry

This soft pastry can be used for steamed puddings, as a pie crust or for dumplings.

100 g (4 oz) beef or vegetarian
  suet
200 g (8 oz) self-raising flour

2 level teaspoons baking powder
$\frac{1}{2}$ teaspoon salt
4 fl oz water

Mix all the ingredients together, make a well in the centre and add sufficient cold water, approximately 4 fl oz, to make a smooth, soft dough which leaves the sides of the bowl cleanly. Turn on to a floured board and knead gently with floured hands until smooth. Roll out to about 5 mm ($\frac{1}{4}$ in) thick.

Shortcrust pastry

200 g (8 oz) flour, sifted
$\frac{1}{4}$ teaspoon salt

100 g (4 oz) margarine or butter,
  cut in cubes
2–3 tablespoons water

Put the flour into a bowl with the salt. Add the fat and rub it into the flour using the tips of your fingers until the mixture resembles fine crumbs. Make a hollow in the centre and add a very little cold water gradually, mixing it with a knife as you go. Use just enough water to form a soft dough – you will probably only need 2–3 tablespoons. Flour your hands and lift the pastry on to a floured surface. Knead it lightly into a ball. Set aside for 30 minutes before using.

Sweet shortcrust pastry

Make as above, but add an extra 25 g (1 oz) butter and 25 g (1 oz) caster sugar to the rubbed-in mixture. Beat 2 egg yolks and stir into the mixture, adding just sufficient water to form a soft dough.

Custard

How one shudders at the memory of school dinner custards, bright yellow made from a packet with a gruesome skin on top. Real home-made custard is something else again and is one of the traditional accompaniments to many of our puddings, including Christmas pudding. If you are worried that, however careful you are, the custard will curdle, stir 1 teaspoonful of cornflour into the beaten egg yolks.

2 egg yolks
300 ml ($\frac{1}{2}$ pint) milk

1–2 tablespoons vanilla or caster sugar

Beat the egg yolks together. Heat the milk until it begins to simmer. Stir a little hot milk into the egg yolks. Strain this mixture on to the milk in the pan and stir constantly over a very low heat – ideally over a pan of simmering water – until the custard thickens. Do not let it boil or it will curdle. Remove from the heat and sweeten to taste.

Vanilla sugar

Invaluable for adding to cakes or sweet dishes, vanilla sugar is made by storing one or two vanilla pods in a jar of sugar. As you use the sugar, replenish it with a fresh supply. The vanilla pods can be used over and over again. Only when they lose their potency do you need to replace them.

Dried peel

The flavour of dried orange or lemon peel gives an intensity to dishes which fresh peel lacks. The peel of Seville oranges with its mixture of bitter sweetness is especially useful.

The most effective way to dry it and retain all the essential oils is to peel the fruit thinly in a coil from stem to base, using a swivel-bladed peeler, and hang the coil on a hook in a warm part of the kitchen. It will gradually harden and over a period of days become sufficiently brittle to be broken into pieces about 2–3 cm (1 in) long. Store these in an airtight jar. Use to flavour soups and stews as well as sweet dishes.

Lemon or orange sugar

A piece of dried lemon or orange peel can be used to perfume sugar. Simply bury a piece in a jar of caster sugar and use when making cakes or sweet dishes.

Scones

An English cream tea is not complete without a plate of freshly baked scones. You can sweeten the scones if you like by adding a tablespoon or two of sugar to the rubbed-in mixture or turn them into fruit scones by stirring in 50 g (2 oz) sugar and 100 g (4 oz) currants. These quantities will make 20–24 scones.

400 g (l lb) self-raising flour,   100 g (4 oz) margarine, cut in
   sifted   pieces
pinch of salt   milk

Heat the oven to Gas 7/425°F/220°C. Put the flour and salt into a mixing bowl and rub in the margarine until the mixture is like fine crumbs. Mix in sufficient milk to form a soft, firm dough – it should not feel in the least bit sticky. (The mixing can all be done in a food processor.)

With floured hands, roll the dough into a ball and put on to a floured board. Using a rolling pin, roll the dough into a piece about 1 cm (½ in) thick. Use a pastry cutter or glass to cut out 5 cm (2 in) rounds. Roll the trimmings out once or twice more, cutting more rounds each time, until all the dough has been used. Place on to greased baking trays. Bake for 12–15 minutes until pale gold and firm. When cool, cut in half and sandwich with butter or clotted cream and jam.

Clotted cream

When I was a child, my grandmother used to make clotted cream with the fresh milk that was delivered, not in bottles but in a heavy churn from which the milkman would ladle out the required amount. The milk came from Devonshire cows and was coloured a creamy yellow. She used to stand a bowl of it on the corner of the stove so that by the next morning a rich crust had formed on the surface, which she would skim off. When we were lucky, my brother and I were allowed to have some on our breakfast porridge or cornflakes. No amount of bought cream has ever tasted so good.

Devonshire claims to make the best clotted cream but then so do Cornwall, Somerset and Dorset and although almost every tea shop in the country offers what they call a traditional cream tea, it is in these counties that the best are to be found, served, of course, with the obligatory scones or splits and lashings of home-made strawberry or raspberry jam.

Clotted, or scalded cream as it is also called, is easy to make, although it does require patience, but it is something to do for fun occasionally. Because the cream is skimmed off the milk we buy today, it has to be made from a mixture of full cream milk and double cream. Once the cream has been skimmed, use the milk that remains to make a rice pudding.

600 ml (1 pint) full cream milk   300 ml ($\frac{1}{2}$ pint) double cream

Pour the milk and cream into a wide-mouthed bowl, cover with a clean tea towel and stand it in a cool place for several hours to allow the cream to rise to the top. After this time, carefully stand the bowl in a large saucepan half filled with water and heat it gently on the stove. Allow the water to simmer gently until the creamy milk has formed a thick, crinkly crust. This will take at least 2 hours.

Once the crust has formed, carefully remove from the heat, cover again and leave to cool. Skim off the crust with a slotted spoon and put into a small bowl. Repeat this process once more. Store covered in the fridge for at least a day to allow the cream to thicken.

Bibliography

Acton, Eliza, *Modern Cookery for Private Families*, facsimile edition, Elek Books, 1966

Anonymous, *Adam's Luxury and Eve's Cookery* (1744), facsimile edition, Prospect Books, 1983

Aylett, Mary and Olive Ordish, *First Catch Your Hare*, Macdonald, 1965

Ayrton, Elisabeth, *The Cookery of England*, Penguin, 1977

Ayrton, Elisabeth, *English Provincial Cooking*, Mitchell Beazley, 1980

Ayto, John, *A Gourmet's Guide: Food & Drink from A to Z*, Oxford University Press, 1994

Bailey, Adrian, *Cook's Ingredients*, Dorling Kindersley, 1990

Beeton, Isabella, *The Book of Household Management*, facsimile edition, Jonathan Cape, 1986

Berriedale-Johnson, *The Victorian Cookbook*, Ward Lock, 1989

Carter, Charles, *The Complete Practical Cook* (1730), facsimile edition, Prospect Books, 1984

Christian, Glyn, *British Cooking at its Best*, J. Sainsbury, 1984

Clifton, Claire, *Edible Flowers*, Bodley Head, 1983

Collins, Christine, *Perfect Puddings*, Faber and Faber, 1976

Costa, Margaret, *Four Seasons Cookery Book*, Thomas Nelson & Sons, 1970

David, Elizabeth, *English Bread and Yeast Cookery*, Allen Lane, 1977

David, Elizabeth, *Spices, Salt and Aromatics in the English Kitchen*, Penguin, 1970

Davidson, Alan, *North Atlantic Seafood*, Penguin, 1986

Farmhouse Cookery, Reader's Digest Association, 1980

Fitzgibbon, Theodora, *The Art of British Cooking*, Phoenix House, 1967

Fitzgibbon, Theodora, *A Taste of the West Country*, Pan Books, 1975

F.K., *The Everyday Pudding Book*, Stanley Paul & Co.

Francatelli, Charles Elm, *A Plain Cookery Book for the Working Classes* (1861), facsimile edition, Pryor Publications, 1993

Glasse, Hannah, *The Art of Cookery Made Plain and Easy* (1747), facsimile edition, Prospect Books, 1983

Green, Henriette, *Food Lovers' Guide to Britain*, BBC Books, 1993

Grigson, Jane, *English Food*, Macmillan, 1974

Grigson, Jane, *Fruit Book*, Penguin, 1980

Grigson, Jane, *The Observer Guide to British Cookery*, Michael Joseph, 1984

Grigson, Jane, *Vegetable Book*, Penguin, 1983

Harris, Mollie, *The Cotswold Country Cookbook*, Chatto & Windus, 1986

Hartley, Dorothy, *Food in England*, Macdonald and Jane's, 1975

Heath, Ambrose, *The Penguin Book of Sauces*, Penguin, 1970

Heesom, Rosemary (ed), *Farmhouse Kitchen*, Trident Television, 1977

Hemphill, R., *Herbs for all Seasons*, Penguin, 1978

Hume, Rosemary and Muriel Downes, *The Cordon Bleu Book of Jams, Preserves and Pickles*, Pan Books, 1972

Hutchins, Sheila, *English Recipes*, Methuen & Co., 1967

Instruction in Cookery: Book of Receipts and Axioms, School Board for London, undated

Jones, Julia and Barbara Deer, *Cattern Cakes and Lace*, Guild Publishing, 1987

Leyel, Mrs C. F. and Miss Olga Hartley, *The Gentle Art of Cookery*, Chatto & Windus, 1974

Mabey, David and Richard, *In Search of Food*, Macdonald and Jane's, 1978

Mabey, David and Rose, *Jams, Pickles and Chutneys*, Macmillan, 1975

Mann, Lyn, *The W.I. Book of Cakes*, Ebury Press, 1985

Parker, Audrey, *A Country Recipe Notebook*, Faber and Faber, 1979

Rance, Patrick, *The Great British Cheese Book*, Macmillan, 1982

Salaman, Redcliff, *The History and Social Influence of the Potato*, Cambridge University Press, 1985

Scott, Shirley and Michael, *Recipes with Herbs*, M. G. Scott, 1985

Smith, Michael, *Fine English Cookery*, Faber and Faber, 1973

Smith, Michael, *New English Cookery*, BBC, 1985

Spry, Constance and Rosemary Hume, *The Constance Spry Cookery Book*, Pan Books, 1972

Spurling, Hilary, *Elinor Fettiplace's Reciept Book*, Penguin, 1987

Stobart, Tom, *The Cook's Enclopaedia*, Macmillan, 1980
Stobart, Tom, *Herbs, Spices and Flavourings*, Penguin, 1987
Sykes, L., *The Olio Cookery Book*, Ernest Benn, 1954
Tannahill, Reay, *Food in History*, Penguin, 1988
The Times Cookery Book, Hodder, 1965
Uttley, Alison, *Recipes from an Old Farmhouse*, Faber and Faber,
    1966
Wilson, C. Anne, *Food and Drink in Britain*, Constable and Co.,
    1973

Index